Perestroika
and
the
Economy

Titles in the Series

NEW DIRECTIONS IN SOVIET SOCIAL THOUGHT
An Anthology

Murray Yanowitch, ed.

PERESTROIKA AND THE ECONOMY
New Thinking in Soviet Economics

Anthony Jones and William Moskoff, eds.

PARTY, STATE, AND CITIZEN IN THE SOVIET UNION
A Collection of Documents

Mervyn Matthews, ed.

THE SOVIET MULTINATIONAL STATE
Readings and Documents

Martha B. Olcott, ed.

SOVIET HISTORIANS AND PERESTROIKA
The First Phase

Donald J. Raleigh, ed.

Perestroika and the Economy

New Thinking in Soviet Economics

Edited by

Anthony Jones and William Moskoff

M. E. Sharpe, Inc.
ARMONK, NEW YORK
LONDON, ENGLAND

For Jane Salk and Bailey Donnally

English translations © 1986, 1987, 1988, 1989 by M. E. Sharpe, Inc.
Translated by arrangement with VAAP, the Soviet copyright agency.
Translated by Arlo Schultz.

Available in the United Kingdom and Europe from M. E. Sharpe,
Publishers, 3 Henrietta Street, London WC2E 8LU.

Library of Congress Cataloging-in-Publication Data

Perestroika and the economy.

    Translation from the Russian.
    Includes bibliographies.
    1. Soviet Union—Economic policy—1986-
I. Jones, Anthony. II. Moskoff, William.
HC336.26.P464   1989   338.947′09′048   89-6147
ISBN 0-87332-569-9

Printed in the United States of America

Contents

Introduction
Anthony Jones and William Moskoff   vii

GENERAL ECONOMIC ISSUES

Restructuring the Management of the Economy
Leonid Abalkin   3

Restructuring and the Enterprise
B. P. Kurashvili   21

The Rebirth of Small-Scale Commodity Production
V. A. Korostelev   45

Competition and Democratization
D. Palterovich   60

The Participation of Working People in the Management
of Production as a Factor in Heightening Labor Activism
E. Torkanovskii   78

PLAN AND MARKET

A New Conception of Centralism
Leonid Abalkin   91

Where Are the *Pirogi* Meatier?
L. Popkova   99

Is It Possible to Be "A Little Pregnant"?
E. Pozdniakov   104

Why Are You Pushing?
O. Latsis   111

The Difficult Road of Cognition
T. Valovaia   116

PRICE REFORM

Product Mix, Price, Profit
  G. A. Kulagin   127

Improving Consumer Prices
  D. M. Kazakevich   145

LABOR INCENTIVES

Employment: Scarcity or Surplus?
  Vladimir G. Kostakov   159

Restructuring the System of Payment of Labor
  L. Kostin   176

Social Development and Economic Growth
  S. Shatalin   195

PROPERTY AND SOCIAL JUSTICE

The Structure and Forms of Socialist Property
  V. V. Kulikov   217

The Distribution Mechanism and Social Justice
  Petr O. Aven   233

BARRIERS TO REFORM

The Reform of the Economic Mechanism
  P. O. Aven and V. M. Shironin   251

Economics and Common Sense
  Nikolai Shmelev   267

About the Editors   277

Introduction

ANTHONY JONES AND WILLIAM MOSKOFF

This anthology is designed to provide a sampling of the new economic thinking that has been developing in the USSR since the mid–1980s. These years have been remarkable ones, both for those engaged in trying to pull the Soviet system out of its torpor and for those outside the USSR who are observing this process.

The decades since the death of Joseph Stalin have seen a dramatic end to the astonishing economic growth rates achieved by the Soviet Union in the 1930s and in the early postwar era. In the 1960s the average annual rate of growth was still about 5 percent, but in the early 1970s it went down to about 4 percent, falling to about 3 percent in the second half of the decade, and then to 2 percent in the first half of the 1980s. The earlier high growth rates were associated with a system of hierarchical and centralized economic planning which mobilized vast resources and concentrated them in selected sectors of the economy, particularly in heavy industry. As an experiment in rapid social, political, and economic change, the Soviet model of industrialization had wrought wonders. It enabled the Soviet Union to move into the first rank of the world's nations as a military power and a pioneer in space, though in many ways it functioned at the economic level of a partially developed country.[1]

Central planning, then, brought the Soviet Union into the twentieth century; but by the end of the 1950s it was a system with rapidly diminishing returns. Its time had passed. It is not as if this went unrecognized in the Soviet Union. Since the early 1960s various attempts—half-hearted ones, most would argue—have been made to reform the system. But it was not until Mikhail Gorbachev came to power in March 1985 that a serious challenge to the status quo was launched.

The essays in this volume, all drawn from the translation journal *Problems of Economics*, provide a sampling of some of the evolving new thinking about the Soviet economy. These pieces by no means exhaust the views held by Soviet economists, but they do document the emergence of a consensus that the existing structures cannot be retained intact.[2]

There has long been a tendency in the Soviet Union to use *ad hominem* arguments when assessing problems. Convenient scapegoats could always be found to absorb the blame for failures to meet planned goals. Even today in the Soviet press it is customary to blame the late Leonid Brezhnev, in not very veiled terms, for "the years of stagnation." But what is currently happening in Soviet economic writing goes far beyond finger-pointing. The past few years have seen a serious effort to confront the real implications of the model of central planning and to ask questions about what Soviet socialism should mean in the last years of the twentieth century.

When we compare recent writings to earlier work in Soviet economics, several important differences are evident. Discussions now pay explicit attention to the social and political preconditions of economic change, and also to the broader consequences of change. There is a growing understanding of the complexity of economic policy making and the ways in which variables interact to produce unintended, and often negative, consequences. A prime example is the new Law on the State Enterprise, a centerpiece of the reform agenda. The law had the proclaimed goal of giving enterprises and their work forces more autonomy, more responsibility for their operations and accountability for their results; but at the same time it left state economic ministries responsible for overall production.[3] Thus, for all practical purposes, the command model was retained, and enterprises remain tied to, and dependent on, state orders. (In late 1988 state contracts reportedly accounted for as much as 90 percent of industrial output.) Nevertheless, the law put managers under pressure to make profits and become financially self-sufficient. Consequently, many enterprises simply raised prices; they did not increase or improve output, as was hoped.

Soviet economists are also becoming more sophisticated in their analyses of the functioning of the economy. In their search for explanations of the snail-like pace of growth and the fall in productivity during the 1970s, they are looking at underlying structural problems rather than writing off every failure to individual malfeasance. Behaviors that were once labeled as deviations or pathologies are now recognized as rational ways for people to operate under prevailing conditions. For example, why is product quality so shoddy? One might put all the blame on incompetent managers or lazy workers. But if one looks at the fact that the enterprise's inputs are allocated by state ministries, and ministries measure enterprise performance in terms of gross output, then a single-minded concentration on gross output to the exclusion of all else is "rational," since only this will ensure that the enterprise will get the resources it needs.

No change is easy, but the task of restructuring a long-established and highly structured system is especially formidable. It is not surprising that Gorbachev and his allies face well-entrenched opponents.[4] Reform means a change in the rules of the game, a break with the old, simplistic notion of growth for growth's sake and production for production's sake. Many groups with vested interests in the old order—most notably the enormous economic bureaucracy—have already demonstrated their recalcitrance. For those whose careers and perquisites are intimately tied to the central planning model, the handwriting on the wall spells out an unpalatable message. Restructuring threatens the bureaucracy's very reason for existence.[5]

Also in the ranks of the unpersuaded are production workers. Reform advocates hold out the promise that reform will mean increased supplies of consumer goods and more income with which to buy them. But the first step is always that workers will have to increase productivity—and lose their job security in the bargain—while the rewards remain distant and uncertain.

Finally, the Soviet "military-industrial complex," long accustomed to enjoying top priority standing in the system, has genuine reason for concern. The defense budget, which has taken an average of 15 percent of Soviet gross national product for many years, will be hard hit if the resources that have been poured into the defense sector are redirected to build the technological base of the civilian economy.[6] In December 1988 Gorbachev startled the world when he announced at the United Nations a planned unilateral cutback of 500,000 troops and a reduction in the number of offensive weapons located in Eastern Europe. From the standpoint of a powerful sector of the system, the implications of this in terms of the resources they can expect are obvious. Whether Gorbachev will have the support to sustain this shift politically is unclear.

Gorbachev has also had to face some unforeseeable problems that severely handicap economic reform efforts. The December 1988 earthquake in Armenia caused enormous destruction and rebuilding will require an estimated 13 billion rubles. Similarly, the accident at Chernobyl in April 1986 cost an estimated 10 billion rubles (almost $17 billion). Both disasters are draining precious resources at a time when the country already faces an enormous budget deficit, estimated at as much as $100 billion.

Another problem that threatens the reform agenda is the resurgence of nationalism and ethnic antagonisms. Of particular importance here is the case of Estonia, a republic in the Baltic region that was singled out as a possible zone of economic experimentation because of its high level of development.[8] Now, Estonian demands for radically increased republic autonomy have become inextricably intertwined with the devolution of economic responsibility, and it will be difficult for Gorbachev to suppress the forces of decentralization in the political realm without endangering his economic goals.

This situation is a complicated one, and promises to become more so. If private enterprise experiments continue to flourish in the Baltic republics, even the state sector in the region will benefit to the extent that investment levels are determined by market forces. But if these resources stay within the republic, not subject to reallocation by the center, then the existing gap in living standards between this region and others, including the Russian heartland, will widen. It is hardly surprising, therefore, that Abel Aganbegian has said that too much movement in the direction of "self-financing for territorial units has perhaps more negative aspects than positive ones."[9]

Looking at how the economy has performed since the reforms began, we find that the record is fairly dismal. In 1986 the economy experienced a 3.9 percent growth rate, its best performance in a number of years. However, it can be argued that this was attributable to the favorable weather conditions for agriculture and to first effects of the 1985 discipline campaign in industry. In 1987, a much fairer test of Gorbachev's efforts, the growth rate fell precipitously to 0.5 percent.[10] While the final figures for 1988 are not yet in, the estimates are not promising. Gorbachev, disturbed by the preliminary figures, told the All-Union Party Conference in June 1988: "Practice has identified the problems that are causing the new economic mechanism to spin its wheels. To some extent, they are connected with the fact that not all of its elements have yet been introduced and that we began carrying out the reform as we went along, as the saying goes. . . .''[11] At the end of September he frankly admitted: ''We are going slowly, we are losing time, and this means we are losing the game.''[12]

When he launched his reform effort, Gorbachev seemed to be relying on a strategy of making existing institutions work better. The emphasis was on squeezing more out of the economy by increasing labor discipline—a policy begun by Andropov. But another important goal was to accomplish a shift from ''extensive'' to ''intensive'' development. Extensive development means doing more, but in basically the same way. Intensive development is a more complicated matter. It involves the introduction of new technologies, as well as a concentration of investment in those branches of the economy where the returns are greatest (rather than as dictated by ideology, political interests, etc.).[13]

It was not until the June 1987 Central Committee Plenum that a commitment to intensive growth was reflected in official economic policy. This marked the break from old approaches and the quickening evolution of economic thought and policy that we have witnessed since that time. Why the change?

The reason seems to have been the realization that the capacity of the system to absorb and effectively use new technology was low. The existing organization of the economy and of the wider society were the problem. Intensive growth would require making room for what has come to be called the ''human factor,'' for ''the wishes, desires, values and interests of the general population to be made an explicit part of the reform process.''[14] Once started down this path, *perestroika* took on more radical implications including the need for much greater decentralization, increased scope for private initiative, and the toleration of economic, political, and social activities that would have been anathema just a few short years ago. In short, what started out as an effort to salvage the practices and institutions of the past now promised to unleash a revolutionary process of change.

To date, the more innovative reforms instituted since mid–1987 have not resulted in qualitative or quantitative improvements in economic performance. The high hopes placed on the new Law on the State Enterprise, which did not go into effect until January 1, 1988, have not been realized, for reasons we have already discussed. Meanwhile, the new cooperatives that opened in 1987–88 have been blamed for high prices and accused of ''speculation.'' The backlash against the cooperatives suggests the persistent ambivalence toward private enterprise in the Soviet Union. On-again, off-again tax requirements and other restrictions have discouraged the development of the cooperative movement.[15] The success of these new ventures is far from assured.

Will the next step be a retreat, or a further, more radical expansion of the reform agenda?

In the essays that follow, Soviet economists articulate their ideas on the Soviet economy, on what needs to be done, and why. We begin with an essay by Leonid Abalkin which succinctly sets out the reasons why restructuring is necessary. According to Abalkin it was clear by the early 1970s that it was the organization of the economy that was hindering economic and social progress. The stagnation of the Brezhnev period did not cause, but only exacerbated what in any case would have been a difficult situation. The Soviet economic system had become a self-perpetuating rather than a productive system. Breaking that cycle is what *perestroika* is all about, but it will require radical change—not only in the ministries, the factories, and the farms, but more generally in political, social, and cultural life.

Whereas in the past Soviet economists uniformly treated existing economic institutions as inevitable, essential characteristics of a socialist economy, in this essay Abalkin goes to the heart of the matter by raising the loaded question of property reform. Who owns, and who should direct the use of, productive property? Without change in the nature of state/public ownership of productive property, Abalkin warns, worker alienation and bureaucratic immobilism will never be overcome. Thus, the issues of democratization, self-management, and enfranchisement of the consumer must be regarded as central.

The selection by Kurashvili takes us to the level of the enterprise. It is here, he believes, that the fate of *perestroika* will be decided. Like Abalkin, Kurashvili thinks reform is long overdue and for that reason all the more difficult. The command system created in the 1920s and 1930s is out of sync not only with modern production technology but also with the aspirations and motivations of its well-educated labor force. Although the use of coercion, characteristic of the early period, declined, nothing "positive" replaced it. Instead, the old system premised on coercion was retained more or less intact, only now it was run on the basis of corruption and collusion. Kurashvili welcomes the new Law on the State Enterprise in principal, but is critical of its "contradictory, half-hearted, intermediate character" as a compromise that preserves administrative methods of management and bureaucratic imperative.[16]

In "The Rebirth of Small-Scale Commodity Production," Korostelev argues that Soviet "gigantomania," the predilection for forming bigger and bigger organizations, has created monopolies in many branches of the economy. The result has been economic stagnation, inflexibility, and nonresponsiveness to the needs of the population. It has also left "dead zones" of products and services needed by consumers but not economically "interesting" to large enterprises. The greater the concentration, the larger the dead zones. Noting the successful operation of small-scale private businesses in Eastern Europe, Korostelev reminds his readers that private enterprise has been operating in the Soviet Union for decades on an illegal or semilegal basis,[17] as "black" and "gray" markets sprang up to serve unmet needs. Unfortunately, this has reinforced the notion that work outside of the state socialized sector is somehow immoral, at best shady and at worst downright criminal. This attitude is now hobbling the progress of officially sanctioned individual and cooperative private enterprise.

These same themes are developed in the essay by Palterovich. Soviet economic theory, he argues, has viewed man "merely as a production worker," with no regard to individuals' needs, interests, aspirations, and moral and material values. It is a mistake not to recognize that the striving for success is "one of the most important properties of the human personality and the motivation behind the productive and social activity of the majority of people" and that competition is "an important element of socialist production relations."

Thus Palterovich rejects one of the keystones of Soviet Marxian economic theory: the assumption that once private ownership of productive property is abolished, people will work willingly in order to contribute to the common good and will derive from this their self-fulfillment. In practice, of course, the Soviet economy has relied heavily on material incentives (along with varying proportions of moral exhortation and coercion) since the 1920s, but always in a backdoor fashion. It has not, however, made good use of the human desire for success, and so, in Palterovich's words, has "lost powerful levers and stimuli for conserving resources, for raising product quality, and for accelerating scientific and technological progress."

But free competition requires democratization at all levels of the society. In the last essay in this section, Torkanovskii makes the case for democratizing the workplace, arguing that enterprises should provide more scope for initiative and more autonomous roles for workers.[18] Although this account is by now a little dated, it remains a useful summary of a set of issues that will have to become more central if the reform is to succeed.

One of the fundamental issues underlying discussions of *perestroika* is the question of plan versus market, command versus demand. The creation of a centrally planned economic system at the end of the 1920s was not simply a developmental strategy; it was also an expression of ideological sentiment quickly enshrined as orthodoxy. The market mechanism was equated with capitalism and—not surprisingly in that era—with chaos and exploitation. To now construct a new Soviet economic order that (either implicitly or explicitly) modifies the role of planning in favor of market forces is to concede a great deal for a regime built on assertions of ideological orthodoxy.

In "A New Conception of Centralism," Abalkin envisions a more limited role for "the center," which in the past has been a "serious obstacle to economic and social progress." Abalkin thinks the center should have a dual role. Its first responsibility should be to define the overall goals of the national economy and to develop a strategy of economic growth. Its second role is to create an environment in which economic actors can function efficiently. The command model will no longer do; the socialist economy must be driven by "the management of interests through interests."

Abalkin argues that production should be determined by the character of consumer demand, not by the state, but he recognizes that the most important consumer in the Soviet Union *is* the state. Abalkin wants state orders to be limited to the most crucial items, but what we have seen so far is that the preeminent role of state orders has remained unchanged.

The question of plan versus the market is the subject of a controversial article published in the literary journal *Novyi mir*. Author Popkova's fundamental point is that plan and market are absolutely incompatible and cannot be mixed. To introduce market economy is to abandon planning and therefore socialism. Those who think otherwise are deluding themselves, for it is not possible to be "a little pregnant." It may be true that market economies have more abundance, but the Soviet Union is committed to the system Lenin put in place and therefore must resign itself to its shortcomings.

Popkova's absolutist formulation of the problem has generated a lively and continuing debate.[19] Pozdniakov, in a response to the Popkova essay, argues that all-or-nothing views are simplistic—and adds that Soviet economics has "long been 'pregnant' with the idea of radical restructuring based on the integral combination of plan and market. . . ."

Latsis objects to the dismal implications of Popkova's argument— that if the Soviet Union does not want to become capitalist, it might as well give up on *perestroika*. Like Pozdniakov, Latsis denies that socialism is incompatible with market principles. This is also the view of Valovaia, who asserts that there is some "optimal combination" of plan and market that can coexist under socialism, and that when it is found, the socialist system will be all the better for it.

It strikes us that a great deal of self-deception runs through this debate. No one questions whether the Soviet system is indeed "socialist" by definition. It is certainly not a model of effective planning, at least in its fullest conception. In any case, if the Gorbachev agenda is carried to its logical conclusions, Soviet economic planning, at least as we have known it since 1928, is doomed.

As long as the issue of plan and market remains unresolved, so too does the question of price reform. It can be argued that the arbitrary way in which wholesale and retail prices are set in the Soviet Union, and then rigidly preserved, is the single greatest weakness of the system, and that economic reform cannot succeed without price reform.

The selections in section three speak to the weaknesses of Soviet price formation, and each makes suggestions on how to rectify the situation. The first author, Kulagin, does not want the state to surrender its prerogative to set prices. He suggests that the state should set the prices of the most important commodities and develop the guidelines for determining the prices of other goods. Since profit should be the basic measure of economic performance, what is important is that prices should be set so as to produce equal profitability.

The next article represents a more radical departure from the status quo. Kazakevich concentrates on the heavy state subsidization of food prices, amounting to billions of rubles each year. While in social terms this may be laudable, he argues, state subsidies have led to enormous distortions in the allocation of resources and the pattern of demand. For example, bread is so inexpensive in the Soviet Union (its price has not changed for three decades) that farmers buy it as feed for their livestock, and then sell meat at high prices in the free market. Kazekevich advocates ending the food subsidies and using the budgetary savings to increase wages, so that in real terms the citizenry will not be worse off. He calls for a "one-time adjustment of consumer goods prices" that can then be fine-tuned to respond to shifts in supply and demand.

In both of these essays, the authors knowingly or unknowingly fail to nail down their own point about the misallocative effects of price rigidity. Certainly the idea that one-time adjustments will lead to allocative efficiency is illusory.

What are the chances for price reform? In a recent interview, Valentin Pavlov, Chairman of the USSR State Committee for Prices, indicated that a proposal on reforming wholesale prices would be ready in June 1989. Pavlov asserted that there was "undoubtedly a need for a reform of relative prices," which "must be accompanied by compensational measures"; but he also affirmed allegiance to price controls and said he would not raise bread prices even if world grain prices rose.[20] That is certainly the kind of news Soviet consumers want to hear, even if it dims the prospects of reform. Obviously, retail prices are as much a political question as an economic one in a socialist economy, and the reformers do not need any more enemies than they already have. The leadership well knows what happened in Poland when the authorities raised food prices.

One of the key problems of the Soviet economy is labor productivity. There is a well-known East European saying about the nature of workers' relationship to their state employer: "We pretend to work and they pretend to pay us." Both essays in the next section grant that there is a good deal of truth in this bitter humor.

It has been long argued that the Soviet Union has a serious labor shortage due to unfavorable demographic trends. But in an essay included here, Kostakov argues that the labor shortage is imaginary, and that the real problem is inefficient use of the existing labor supply. There are too many people working where they are not needed—for example, the redundant workers kept on at an enterprise to be available for "storming" to meet quotas at the end of a production period. Kostakov estimates that there is in fact a significant labor surplus in the Soviet Union, and that the emphasis on demographic explanations has sidetracked researchers from addressing the underlying reasons for the ineffective use of labor.[21] One obvious problem is that there is not much incentive to work hard if there is nothing to buy with one's income. But

Kostakov also gives attention to noneconomic factors. The younger generation of Soviet workers has a different set of aspirations and their concerns about the workplace need to be addressed.

Leonid Kostin's essay is a catalogue of what is wrong with the current system of rewarding labor, from the norms that are used to assess the value of labor and the sources from which wages are paid, to the structure of the bonus system. He concludes his indictment of the existing system of remuneration with a call for a ''radical restructuring of wages'' to reflect differences in ability and performance.

The concern raised by proposals like this is that greater dispersions in wages will aggravate existing inequalities and undermine notions of social justice in a society where wage ''levelling'' has long been the norm. On this count Shatalin argues that a clear distinction must be made between wage differentials, which provide incentives, and social consumption funds, which play a role in distributive justice.

Another concern is that if unprofitable production is shut down and redundant workers are released, unemployment, already estimated to be around 3 percent,[22] can be expected to rise, at least in the near term. In the early 1930s the Soviet government declared that it had achieved full employment. Even if that has not always been strictly true, a job has long been regarded as a fundamental right—and duty—of every Soviet citizen. Now it has been predicted that as many as 16 million workers will be released from their jobs by the year 2000.[23] The official position is that no one need fear the painful consequences of unemployment that are familiar in the West; that plenty of jobs are available in production and in the new cooperatives; and people will be aided in getting retrained and finding jobs.[24]

Handling popular fears that economic reform will undermine people's security, and balancing the concern for efficiency with the promise of equity, may be one of the most delicate tasks the reformers face.

Section five looks at the related issues of property ownership and social justice. Kulikov provides a very useful summary of many of the issues involved in rethinking the status of property—one of the most sensitive issues in the Soviet system. Official policies on private property have changed many times over the decades, lurching back and forth between intolerance and qualified tolerance. Recent policies have been the most tolerant since the 1920s (virtually all of the legal restrictions Kulikov mentions have now been lifted), but the situation has not stabilized. Large segments of the population, not to mention officialdom, are ambivalent at best about private enterprise; cooperatives, private businesses, and peasant markets have been subjected to attacks. Although the success of these endeavors is crucial to the success of *perestroika*, the new entrepreneurs are operating in a risky environment and without guarantees that their legal status is secure. If private initiative is to be institutionalized, people must be given some firm basis for believing that they will not lose everything they have worked for (or worse) if the leadership changes or the ideological winds shift.

The economic reforms are already having an effect on income distribution in the USSR, and this has sparked a stormy debate on the "justice" of the changes. Aven's article from *Kommunist*, based on letters to the editors of the Party journal, and the response of an economist to the concerns raised, highlights the complexity of the human issues involved in *perestroika*.

Finally, the essays in section six provide very outspoken evaluations of the reforms, their conception, implementation, and progress. The analysis by Aven and Shironin, probably the frankest statement to be found in this volume, is especially critical of contemporary Soviet planners and economists. Soviet economics has been shaped by the command economy model. Its restricted conceptual apparatus has left unexamined the economy's most basic structures. The authors' view is that the reforms have not been properly thought out; that the current understanding of how the economy actually operates is not sophisticated enough to provide the basis for an effective reform strategy. Most of the previous attempts at reform in the USSR and in other socialist societies have ended in failure, and the authors seem to feel that this one may fail as well.

What is needed, they suggest, is not a better and more tightly defined program, but rather an openness to what they refer to as an array of possibilities, a "system of potential answers." In other words, economic reform is too important to be left to economic policy makers. The various interest groups in the society must be permitted to bargain and maneuver; they must be involved in decision making, not simply regarded as pawns in the implementation of centrally mandated policies. Only a negotiated program will have a chance of success. What, exactly, should be done to accommodate those who want no change of any kind they do not say.

The essay by Shmelev which concludes this volume is a succinct account (by one of the Soviet Union's most outspoken and radical supporters of *perestroika*) of the current status of the reforms. It was written in response to a long article by another well-known writer about economic issues, Vasilii Seliunin, which lambastes economic planners and administrators for stubbornly clinging to the goal of growth at any price (even when it is wasteful of resources and threatens the environment) and for continuing to assess economic performance in terms of aggregate growth rates.[25] The goal, he states, must be to increase the amount of goods that people can actually buy and use, not just to produce figures in economic reports. What is needed is less interference from above and more scope for demand from below. In Seliunin's words, "Man is the ultimate goal of the economy. Man is the sun around which the economy should revolve."

In Seliunin's view, to judge *perestroika* in terms of overall growth rates will doom it to failure, for it will not be possible to increase output while making the transition from a centrally planned command economy to a more consumer-oriented, demand-driven system:

> [The] overall growth rate will be minimal and possibly even negative. There is no other solution. Either acceleration, understood as increasing the volume of production, or restructuring. . . . There is no third possibility and so it is necessary nevertheless to choose.

Shmelev, who is in general agreement with Seliunin's analysis, deplores the continuing reluctance to give up on the old system and to embrace economic rationality. Like Seliunin, he is scathing about the enormous waste of products and resources, of skills and manpower, and the failure to produce what people need and want to buy.[26] He points out the disabling contradictions in the new Enterprise Law, which has left the economic ministries and the enterprises locked in a death grip.

In this *cri de coeur* we see how difficult it is to effect change. Even in the face of the boldest challenge to the system of centralized planning since it was first instituted by Stalin, the system has kept its hold.[27] Soviet economists themselves are having to struggle to change, to push back the boundaries of debate and to develop the tools they need to do their work.

In spite of the seemingly open and free-wheeling manner in which ideas and programs are being debated by Soviet economists, they too are still hobbled by the habits of the past. Even a cursory reading of the economic literature prior to the mid–1980s shows how very narrow were the limits within which discussion was conducted; as the Party line changed, so too, in concert, did the stated views of economists. And to a significant degree, this is still the case. Economists do not challenge the premises of *perestroika* (at least not in print), but confine themselves to more or less strongly worded praise or criticism of specific aspects of restructuring.

In reading these and other articles by Soviet economists, we need to be sensitive to the context within which they are being written. Some economists have shown great personal courage in boldly expressing views which not long ago might have cost them dearly. Given the uncertain future of the Gorbachev reforms, they still must weigh every word. We can only wish them well.

Notes

1. Astonishingly, one Soviet economist recently stated that, in terms of per capita consumption of goods and services, the Soviet Union now ranks between 50th and 60th among the world's countries. See *Current Digest of the Soviet Press* (hereafter CDSP), vol. 40, no. 39, October 26, 1988, p. 27.

2. Although Party politicians ultimately control the reform process, economists have become very influential in the USSR, both as opinion makers and as policy advisers. See Anders Aslund, "Gorbachev's Economic Advisers," *Soviet Economy*, 1987, no. 3, pp. 246–269. Articles by the more outspoken economists quickly become collectors' items, given the relatively limited printings of the magazines and journals in which they appear. See CDSP, vol. 40, no. 17, May 25, 1988, p. 25.

3. CDSP, vol. 40, no. 35, September 28, 1988, p. 23.

4. For a collection of interesting articles on the foes of reform see CDSP, vol. 40, no. 16, May 18, 1988.

5. Thousands of bureaucrats have already lost their jobs, and there are apparently plans to reduce bureaucratic ranks (which include some fourteen million people) by up to 50 percent. See CDSP, vol. 40, no. 4, February 24, 1988, p. 4.

6. There is great interest among Soviet economists in the issue of conversion from military to civilian production, and clearly this is the policy of the Gorbachev leadership. But, given the highly specialized nature of much of the defense industry, conversion would be not only difficult but also potentially very disruptive, as it would be in the United States. See Leo Reddy, "Winding Down the War Machine," *The New York Times*, December 20, 1988, p. 27.

7. See John Tedstrom, "Recent Trends in the Soviet Economy: A Balance Sheet," Radio Liberty *Report on the USSR*, vol. 1, no. 5, February 3, 1989, p. 14; and statements by Oleg Bogomolov in *Argumenty i fakti*, 1989, no. 3.

8. See "Conformist Communists Propose Turning Estonia into Closed Economic Zone," Baltic Situation Report/7, Radio Free Europe Research, October 28, 1987. Ethnic issues aside, regional and local demands have been burgeoning under *glasnost'*. One focal point of concern is the environment, as in the battle over the building of a huge hydroelectric station on the Lower Tunuska (see CDSP, vol. 40, no. 36, October 5, 1988, p. 19) or the desertification of the Aral region and the debate over river diversion (see James Critchlow, "Desertification of the Aral Region: Economic and Human Damage," Radio Liberty Research Report, RL 392/87).

9. Quoted in Philip Hanson, "Economic Decentralization and the Nationalities Issue," Radio Liberty Research Report, RL 127/88, March 15, 1988.

10. John Tedstrom, Radio Liberty Research Reports RL 496/88; Central Intelligence Agency, "Gorbachev's Economic Program: Problems Emerge," June 1988, pp. 3, 23.

11. CDSP, vol. 40, no. 26, July 27, 1988, p. 8.

12. *The New York Times*, September 25, 1988, p. 1. In what may have been an attempt to put his own economic performance in perspective, Gorbachev claimed in February 1988 that the only reason that the economy seemed to be growing in the mid–1980s was that world prices for Soviet oil were high and sales of alcohol within the USSR were rising. If one discounts these, he said, then there has been no increase in national income for almost twenty years. See Elizabeth Teague, "Gorbachev Tells Plenum Soviet Economy Has Stopped Growing," Radio Liberty Research Report, RL 74/88, February 27, 1988.

13. See T. Anthony Jones, "Changing Course: Social Organization and New Technology in the Soviet Union," in Richard Simpson and Ida Simpson, eds., *Research in the Sociology of Work*, vol. 4, 1988, p. 207.

14. See CDSP, vol 40, no. 14, May 4, 1988, p. 17, and vol. 40, no. 28, August 10, 1988, p. 23. According to *FAKT Bulletin* (Moscow, 1988, p. 2) there were 30,000 cooperatives in the USSR in October 1988, with more than 2,500 in Moscow alone. However, figures in the Soviet press vary widely, and so the actual number of cooperatives in existence remains a mystery.

15. See Tat′iana Zaslavskaia, "The Social Mechanism of the Economy," *Soviet Sociology*, Fall 1987, pp. 29–42; and "Social Justice and the Human Factor in Economic Development," *Problems of Economics*, May 1987, pp. 5–26.

16. For a translation of the full provisions of the law, see CDSP, vol. 39, no. 30, August 26, 1988, pp. 8–13, and no. 31, September 2, 1988, pp. 10–17.

17. For translations of the Soviet laws on private enterprise, see CDSP, vol. 38, no. 46, December 17, 1986, pp. 1–8.

18. For an account of the work democratization literature in the Soviet Union, see Murray Yanowitch, *Work in the Soviet Union: Attitudes and Issues* (New York: M. E. Sharpe, 1985).

19. In addition to the responses considered in this volume, there is a lengthy discussion in CDSP, vol. 40, no. 35, September 30, 1987.

20. *Moscow News*, no. 43, October 30–November 6, 1988, pp. 8, 9.

21. For a discussion see William Moskoff, "The Soviet Urban Labor Supply," in Henry W. Morton and Robert C. Stuart, eds., *The Contemporary Soviet City* (M. E. Sharpe, 1984), pp. 65–83.

22. N. Shmelev, "Advances and Debts," *Problems of Economics*, February 1988, p. 21.

23. CDSP, vol. 40, no. 4, February 24, 1988, p. 4.

24. For the official Soviet analysis of the resolution "On Ensuring the Effective Employment of the Population, Improving the System of Job Placement and Increasing Social Guarantees for the Working People," see CDSP, vol. 40, no. 4, February 24, 1988, pp. 1–4. For a Western analysis, see Aaron Trehub, "Joint Party-Government Resolution on Employment," Radio Liberty Research Report RL 46/88.

25. A translation of Seliunin's article, "A Profound Reform or the Revenge of the Bureaucracy?" appeared in *Problems of Economics*, March 1989.

26. Shmelev is a strong advocate of borrowing money from abroad to import consumer goods as a stimulus.

27. For an economist's account of Stalin's harmful influence on Soviet economics, see CDSP, vol. 40, no. 18, June 1, 1988, p. 12.

General
Economic
Issues

Leonid Abalkin

Restructuring the Management of the Economy

A Continuation of the Work of the October Revolution

The restructuring of the management of the economy is an integral part of the program for the qualitative modernization of socialism. It is revolutionary in spirit, in depth, and in the scale of its transformations, and it is the most radical reform of the system of management undertaken since the construction of socialist society in our country.

As noted at the June 1987 Plenum of the CPSU Central Committee, "the restructuring that is underway in the nation is a direct continuation of the cause of the October Revolution, the consistent implementation of ideals inscribed on the banner of the revolution." "It is specifically in the development of socialism and in the continuation of the ideas and practice of Leninism and the October Revolution," stated M. S. Gorbachev in the report "October and Restructuring: the Revolution Continues," "that we see the essence of our current affairs and concerns, our primary task, and our moral obligation."

Russian text © 1987 by "Pravda" Publishers. "Perestroika upravleniia ekonomikoi—prodolzhenie dela oktiabr'skoi revoliutsii," *Voprosy ekonomiki*, 1987, no. 12, pp. 3–13.

The author is a correspondent member of the USSR Academy of Sciences and is director of the Institute of Economics of the USSR Academy of Sciences.

This article is based on a report presented at a session of the Academic Council of the Institute of Economics of the USSR Academy of Sciences on October 29, 1987.

The need for the radical modernization of the system of economic management

The revolutionary modernization of the system of management, the break with existing methods, and the transition to a qualitatively new model of the economic mechanism must have deep-going foundations. This is all the more important because in the last seventy years, the Soviet Union has achieved enormous successes both in its economy and in other spheres of social life. All our achievements can be attributed to the enormous advantages of the socialist system and the principles of planned economic management. However, today we speak specifically of a fundamental restructuring, of the radical reform of existing forms and methods of management. V. I. Lenin repeatedly emphasized: "Again and again, we shall have to improve our work, redo it, start from the beginning. Every step onward and upward that we take in developing our productive forces and our culture must be accompanied by the work of improving and altering our Soviet system—we are still low on the scale of economics and culture. Much will have to be altered, and to be 'embarrassed' by this would be absurd (if not worse)."[1] ". . . We shall have to do this many a time in every sphere of our activity, finish what was left undone and adopt different approaches to the problem."[2]

Radical reform of the system of management is necessitated first and foremost by the entry of the economy into a qualitatively new stage of development and by change in the conditions of expanded reproduction. By the early seventies it became obvious that the existing management techniques were too confining for the national economy, which has grown in scale many fold. They had begun to restrain the further progressive development of the economy and to inhibit social progress. Even without subsequent serious difficulties and negative phenomena, profound qualitative reforms in the system of management techniques would be inevitable nevertheless, even though the character and shape of these reforms would be different from those presently required.

At the same time, the revolutionary modernization of the system of management and of all public life is necessitated by [the appearance] in the past of serious deformations in the socialist economic system, production relations, and the methods of planned management. These deformations substantially weakened and in a number of cases undermined the enormous potential and advantages of the socialist economic system and led society to the point of stagnation and the brink of crisis.

The urgent need today is for a specifically revolutionary, uncompromising struggle against such deformations, against any and all deviations from the norms and principles of the socialist organization of society. We want more socialism not because it did not exist in the past, but because there was too little of it.

As emphasized at the joint ceremonial session of the CPSU Central Committee, USSR Supreme Soviet, and Supreme Soviet of the RSFSR on the occasion of the seventieth anniversary of the Great October Socialist Revolution, restructuring is intended not only to correct the stagnation and conservatism of the preceding period, but also to overcome historically limited, outmoded aspects of social organization and work methods. This means investing socialism with the most sophisticated forms corresponding to the conditions and needs of the scientific-technological revolution and the intellectual progress of Soviet society. This will be a relatively long process of revolutionary modernization of society that will have its own logic and stages.

It is quite obvious that accomplishing these urgent tasks will be impossible without a serious interpretation of the experience and lessons of history. It should be emphasized that progress in economic theory is altogether impossible without historical analysis. If research is based not on dogma but on facts, there will be no other source of theoretical generalizations than the interpretation of historical experience. A reliable way of strengthening the relationship between economic theory and life, and a necessary condition and guarantee of the successful solution of modern problems is the study of the lessons and practical experience of socialist management.

Analysis of historical experience confirms the close interrelationship between the present restructuring and the cause of the October Revolution. Such a relationship can be seen first of all in the goals and ultimate ideals of their revolutionary reforms. It is confirmed by their scale and complexity, by their orientation toward the social energy of the masses, and by their consistent democratization of management. Naturally, when we establish a close interrelationship between the present restructuring and the reforms effected by the October Revolution, it is wrong to equate these processes mechanically, as they are by no means identical. It is important to see the uniqueness of modern tasks and their differing nature from those that had to be addressed in the initial and subsequent stages of socialist construction. It is naturally also inadmissible to copy the forms and methods of the reforms that were carried out during this period of time.

The goals and nature of restructuring

The sense and goals of restructuring are associated with the strengthening of the positions of socialism, with the more complete utilization of its historical advantages, with overcoming everything that inhibits and restrains socioeconomic progress. The relationship between the current restructuring and the goals and ideals of the October Revolution can be seen in this regard. The conception of the orientation of restructuring as a process in the progressive development of Soviet society must serve as a reliable reference point in addressing a wide range of theoretical and practical questions.

The current restructuring is of an integrated nature and embraces the nation's economy, sphere of social relations, and political and intellectual life. In this complex of reforms, there are no questions that are unimportant or of secondary importance. Naturally, economic reforms, the raising of the economy to a qualitatively new level, and the restructuring of the system of management have a decisive part to play. However, as shown by the experience of history, including the history of economic reform in the sixties, radical reforms in economic life are impossible without fundamental changes in the political, social, and cultural spheres.

An important feature of the restructuring is that it combines continuity and faithfulness to management principles used throughout the seventy years of Soviet power with a truly innovative and creative approach to the solution of new problems and the decisive break with everything that impedes further development. Here is manifested dialectical negation, which discards the old while preserving everything of value in it, and which is characteristic of social progress.

The combination of continuity and innovation is a question that is associated with the clear differentiation of principles and methods of management. The principles express the permanent pillars of the socialist economy. They are not subject to short-term change. Of course, this conclusion, like any other, should not be made an absolute. With the accumulation of historical experience, the principles themselves, as the guiding principles of economic activity, are enriched and developed, but they retain their unified general socialist content in all stages.

The methods of socialist management, unlike the principles, are volatile and changeable. They cannot be uniform for various historical stages or for various conditions. All forms and methods of management, unlike principles, inevitably age. The retention of obsolete methods leads to the economic mechanism's loss of its inherent dynamism and to stagnation in the economy. Over time, with the intensification of the contradiction between changing conditions and obsolete methods of management, economic relations and socialist management principles become deformed (bureaucratization of planning, formalization of cost accounting, the development of egalitarian trends in distribution, etc.).

The break [with old] methods of management and the transition to qualitatively new methods are an important law of economic progress and an indispensable condition to mastering the very rich potential and advantages of the socialist system for the planned management of the economy. As the experience of history has shown, this is a very complicated matter. The old methods are tenacious, and with the aid of their unique capacity for mimicry can last for a very long time when disguised under new names (especially when organizational structures and political institutions remain the same). Such adaptability presents quite a serious danger to every major reform.

Such phenomena can also be found today in the initial stage of the wholesale restructuring of the system of economic management. They are manifested in attempts to preserve the system of detailed regulation of production targets—a system repudiated by practice—

under the guise of the state order, to adapt economic norms to old forms of planning, and to emasculate the real content of self-financing. There is nothing unexpected in this. The modern situation only confirms the lesson of history: if there is to be serious success, we must struggle for the new tenaciously and stubbornly.

Restructuring requires overcoming the braking mechanism. In the given instance, we are referring not simply to a model but to a real and quite complex problem that is indeed a mechanism with links that are well connected to one another. Its essence is that the deformations of production relations that arise for a number of reasons, some of which have stemmed from the uniqueness of historical conditions in the nation's development, have over time acquired the features of inherent aspects of socialism. This has found reflection in economic theory, which has elevated the existing situation to the rank of an objective necessity. Deformations have thereby acquired "scientific" justification and have led to the appearance of serious flaws in theoretical views and conceptions.

Such principles of economic theory have formed the basis of the social consciousness, views, and convictions of more than one generation of Soviet people, and party, state, and economic leaders. These views in turn underlay the implementation of practical measures that reinforced the existing deformation of production relations and resulted in attempts to solve problems by using obsolete management techniques. The circle was completed and the braking mechanism proved to be a kind of self-reproducing system, all elements of which reinforced one another. From this it follows that overcoming the braking mechanism will not be an easy task. Meeting this goal requires a large number of measures and a considerable amount of time. At the same time, it is obvious that without this, it will be impossible to ensure the success of restructuring and to realize its objectives.

Principles of political economy in the restructuring of economic management

The clarity of theoretical positions and the thorough scientific substantiation of decisions and practical measures acquire great importance in the implementation of economic reforms, especially if they are of a radical nature. Here it is inadmissible to operate by trial and error, relying on common sense and having no precise theoretical conception.

Among the most important theoretical principles underlying the conception of restructuring of economic management it is necessary to single out the enrichment of notions of the very character and type of social progress. It is clear today that economic progress is not an independent phenomenon, but is closely linked to deep-going qualitative changes in the political, social, and cultural life of the nation. Only with the integrated, coordinated solution of problems that arise in the given spheres of life will it be possible to effect major changes in the economy. This does not in any way reject the decisive, fundamental character of changes in the economy. But under this interpretation, the very base is viewed not as an isolated sphere of public life, but as a link and component part of a unified, whole system of social reforms.

The integrated character of restructuring, as highlighted by the party, substantially distinguishes the present approaches to the resolution of current problems from the reform of the sixties, which tried to bring about radical improvements in the national economy exclusively through changes in the economic sphere. For this reason alone, it was in principle impossible to achieve a far-reaching improvement of the nation's economic situation.

Economic progress does not follow a straight line. All progress is a complex, contradictory phenomenon. Hence the possibility of zigzags along the path of its development, or "waves" which characterize the uniqueness of processes in social life and the variability of progressive reforms. It is also necessary to consider the possibility of dead-end directions or branches of social development. Sooner or later, movement in such a direction inevitably leads to stagnation and requires a decisive, radical break in order to return society and its economy to the path of forward progress.

Social progress in general, and economic progress in socialist society in particular, always occurs in struggle through overcoming the resistance of obsolete forms and conservative views. The historical experience amassed in seventy years of socialist construction shows that forms of economic relations and management techniques inherited from the past and alien to socialism are not the only inhibiting forces. Socialist production relations themselves in their concrete forms can continuously age, lose their stimulative role, and become a brake on social progress. Socialist but obsolete forms of production relations can be an inhibiting factor. An understanding of this circumstance will provide the necessary reference points required to locate the avenues of reform and restructuring.

An important feature of economic progress is the fact that it leads not to the simplification of economic life and its structures, not to the uniformity and unification of economic forms, but to the increasing complexity and natural increase in the diversity of forms of organization of economic life and management techniques. We can no longer picture things in a way that suggests that economic progress means the gradual elimination of various forms of public property or that it can be equated with an increase in the share of the state form of ownership of the means of production. On the contrary, as society matures, the forms of ownership (basic, derivative, and secondary) become more complex and diverse and incorporate numerous transitional forms.

It is equally wrong to view economic progress as movement toward the transition to ever larger enterprises and economic complexes as a form of a unilinear dependence. On the contrary, the very forms of production organization and types of primary links are becoming more diverse, which presupposes a flexible combination of large, medium-size, and small enterprises and associations of various types, including production, science-production, and production-trade enterprises and associations, etc. Various types of voluntary associations and associations of producers for the performance of joint functions are also possible. The forms of organization based on cost-accounting principles are becoming more complex and numerous because we are no longer searching for uniform ways of organizing cost accounting, without regard to the size of enterprises, branch specifics, and the uniqueness of their activity in different spheres and regions of the nation.

Finally, it must be emphasized that economic progress in socialist society requires the combination of both evolutionary and revolutionary forms. Their combination in a certain way and their consecutive replacement of one another are a natural aspect of the progressive development of the socialist economy. The need for revolutionary change develops when qualitative, deep changes occur in the economic base itself, in the productive forces, and in the type of expanded reproduction, and when pressing problems in socialist society are postponed rather than promptly resolved, i.e., when they become stratified, thereby dramatically aggravating all the contradictions in the economic system.

A central place among the theoretical underpinnings of the present restructuring of economic management belongs to the new understanding of public ownership, its multidimensionality, its complex internal structure, and the mechanism characterizing its economic realization. The elimination of such painful phenomena as the alienation of the worker and the work collective from management and the decision-making process, and the need to eradicate the bureaucratism that has afflicted the entire system of economic management is ultimately associated with property reform. The real content of democratic institutions and procedures and the transition to real self-management in society and the economy are also associated with the development of property relations.

The question of developing other forms of ownership in addition to the state form is attracting the attention of scholars and the public. It has become clear that all these forms are natural for the present stage of socialist development and that they ''work'' for the final goal—the improvement of the life of the people and the more complete satisfaction of their needs. However, this is not the most important or most difficult question in property theory, even though here too there is still much that has to be reinterpreted both in a theoretical sense and in the practical implementation of projected measures, in particular, in methods for regulating incomes, prices, etc.

The most complex and difficult question is how to secure the effective functioning of the state sector of the economy, how to secure the real and not formal coupling of the worker to the means of production, how to overcome the alienation, the ''no-man's-land'' character of state property, the indifferent attitude of the worker and the collective toward public property. How can the worker be instilled with a truly proprietary attitude toward social production? The development of full cost accounting, the introduction of self-financing principles, the transition to self-management on the scale of work collectives and territories—this is the search for effective forms of realizing public property and a functional mechanism appropriate to it. There are still many unresolved problems here on which must focus the political economy of socialism. At the same time, today it can be said that the purely formal character of socialist socialization of the means of production is manifested in the indicated processes (alienation of the worker from the management process, absence of the feeling of proprietorship, etc.). As regards the nature of property, it is not a "no-man's-land" in the strict sense of the term. However, the result of the alienation of the worker and the work collective from actual management is that the functions of the owner are usurped by various management organs. Therein lies the economic basis of bureaucratism. Property relations must be filled with real economic content, which will mean the actual socialization of production that began seventy years ago.

The restructuring process is inseparable from the activation of the social energy of the masses, which is only possible on the basis of the powerful driving force of economic processes. The theoretical interpretation of the subject matter of interests, their complex internal structure, and modes of expression and implementation occupies an important place in the theoretical substantiation of the system of management.

Economic science until now has been limited to [expounding] very primitive ideas about the three-part structure of interests: society, the collective, and the individual worker. In reality, the structure of interests is much more varied. In addition to primary interests, there are secondary and derivative interests that arise as a result of the social division of labor, including the isolation of management structures. There arises the complex problem of representing interests. In time, management bodies that are created to perform certain social functions, to express and protect common interests, acquire their own interests that may significantly differ from society's interests.

The necessary methodological approach to this problem was articulated by the founders of Marxism. Friedrich Engels wrote: "Society generates certain common functions that are indispensable to society. The pertinent people form a new branch of the division of labor *within society*. They thereby acquire special interests even vis-à-vis those who authorized them: they become independent toward them. . . ."[3] Each link in the complex hierarchical structure of management tries to identify and represent its own special interests, which are generated by their place in the social division of labor, with the interests of the state. Therein lies one of the deepest roots of existing bureaucratism.

The underassessment and denigration of the role of the individual is one of the serious problems in this regard. The individual and the human personality are frequently lost behind abstract conceptions of the good of society and improvements in the life of the people. Our traditional logic, which seems impeccable to the majority, is that the increased effectiveness of production and the higher level of well-being on the whole creates better conditions for each individual person. At the same time, it would seem that the founders of Marxism applied quite an opposite logic. It is they, as the theorists of real socialist humanism, who advanced the formula that the all-around development of the individual and his well-being are the prerequisite (specifically the prerequisite, not the result) to the free, comprehensive development of society. The sense of this formula is not to make them mutually exclusive, but to view society as a living aggregate of real individuals with their own features and personal uniqueness, not as a faceless mass or an aggregate of obliterated individualities. Professing a concern for the common good while ignoring individuality is one of the most serious distortions of the essence of the socialist ideal and the starting point of the bureaucratization of management.

The new conception of centralism and economic competition

The new conception of centralism is also based on wholesale reform of the system of managing the economy. The question of what the basic link of the national economy—the enterprise or association—should be and how it should function has been sufficiently formulated to date. This is reflected in numerous documents and state acts that define the position of the collective as the proprietor of means of production assigned to the enterprise and the position of the enterprise as a socialist commodity producer operating according to the principles of full cost accounting, self-financing, and self-management.

Considerably less attention has been devoted to the development of new approaches to the centralized management of the economy. However, it is clear that such fundamental questions as the transition to a new generation of machines, technological breakthroughs, the structural reorganization of the national economy, and changes in investment policy cannot in principle be decided at the level of the basic link. Their implementation requires serious modernization and increasing the effectiveness of the methods of centralized management. In connection therewith, formulating the new conception of centralism is regarded as one of the top-priority tasks of economic science.

Here it is important not to confuse the objective with the means. The formulation of the question of what is better—more or less centralism—just like the question of which is better—more or less independence—is in principle incorrect. Neither centralism nor independence is the objective. They do not possess the property of a target function, and therefore, as they develop it is impossible to judge whether this is good or bad.

The target function is given by the socioeconomic system. It is connected with the increase in the effectiveness of production, with the growth of labor productivity, with the improvement of product quality, and ultimately with the betterment of people's lives. Centralism must be broadened or narrowed to the extent that it promotes the optimal attainment of the objective or that it corresponds to the demands of socialism.

A distinguishing feature of the new conception of centralism is the understanding that it must be realized with the aid of economic methods. Economic methods proper are not a supplement to centralism but are an internal aspect of centralized planned management of the socialist economy, its intrinsic content. Economic methods are a form of realization of centralized planned management that is appropriate to socialism; they are the management of interests through interests.

In the modern conception of centralism, a large role belongs to state orders, norms, and the system of direct economic ties. While production is for the most part oriented toward the consumer, toward the better satisfaction of his needs, priority belongs to the satisfaction of society's needs. The state order is the mode of satisfaction of priority, especially significant, strategic, and socially important needs. It accordingly has a restricted sphere of application and must secure priority for the producer and must as a rule be placed on a competitive basis.

The assignment of control figures of a nonobligatory nature and the elimination of their administrative character are also of fundamental significance in the new conception of centralism. The control figures orient the producer, especially the enterprises, toward the changes that society intends to make, and they inform work collectives of changes in the structure of production, on rising or declining demand for certain types of products. Therefore they perform a new (hitherto unknown) orientational-informational function in planning. Such instruments of centralized management as norms, ceilings, prices, taxes, financial and credit instruments, etc., also have a new look in the given conception.

The question of the very structure of economic management bodies, which are not by any means identical with state administrative bodies, is also fundamentally important. Economic management bodies proper are needed only to the extent that they promote the better, more effective work of the primary links of social production. The point here is not that central and middle-level management bodies should delegate some of their rights downward—to enterprises and associations. It appears here that logic dictates the direct opposite. Economic management bodies must implement the functions and types of activity that the producers themselves either are unable to perform or cannot perform effectively. In other words, they must be created as being born of the common interests of producers and must fulfill the functions that are delegated to them from below by the work collectives of enterprises and associations. Economic management bodies express their common interests and are necessary only as long as they promote the optimal satisfaction of joint needs. Otherwise they become a superfluous bureaucratic incrustation on the economic system. They cease to be a driving force and instead become a brake on economic progress.

One more part of the theoretical underpinning of the restructuring of the system of management arises from formulation of the questions involved in economic competition, in the development of the socialist market, in the elimination or at least attenuation of monopolistic trends in the national economy

It is crucially important to emphasize that commodity-monetary relations, the market, and competition are categories that have a certain general economic content independent of the social specifics of a given social system. Naturally, in every society they are included in the unified system of production relations and are invested with a specific social content that is characteristic of a certain mode of production. Nevertheless, it is also necessary to recognize their general social nature, i.e., the dual content of the given relations and categories. Therefore, the development and broad use of commodity-monetary instruments, the activation of market relations, and increasing the role of economic competition do not in any way mean a return to the past or the borrowing of bourgeois management techniques. We have in mind the use of functions, under new conditions and in a new social environment, that are inherent in these conditions as general economic phenomena. Arriving at such a conception involves overcoming the underassessment of these categories and their neglect.

The use of the market will make it possible flexibly to regulate economic processes, to simplify relations between producers and consumers, and to ensure freedom in the selection of partners, including the selection of suppliers. The very freedom of choice as an element of the socialist market will make it possible to activate a powerful lever—economic competition, including competition between state enterprises as well as between state and cooperative enterprises. After all, the creation of cooperatives stems not only from the necessity of filling the breach that originates in state trade, in public catering, and in the service sphere. They must ensure healthy competition. They must give the consumer the right to choose the sphere and form of realization of their incomes and ways of satisfying needs. The sense of economic competition ultimately consists in the better and free satisfaction of public and personal needs.

All this naturally requires resolute struggle against monopolistic trends and phenomena that inevitably lead to inhibition and stagnation. Lenin called attention to this aspect of monopoly, emphasizing that any monopoly, and not only one based on private ownership, is a factor of stagnation.[4] Economic competition has numerous forms of manifestation. They first of all include competition for the best satisfaction of needs and the struggle for the customer. Competition must be widely developed in the scientific-technological sphere, overcoming the monopolistic situation of individual research groups, institutes, and scientific collectives. The most important decisions in the scientific-technological sphere must as a rule be adopted on a competitive basis. Economic competition must also be applied to the utilization of state resources, including credit.

Practical measures that are implemented in the restructuring process must be based specifically on this new understanding of the role of the market, economic competition, and the activation of the driving forces of scientific-technological, economic and social progress in this regard.

Problems and contradictions in the initial stages of restructuring

The restructuring of economic management will be a long, complex process. It is impossible to count here on an immediate return, on rapid change. The objective need arises for a certain "transitional period," in the course of which elements of the old and the new will inevitably be combined in economic management. It is also clear that the new cannot be affirmed easily and without struggle, without overcoming the resistance of inhibiting forces. In supporting the program for restructuring economic management in his final works, Lenin said that in order to realize the given tasks [I know that] "devilish persistence will be required, that in the first few years at least work in this field will be hellishly hard. Nevertheless, I am convinced that only with such effort shall we be able to achieve our aim, and that only by achieving this aim shall we create a republic that is really worthy of the name of Soviet, socialist. . . ."[5]

M. S. Gorbachev's report "The October Revolution and Restructuring: the Revolution Continues" contained fundamentally important evaluations of these questions. It noted that notwithstanding the broad support for the reforms by the working people, it would be wrong not to see a certain strengthening of the resistance of the conservative forces that view restructuring as a threat to their selfish interests and goals. And this is manifested not only in various management links but also in work collectives. The forces of conservatism can be expected to exploit any difficulties in order to discredit restructuring and evoke the dissatisfaction of the working people.

One of the important contradictions of the initial stage of restructuring consists in the fact that the new tasks as a rule have to be realized within the framework of the old organizational forms and with the old cadres. Unfortunately, there is no other avenue to take. This requires a sufficiently clear understanding [of the objectives] and also the creation of a broad "people's front" of restructuring, the unification of all healthy, progressive forces around the goals and tasks of reform. Only in this way will it be possible to resolve the indicated contradictions and to break down the resistance.

Of course, it must be kept in mind that in the initial stage, in the absence of the necessary democratic traditions and experience, certain costs are inevitable. But to fear them, to try and insure against all contingencies is completely unjustified, since such an approach will doom us to passivity and sluggishness. Unfortunately, here, too, we encounter today what Lenin noted back in the first years of Soviet power, specifically, the fact that our revolutionary boldness and readiness for all large-scale reforms, for radical change in the economic and social sphere combine with amazing timidity as regards very minor reforms in office routine.[6] Learning this lesson of the past, the lesson of our entire historical experience, is important today so that we do not repeat it, so that we do not stop in the face of bourgeois impediments that seriously weaken the social activism and energy of the masses.

The danger of illusions and the subsequent disappointment associated with them is one of the problems in the initial stage of restructuring which can seriously weaken the activism of the masses in the struggle for it. We must always be realists in all things, we must see what can be done in a short time and what cannot be done.

The experience we have accumulated in the years of implementing socialist reforms shows that together with the formulation and solution of large-scale problems, there arises the heightened danger of simplistic utopian views in science and in everyday thinking. In the words of Lenin, "great historical tasks frequently give rise to great visions, which develop side by side with many small, unsuccessful dreams."[7] Utopianism is generated by new problems in the absence of the corresponding knowledge and by the striving for the earliest possible attainment of the objective. At the present time, utopianism is associated with simplistic views of acceleration—our country's speedy attainment of the leading edge of scientific-technological progress and the fastest possible restructuring of social relations. Utopian notions ignore transitional stages; they present transitional forms as final goals and as the corresponding results. Utopianism frequently originates from the exaggeration of the potential of legislative power and the notion that the adoption of a decree or law almost automatically leads to corresponding practical reforms.

No less a danger is presented by so-called excesses, when attempts are made to solve new problems with old, traditional methods or to extend new methods to spheres in which they are not applicable. We are encountering this today. It is sufficient to cite the excesses committed in the fight against unearned income, which not only diminish the energy of reforms but also discredit restructuring in the eyes of the broad masses.

Comprehension of the lessons of historical experience is called upon to provide us with theoretical armament and to arouse the social energy of the reforms. The inspiring goals of the October Revolution serve as a mighty incentive to carry out the program for the restructuring of Soviet society, to raise it to qualitatively new levels of economic and social progress.

Notes

1. V. I. Lenin, *Polnoe sobranie sochinenii*, vol. 44, p. 224.
2. Ibid., vol. 43, p. 231.
3. Karl Marx and Friedrich Engels, *Sochineniia*, vol. 37, p. 416.
4. See Lenin, vol. 27, p. 397
5. Ibid., vol. 45, p. 392.
6. Ibid., p. 400.
7. Ibid., vol. 39, p. 411.

B. P. KURASHVILI

Restructuring and the Enterprise

Whether restructuring becomes a deep socioeconomic and political reform or just one more superficial administrative reorganization depends primarily on the degree to which there is substantive change in the enterprise's status in the economic mechanism. We understand the economic mechanism to mean the regulatory subsystem of the economic system that incorporates state management of the national economy, production self-management of enterprises, and in part the spontaneous regulation of economic relations.

Why is the objective necessity of restructuring beset by losses of tempo and scale? In our view, this is the result of the negative aspect of the "human factor": the lack of professional and psychological preparedness of the administrative apparatus for modern methods of management, and the temporary, not entirely favorable correlation of "reformers," "semireformers," "semiconservatives," and "conservatives" in this apparatus. The lack of theoretical clarity on the economic and legal principles of the new economic mechanism is another factor. Therefore, the discussion of these principles and the construction of a theoretical economic-legal model of the status of the enterprise in this economic mechanism remain an urgent matter even after the adoption of the Law on the State Enterprise.

Russian text © 1988 by "Nauka" Publishers and "Ekonomika i organizatsiia promyshlennogo proizvodstva." "Perestroika i predpriiatie," *Ekonomika i organizatsiia promyshlennogo proizvodstva,* 1987, no. 10, pp. 3–30.

The author holds a doctor's degree in juridical sciences and is affiliated with the Institute of State and Law of the USSR Academy of Sciences, Moscow.

This article is published for the purposes of discussion.

Basic features of the existing mechanism
and their sources

What do we understand the old status of the enterprise to mean? From what should we proceed when we reject one and preserve another in order to create that which is new? Let us turn to the thirties when a different economic mechanism was formed and took the place of the mechanism that developed under NEP [New Economic Policy]. NEP was not only a ''new'' policy (which superseded War Communism) but was a normal economic policy as well. In the words of V. I. Lenin, it was introduced in this capacity ''in all earnestness and for a long time to come.'' The most important aspect of NEP was not the NEPman [the private trader who flourished during the NEP period] nor even *prodnalog* [tax in kind in the form of foodstuffs], but was rather cost accounting in combination with state planning.

In theory, NEP could, by undergoing gradual modification, secure the construction of total socialism and function in the stage of its maturity. But history deemed otherwise. The specific conditions, particularly the mounting threat of military attack by imperialism, forced the curtailment of this normal economic policy and its replacement with an extraordinary policy. It can be debated whether the extraordinary policy was historically necessary or whether it was voluntaristically foisted on the nation by the erstwhile political leadership. No matter what the outcome of this debate, it remains an incontrovertible fact that the extraordinary economic policy replaced NEP and that within its framework there formed an economic mechanism which in the thirties and forties fully performed (unfortunately at a dear price) its historical mission of ensuring the survival and consolidation of socialism in the USSR and promoting the formation of the world socialist system.

In the fifties it became objectively necessary to replace the second (after War Communism) extraordinary policy with the second (after NEP) normal economic policy. The need for this abrupt change was acknowledged in economic discussions in the early fifties. But three decades passed, and the given historical task was still not realized. What is more, it is only now being seriously posed under the name of restructuring [*perestroika*]. Two generations of political leaders were unable to rise to the level of this task and left a debt-encumbered legacy to their successors. The ignoring of objective regularities of development over a period of thirty years proved costly to society and formed a powerful inert system of social relations and social forces behind them which is now considerably more difficult to change than it was in the past.

In our view, the postwar economic mechanism, especially in the seventies and first half of the eighties, externally closely resembles the economic mechanism of the thirties and forties in its basic features, but unfortunately, it has lost its systemic nature and together with it its effectiveness. *The present economic mechanism has turned into an internally uncoordinated, distorted external semblance of the mechanism of the extraordinary period of development.*

The changes that have been made in it in the last thirty years do not compare in any way with those that occurred in the process of development of the socialist mode of production. *First of all, two fundamental changes have not been properly taken into account: the dramatic rise in the skill level and in the cultural and educational makeup of the work force, and the natural change in the motivations behind their economic behavior.* The reference is to the change from self-sacrifice in labor, from minimum demands on the level and differentiation of consumption that typified the extraordinary conditions, to a larger share of material interests, persistent demands for the consistent implementation of the principle of just socialist distribution of material and nonmaterial goods according to one's labor.

Thus, the economic mechanism was not adapted not only to these profound and complex changes but even to relatively simple and obvious changes—the manifold growth of the scale of the national economy and its intensification based on advances in scientific-technological progress. Both one and the other exclude the possibility of rational management when it is extremely centralized and when the initiative and creativity of the managed are rigidly restricted.

The stability of socialism and the consolidation of the positions of the USSR in the international arena were already secured. It demanded work, inhuman effort, mass asceticism, and the people's understanding of the need for a strict, authoritarian political regime, which in principle cannot be eternal under socialism. At the same time, we were absolutely unable to rid ourselves of many methods of management that were characteristic of the "besieged fortress" but that became incomprehensible, senseless, and unnecessary and that hindered the spiritual life and social activism of citizens once the "siege had been lifted and the enemy had been thrown back."

The enormous creative potential of socialist society was driven into the channel of merely fulfilling tasks (always necessary but not sufficient), and innovative ideas regarding avenues of the future development of socialism were suppressed, not supported. The semistagnant development of the economy generated a noncreative atmosphere in public life. This atmosphere in turn tended to perpetuate the obsolete economic mechanism. Everything was supposed to begin with the economy, but it did not begin, even though some things were, naturally, accomplished.

Broadly speaking, in what way was the adaptation of the economic mechanism to the fundamentally new conditions of social development expressed? The changes have been primarily in two directions. First, the scale of application of coercive measures has attenuated and diminished. [But] this correct line of development could not in itself produce a breakthrough. It had to be combined with a positive program. This was generally understood. The second direction called for positive changes in the economic mechanism. Their general character was correctly understood: the need was not for the one-sided realization of the principle of democratic centralism but for reform; not for the weakening but for the reform of the centralist principle, the strengthening of the democratic principle, and the expansion of the rights of enterprises.

But a specific, satisfactory solution to this twofold, dialectically contradictory problem was not found in the last thirty years. This was one of the most painful dramas in the history of socialism. This explains the *value of the experience derived from the failures that accompanied the search for this solution. If we fail to understand this [experience] and if we continue in the same spirit, the painful drama of socialism may become a tragedy.*

In our view, the most salient feature derived from the unsuccessful search for the new economic mechanism consists in the attempt to design it on the basis of mandatory planning. There was the certainty (or merely the appearance of certainty) that it was unshakable. Everything else was judged on the basis of this premise. As a result, the economic mechanism that formed in the mid-eighties was not devoid of logic—not so much socioeconomic logic and the logic of interacting interests as command logic (orders and their execution), which was close and understandable to the managerial apparatus. But economics is not considered to be this kind of logic!

The weaknesses of the present economic mechanism and its lack of correspondence to the times are not so obvious. This explains the tenacity of the illusion that the mechanism itself is not bad but that the cadres are deficient in their mastery and use of the mechanism. *Many believe that cadres and not the system of management decide everything today as in the past.* But why did this system foster good-for-nothing cadres? This question is not usually asked. Instead there are references to fortuities or to the fact that the wrong people were at the helm at a certain time. From this subjective idealistic judgment (which, however, is not devoid of a certain degree of persuasiveness), it is concluded that it would be well to try once more to extend the life of the customary economic mechanism (naturally after improving it) rather than embarking on the difficult, risky road of its restructuring.

The other argument against such a position is to look the truth in the eye, to see the hidden weaknesses and vices of the obsolete mechanism and, above all, to approach it with the rigorous criterion of revolutionary socialist practice. Is it enough apologetically to exploit the customary criterion? Does the economic mechanism guarantee the attainment of success in comparison with the past? Such successes come even when development is semistagnant. Today's level is naturally higher than ever before in the past. This is good, but it is not enough. The time has come to proceed from another criterion worthy of a mighty socialist power: Do the successes correspond to the nature and potential of socialism; can the existing economic mechanism ensure our historically natural superiority over the developed capitalist countries and leading positions in the world economy?

We repeat that the present economic mechanism is an eroded semblance of the mechanism that existed under the extraordinary conditions of development. Both—the prototype and the semblance—are based on mandatory state planning, on the assignment of plan targets to enterprises ("industrial allocation" [*promrazverstka*]). However, mandatory planning today is much weaker. It has in fact ceased to fulfill its integrating functions satisfactorily and reliably. It is incapable of withstanding the disorganizing force of departmental parochialism, the unnatural dominance of producer over customer, and the abuse of formal indicators. Departments (especially "cost-accounting" departments) do not so much oversee enterprises as become one with them and help them to obtain group benefits at society's expense.

The obsolete economic mechanism and the unsatisfactory system of managing the national economy have engendered a host of economic anomalies. They include the disproportionality and imbalance in the production of interconnected products; structural skewness in the production apparatus to the detriment of the branches that predetermine technological progress and the rapid "nonevolutionary" growth of labor productivity; the chronic scarcity of one product and the constant overproduction of another; the incompleteness, inefficiency, and unreliability of material-technical supply; the rapid growth of above-norm inventories and their immobilization; the striving for self-sufficiency in production, which compensates for flaws in supply; the underutilization of the advantages of specialization; the substantial underutilization of equipment; the uneconomical expenditure of material and financial resources; unjustified new construction; protracted construction; delays in the assimilation of new capacities; the untimely installation of equipment; the wasteful, frequently predatory exploitation of natural wealth; the low quality of the greater part of the output of many branches, which is "compensated" by the increase in the volume of production; the lack of substantiation and unbalanced nature of many wholesale and retail prices; the padding of performance figures and other falsifications of primary accounting data that compromise the authenticity of statistical data; the static, backward product mix; technological conservatism—slow or ostentatious introduction or even the undisguised nonintroduction of scientific-technological advances; the adverse structure of foreign trade (the predominance of raw materials and semifinished goods in exports, much like underdeveloped countries, and in imports—finished goods that we can produce more profitably ourselves); weak differentiation in pay; unwarranted leveling at enterprises and in the work force, resulting in the undermining of labor morality and the fostering of a sense of dependency; the largely artificial shortage of labor resources; personnel turnover; and mass theft in production.

Behind each of these manifestations of insane, unrestrained mismanagement are many billions [of rubles] in damage in the form of direct losses and lost profits. In general, the damage involved is comparable in magnitude to the national income. Because of mismanagement, our level of labor productivity is 2-3 times lower than that of the developed capitalist countries. As sociological research shows, "scarcely one-third of the entire work force is working as hard as it can."[1] It is difficult to measure the moral and political damage, but the extent of it is clear. Only the great vital force of socialism is saving our country from general crisis. This is what we have come to! This is the bill that the people and the party can and should submit to the obsolete economic mechanism, and hence also to advocates of its "improvement," which in fact amounts to its perpetuation.

A step forward

The June 1987 Plenum of the CPSU Central Committee formulated and resolved questions relating to the radical reform of economic management more systematically and concretely than heretofore. There is no need to exaggerate or understate the role of its decisions. As M. S. Gorbachev stated at the plenum, "they provide fundamental guideposts for the restructuring of the economy. Of course, much is still suggested by practical experience. Actual events will give us a deeper understanding of restructuring. New problems and many difficulties await us. There is no guarantee that we will not make mistakes. . . ." In other words, the ongoing changes are only a certain stage in a long and complex process.

Even with the adoption of the Law on the State Enterprise (Association), restructuring does not go beyond the framework of the initial stage. From the standpoint of the future of the Soviet economy, it is rash and dangerous not to see the contradictory, half-hearted, intermediate character of the legislative decisions that have been adopted. They are the fruit of a temporary compromise between radical and conservative approaches, between initiators of cardinal reform and the inert, bureaucratized management apparatus that uses "restructuring" phraseology to mask its conservative positions and suggestions.

The Law on the Enterprise proclaims and strengthens new or newly understood principles and elements of organization of socialist management. They include the definition of the enterprise as a socialist commodity producer; the use of public property by the work collective "as the proprietor," a separate part of which is "owned" by the enterprise; the customer's priority in economic relations; the consistent implementation of the principle of distribution according to one's labor at the enterprise level, and in connection with this the economic competition of enterprises for the satisfaction of concrete social needs; full cost accounting; the distribution of income between society and the enterprise on the basis of economically substantiated norms; the restriction of monopoly and the halting of attempts to abuse monopoly powers; the broad self-management of work collectives; the right of enterprises to make any decision that does not contradict legislation at its own initiative and without special permission ("everything that is not forbidden is permitted"); the enterprise's acquisition of materials (including means of production) through direct ties and wholesale trade; the application of contract prices; independence in establishing cooperative and integrative relations with other enterprises; and the independence of enterprises to engage in foreign economic activity.

All these provisions are extremely important. However, their practical significance is diminished by the fact that they are in many cases not expressed in sufficiently concrete terms. More than half of the Law consists of theoretical judgments, wishes, and indefinite prescriptions. Its "deeds"—legal norms—do not by any means always correspond to its "words." Many norms essentially preserve elements of the obsolete economic mechanism and block radical changes in it. This applies first of all to the system of planning. The Law would seem to depart from mandatory planning. Article 10.3 states that control figures "are not mandatory and must not hinder the work collective in the formulation of its plan, and must give it wide latitude in making decisions and selecting partners in the process of concluding economic contracts." It might seem that control figures merely orient the enterprise in an economic situation. But in accordance with Article 9.1, control figures are "assigned" to the enterprise by a higher body and are "conveyed" to it. It is more than likely, depending on the reaction of an enterprise to the given control figures, that the higher body will make decisions that are favorable or unfavorable to the enterprise on the basis of economic norms, on the basis of centrally allocated material-technical supplies (this "rationing system" will not soon relinquish its dominant place to wholesale trade), on the basis of the surviving, as it follows from Article 15.3, "serfdom"—the system of assigning customers to suppliers; and on the approval or nonapproval of the elected enterprise manager in his post. In a word, enterprises "have nowhere to go" and will accept the control figures that are conveyed to them just as they accepted the mandatory plan targets before the Law. One can be certain that the apparatus that developed and conveyed the control figures to the enterprise "will not allow" its works, which justify its very existence, to "come to naught," even if these control figures are economically absurd. The "replacement" of obligatory plan targets by formally nonobligatory but actually obligatory control figures is perceived as the transition from open to shameful mandatory planning. To be sure, within a slightly restricted framework, since control figures are conveyed to the enterprise once in five years, while annual plans are "formulated and approved by the enterprise independently, based on its five-year plan and the economic contracts that are concluded"; the control figures include a substantially smaller number of indicators compared with those contained in the plan.

Or let us take another innovation—the state order that is given to the enterprise. The step forward here consists in the fact that the order is given not for all output (as was the case in the plan) but for the part that is necessary primarily to realize public and social tasks, to fulfill scientific-technological programs, to strengthen the nation's defense capacity and economic independence, for the delivery of agricultural produce, and for the activation of production capacities and facilities in the social sphere financed by state centralized capital investments. What is more, state orders "must provide for the reciprocal responsibility of the parties—the producer-supplier and the customer." It is true that the parties do not have equal rights. The enterprise may not reject state orders that are economically unprofitable to it. According to Article 10.3, they "must obligatorily be included in the plan" which is "independently" formulated and approved by the enterprise. Such is the independence that is measured off for the enterprise. The proclaimed transition from predominantly administrative to predominantly economic methods of management has not reached too far as yet.

In addition to changes in the system of planning, this transition requires cost-accounting relations that are "horizontally" and "vertically" harmonious. They are based on the legislative recognition of the economic competition between enterprises and their socialist labor competition. In its unity with comradely cooperation, it incorporates the inner driving force behind socialist production. The greater the latitude of the objective laws governing commodity-monetary relations, the more complete and consistent will its action be.

Under socialism, commodity-monetary relations alone ensure the sufficient equivalent exchange between enterprises under the conditions of the division and cooperation of social labor. Without such exchange, there can be no distribution on the basis of one's labor. It is time to admit that in the foreseeable future as well there will not be another mechanism that would guarantee the equivalence of exchange. State government is not suited to this function and does not have adequate means to discharge it.

Under the extraordinary conditions that existed at one time, the state assumed the distribution function not by any means for the purpose of securing equivalent exchange and thereby distribution according to labor, but rather it did so for opposite reasons for which it was specifically suited. Then (and indeed now, only on a different scale) the state ensured by official decree the necessary nonequivalence of exchange for the satisfaction of national interests. Equivalent exchange and commodity-monetary relations were relegated to the background in order to transfer resources from agriculture to industry, and within industry—from light to heavy industry, from civilian industry to the defense industry. As a result, only incomplete, book-keeping cost accounting, which at best has a resource-saving effect, was possible.

Today this is not enough. There must be room for economic competition. Specifically economic competition and not competition in the sphere of clever account-padding, obtaining nonintensive plans, jacked-up prices, and scarce resources by playing up to the higher-ups, which is what some enterprises owe their "percentage" successes to today. Thus, there is need for an arbiter who will objectively and impartially sum up the results of economic competition. It can only take the form of the socialist market, whose success in coping with this task is inversely proportional to the state's interference in its functioning, in the honest competitive struggle of enterprises.

When the state proclaims and formulates full cost accounting, it thereby restricts its distributive function to the necessary minimum and basically relies on the controlling mechanism of economic self-regulation. This is how it is in principle. But the matter becomes more complex with the transition from the old to the new economic mechanism. The old economic mechanism, which deliberately disrupted the equivalence of exchange through price policy, led to the general and deep disorganization of the system of prices. An economically substantiated system must now be formed. Without such a system, full cost accounting, economic competition, and socialist competition may undeservedly and unjustly elevate certain enterprises while bringing others to the verge of bankruptcy. This danger must be recognized, even though it is clear that in the transitional period, restrictions on full cost accounting are inevitable and they are envisaged in the Law on the Enterprise.

In accordance with Articles 3.1 and 14.4, the wage fund is formed both according to the residual principle (which is natural for truly full cost accounting) and according to the normative principle, i. e., at the discretion of the higher authorities. It is assumed that the state will extend the first or second variant to branches and enterprises with regard to the different economic conditions of their activity. The normative principle is applied in the event of dubious prices, a monopolistic situation, scarcity, and other factors that preclude honest competition. At the same time, the wage-fund-formation norm assigned to the enterprise will be based not so much on normal branch profitability and rent adjustments [*rentnye popravki*] as (we should not close our eyes to this) an attempt to make it fit the "sufficient" wage level. Distribution based on the results of economic competition will give way to conventional distribution "from above," and "full" cost accounting will become a mere makeweight of such distribution.

The shamefully preserved mandatory planning and the very conditional, if not sham, fullness of cost accounting are in our view the basic shortcomings of the Law on the Enterprise. They require explanation. Like any compromise solution, the Law reflected the correlation of advocates and opponents of reform and the measure of partial and temporary coincidence of their interests and goals. For radical reform, it is unquestionably preferable that the Law immediately reinforce the final goal of the new economic mechanism. However, in the existing situation we can also be satisfied with an intermediate model just as soon as it meets the conditions of the transitional period and helps to overcome what the June 1987 Plenum of the CPSU Central Committee called "precrisis forms." Naturally, such a content of the Law prescribes that it will short-lived. But there is all the more basis for creating over time a truly stable law, a law that is more perfect from a legal standpoint.

Shameful mandatory planning and "limited-full" cost accounting in large measure mean the preservation of administrative methods of management, and thereby the existing bureaucratized management apparatus which is the main carrier of conservative tendencies. This is the most dangerous element of compromise. We should recall, however, that the Bolsheviks once resorted to such a compromise—the Brest-[Litovsk] Peace [Treaty]—and their confidence that it would be repudiated by the turn of events proved to be justified.

The Law on the Enterprise could also be better, but let us be realists: the Law has already been adopted. Its practical implementation will take place in the struggle between advocates of restructuring—for the most part, work collectives of leading enterprises, their managers, and progressive management apparatus personnel—and its opponents. The general principle in the Law and certain tangible movements or at least motions in the direction of the new, optimal economic mechanism give advocates of restructuring support such as they never had before in the struggle for reform. The Law therefore represents a step forward in our development. While it offers no guarantees that the old economic mechanism will not be restored, it makes it less likely and lays the foundation for subsequent steps, including the formation of a new system of planning and the cost-accounting relations corresponding to it.

Toward a new planning system

Which relations will have to be regulated first of all? The relations between the state and enterprises regarding the planning of their activity, and relations relating to the realization of cost accounting. The former predetermine the latter. It is not for nothing that the planning system is called the heart of management.

Our bitter thirty-year experience of semistagnant development, which included correct but unfortunately half-hearted measures exemplified by the "semireform" of 1965, a host of relatively unproductive, partial measures, and the experience of socialist countries, permit us to say that not mandatory, but orientational, indirect, regulative planning must become the dominant form of state planning of the activity of enterprises.

What is its essence? Let us examine it from the enterprises' standpoint.

The state determines the levels of production of various products, the basic directions of development of production, and its progressive structural changes, and it conveys the appropriate targets to organs that manage the national economy and allocates the corresponding material and financial resources to them. The organs of management do not distribute their targets among enterprises but only orient them by encouraging the production of those products that are declared to be priority items based on the economic conditions that have formed for the plan period.

Enterprises independently devise and adopt plans governing their activity (basic and subsidiary, specialized and nonspecialized, but technologically and economically profitable). These plans are based on a portfolio of orders that have been concluded, in particular, with state organs on an equal basis. Higher organs conclude contracts with enterprises that define the directions and conditions of state incentives for production classified in the priority category during a given plan period. These contracts concern centrally allocated materials and equipment, subsidies for capital construction or the reconstruction of production, the granting of credit, etc. A plan that meets society's needs is formed in this way. It is registered by a higher organ. Registration is not the same as approval. The refusal to register a plan does not revoke it but only deprives an enterprise which insists that its plan is correct of state support.

Let us now examine the essence of regulative planning from the state's position. Will not regulative planning be weak, flawed, "planless" [*besplanovyi*]. In our view, it will not. The denial of the effectiveness and the very possibility of regulative planning as the state-power determination of the parameters and perspectives of production attests to insufficient knowledge and in some cases to speculation on the lack of knowledge. Denial on the basis that these parameters and perspectives are not directly prescribed from top to bottom but are ultimately attained through the state-regulated economic mechanism, which also includes "shadowy" and spontaneous aspects that cannot be eliminated from economic life (therefore, the given form of planning can be called regulative, even though other names are not excluded).

State centralized regulative planning has certain advantages over mandatory planning. First, regulative planning has a healthy information base: summarized data on preplan agreements between enterprises which reflect both social needs—the sum of orders—and the production potential—accepted orders, refusals, unutilized capacity. Today, at a time when enterprises are interested in lower plan targets, this information is hopelessly distorted.

Second, the state is relieved of the necessity of overseeing everything. It knows where society's needs are satisfied even without its intervention in the process of economic self-regulation. And hence it can concentrate its efforts in areas in which such intervention is actually necessary.

Third, when the state has a stronger sense of the objective nature of economic processes and fewer temptations to engage in economic voluntarism, it can calculate the directions and methods of its influence on production more precisely. In some cases, this will take the form of credit, ensuring the better utilization of production capacities and their modernization; in others, it will mean the creation of new capacities oriented toward revolutionary change in production and the uneven growth of labor productivity. It is specifically in investment policy and in the formation of new enterprises and entire branches that the state unconditionally plays the leading role, since it can mobilize the enormous resources that are concentrated in its hands.

Consequently, the strategic role of the state in economic development is secured entirely by regulative planning. It is true that it is secured in a different way than in the case of mandatory planning, but that is another matter. The state uses mandatory planning under extraordinary conditions to subordinate production (to the extent that this generally possible) to the laws of political struggle, to the attainment of political objectives that are characteristic of the given conditions. Lenin's well-known thesis regarding the precedence of politics over economics is realized thus. Given this approach, the state intervenes in the economic process (to the extent that this is possible without destroying its foundations) imperiously and abruptly, breaking and bending it to a certain degree and authoritatively directing production by assigning plan targets that must be unconditionally met. While this does not mean the revocation of economic laws, their action is nevertheless restricted and they are in a sense relegated to a secondary position.

By applying regulative planning, the state deliberately involves itself in the economic process, draws on the support of its laws, formulates economic policy on the basis of the use of these laws, and consequently subordinates economic policy to itself. While sharing the privilege and burden of planning with enterprises, it not only does not lose its strategic role, but on the contrary, performs it optimally under normal, nonextraordinary conditions. Probably the only one who fails to see this is the one who is very nostalgic for the difficult but heroic past, the one who closes his eyes to the fact that only the external effects remain from the former effectiveness of mandatory planning.

How can the adoption of maximally intensive plans be secured? Mandatory planning merely exerts pressure on the enterprises. Regulative planning creates economic conditions that themselves incontestably force the collectives to adopt intensive but realistic plans, since their well-being depends entirely on this and not on the percent of fulfillment of plan targets. Regulative planning is capable of eliminating work for "percent" from economic life, since the selfish manipulation of percent will make no sense. But if the economic conditions themselves motivate enterprises to work honestly and intensively, the slightly altered words of a person in the serial "The Investigation is Being Conducted by Experts" can be applied to mandatory planning: What the hell do we need this pressure for?! . . . We can concentrate on the organization of fruitful cooperation between the state and enterprises in the normal planned process.

The basic advantage of regulative planning over mandatory planning is that it is democratic. This is not only ideologically and politically good, it is also economically beneficial as well. The subjects of planning (the state and enterprises) through their collaboration reveal the advantages and conquer their weaknesses. How? The state apparatus, if it fulfills its purpose and does its work, constantly studies common and future social needs and forecasts their dynamics. The enterprise, on the other hand, is closer to the current detailed needs of its specific customers—its clients. Each subject of planning makes decisions in areas where it is better informed and hence stronger. And where it is weaker, it merely expresses its opinion, which, to be sure, is not devoid of normative content. That is, each has its advantages in areas where it can do the general work better than the other. At the same time, the state, by nature of the questions addressed by it and by virtue of its right to dispose over considerable resources, plays the leading role and determines the strategy of development. Its purpose, in our view, consists specifically therein and not in the demonstration of its "capacity for issuing directives."

Regulative planning is organic to socialism and is on the whole incomparably more effective economically than mandatory planning. Socially, this form ensures better than any other the high social activism of the working people, their creative participation in the management of the enterprise and society's affairs in general. Regulative planning as the predominant (but not exclusive) form of state planning is inseparable from the development of socialist democracy and socialist self-government. Without it, these concepts become meaningless declarations that are devoid of vitality.

Does this mean that mandatory planning has to be abandoned entirely? Clearly, it does not. It is characteristic of extraordinary conditions but may have advantages over regulative planning even under normal conditions. Branches of the national economy differ from one another as objects of planning. It is our perennial misfortune that we do not reckon with this objective reality. And even if we recognize it, we try to "consider" differences in branches eclectically, squeezing into mandatory planning amendments and supplements that contradict its nature and corrupt it. As a result, we have an amorphous "universal" form of planning that does not satisfy the needs of the national economy, that does more to disorganize than organize it. It remains afloat only because it is pleasant to the ear and "creates work" for the government apparatus.

The goal of the state is to organize the national economy as a unified whole, to secure the common and long-range interests of society. With respect to most branches, this can, in our view, be best achieved on the basis of regulative planning; with respect to a few branches, it is best achieved on the basis of mandatory planning. This is to say that we are discussing the partial retention of mandatory planning. It must be regarded as a necessity, not a virtue; we must abandon it where possible and tolerate it where necessary.

Under present international and production conditions, it seems premature and frivolous to abandon mandatory planning in the defense industry, fuel and energy industry, and in transport. Why specifically in these branches? In them, it is as yet practically impossible to abandon the monopolistic position of the producers. And hence it is dangerous to give them broad independence in the area of planning, to allow them into the "garden" of full cost accounting where they will invariably exploit the advantages of their situation. What is more, in the interests of the national economy these branches have the general obligation to develop with guaranteed stability and at a relatively more rapid pace. The state can ensure this by efficiently maneuvering resources and resorting to the necessary costs. Nor can we fail to consider the fact that these branches require production discipline that is uniform on a national scale (essentially a semimilitary discipline). It can more easily be secured with the aid of mandatory planning. The natural question is: Who would want to work in these branches that are clearly the losers compared with those that are converted to full cost accounting? People desiring to work in them will be found if they are assured significant material and social compensation.

When we speak about the partial retention of mandatory planning, we are thinking not of the existing weakened, eroded mandatory planning that has become one of the main reasons for economic anomalies and semistagnant development, but effective, viable planning in which all directives (plan targets) are rational and economically substantiated and their unconditional fulfillment is secured by the sufficiently precise measurement of the actual performance of collectives. For a restricted sector of the national economy, the state is entirely able to organize precisely this kind of mandatory planning.

In industries whose sophisticated products cannot be adequately measured with the aid of formal indicators, the effectiveness of mandatory planning is secured through rigorous oversight by the customer. If the client is especially interested in the impeccable quality of the products that are produced for him and if the permanent representative at the supplying enterprise regularly monitors the quality of the entire production process (from the start to final inspection and testing), it can be hoped that the gross output indicator and other indicators will be honest. It is practically impossible to organize such oversight in all branches. For all the positive significance of the newly introduced State Acceptance of Products [*Gosudarstvennaia priemka produkstii*], it cannot replace oversight by the customer.

The effectiveness of mandatory planning in the fuel-energy industry and in transport is secured by the fact that their final product is relatively simple in its qualitative characteristics and is adequately expressed by formal indicators.

For the sake of completeness of the planning system and of expanding the possibility of maneuvering in short-term economic policy, it is clearly advisable that regulative and mandatory planning be supplemented by yet another form—limited mandatory planning. The essence of it is that plans independently adopted by the enterprise are not registered as in the case of regulative planning but are confirmed by a higher organ. This procedure brings it closer to mandatory planning. The difference is that the enterprise compiles plans not according to planned allocation but rather on the basis of a portfolio of orders. It would be well to use limited mandatory planning as a temporary form (in carrying out normalization measures at enterprises that are functioning poorly under regulative planning) and as an intermediate form (with the gradual conversion of branches and enterprises from mandatory to regulative planning).

In our period of constructive criticism, it is desirable to give economic and legal recommendations a normative form that is amenable to practical evaluation. The enterprise's status in the new planning system can be presented in the following form.

1. In accordance with the principle of democratic centralism, the enterprise is given plan independence, which ensures the concrete accounting of economic conditions and initiative and enterprise in satisfying the customer's interests. This independence is restricted by the state within the limits necessary for the satisfaction of public interests on a priority basis.

Depending on branch affiliation and other conditions, the enterprise functions in a general (regulative), temporary (limited mandatory), or special (mandatory) regime of centralized state planning.

2. An enterprise that operates in accordance with the legislation in the general regime of state planning independently formulates and approves the plans governing its activity. State organs do not assign it mandatory plan targets. Plans are based on the orders of customers and decisions of state organs on concrete measures to

stimulate the production of priority products.

At the beginning of the planning process, the enterprise, on the basis of its portfolio of orders, compiles preliminary drafts of five-year and one-year plans and a survey of rejected orders (together with an indication of the reasons) and a tentative statement of unutilized capacities. Within the legislatively established period, it submits these documents to a higher organ so that it may summarize the existing economic situation and take it into account in the process of formulating five-year and one-year plans for the economic and social development of the USSR.

Upon receiving information within the specified period from the higher organ on the possibility and conditions of planned state-stimulated production of certain products, the enterprise concludes contracts independently: with clients—state organs, enterprises, institutions, and citizens—on the economic and other conditions of fulfillment of their orders; and with a higher organ on tax exemptions, subsidies, credit, the supply of centrally allocated materials or other economically justified aid rendered to the enterprise in accordance with the state plan in connection with the enterprise's participation in the production of priority products. Products not designated as priority are produced by the enterprise without the assistance of the state.

On the basis of concluded contracts, the enterprise formulates and adopts five-year and one-year plans for its activity and submits them by the specified deadline to a higher body for registration. Appended to the plans are surveys of rejected orders together with an indication of the reasons for the rejection; a statement on unutilized capacities; and (with the agreement of the higher organ) a list or copies of contracts concluded with customers.

3. If the higher organ refuses to register the plan because of its orientation toward the production of obsolete products, the application of obsolete technology, the shipping distance, or for other reasons, the enterprise either corrects the plan and amends the contracts or informs the higher organ of the considerations by virtue of which it will fulfill the plan at its own risk without calling upon the state for assistance in the event of adverse consequences. Based on the decision of the higher organ, which is approved under the procedure of subordination and which may be disputed in State Arbitration, an enterprise may be temporarily converted (for a period no longer than two years) to the state planning regime, which is analogous to the general regime with the exception that registration is replaced by the enterprise's indepen-

dently adopted plan according to the procedure for its approval by a higher organ.

The enterprise is in a temporary (limited mandatory) regime of state planning: in the initial period of its activity; if, in connection with the unprofitable operation of the enterprise or serious breach of legislation by the enterprise, the higher organ will carry out normalization measures at the enterprise, taking upon itself the direct management of its activity; with the gradual conversion of the enterprise from special to the general (regulative) regime of planning.

4. At the behest of the USSR Council of Ministers, the USSR Supreme Soviet, or its Presidium when necessary, applies the special regime of state planning to individual branches when the higher organ establishes mandatory plan targets for enterprises and defines the basic conditions governing the delivery of products to customers. The decision to extend the special planning regime to a branch specifies the indicators that will be used to evaluate the fulfillment of mandatory plan targets and forms of direct oversight over product mix and product quality by customers and the state.

Enterprises operating under a special state planning regime submit to the higher organ within the specified time their plan proposals, which take into account existing direct ties with suppliers and customers; on the basis of mandatory plan targets, enterprises formulate the plan governing their activity; after the approval of the plan by the higher organ, enterprises conclude economic contracts.

The measure of cost accounting

The legislative securing of cost-accounting principles and of the specific norms ensuring its realization is of exceptional importance. The appropriate groundwork has already been laid. There is a vast body of normative material and scientific literature in which all substantive features are directly reflected or else are skirted on the basis of considerations inherited from the extraordinary period of development (but it is clear that they are purposely skirted). The time has come to summarize at the new normative level all advances of economic and legal thinking in this most important sphere.

In our view, the essence of cost accounting in enterprise activity is quite fully expressed by the following principles.

—The well-being of the work collective is based exclusively on the rational use of public property that has been transferred to, or is in, its possession, on its zealousness, economic initiative and enterprise, and on justified economic risk.

—Assuming the conscientious labor and rational self-organization of enterprises, the economic conditions ensure them income sufficient to satisfy the rational needs of their work force and for the development of production on the basis of self-recoupment and self-financing.

—Part of the enterprise's income that is established with regard to social needs and economic conditions goes to the state for the satisfaction of social needs.

—Economic relations between enterprises are based on equivalent exchange in commodity-monetary form. They voluntarily and gratuitously help one another in the event of natural disasters, accidents, unexpected changes in business conditions, etc.

—The remuneration of the work force depends on the economic performance of the enterprise, and especially on the level of labor productivity and on the lowering of production costs at a given enterprise compared with socially necessary costs.

—In the management of enterprises, the state, in addition to one-sided, imperious but economically substantiated decisions, makes maximum possible use of economic methods that are expressed in commodity-monetary relations of state organs and enterprises. The enterprise may appeal to the state for assistance (loans, subsidies) in reconstruction, in the expansion of production, and in other socially necessary work that costs more than the enterprise itself is able to pay.

—Cost-accounting relations between enterprises and between enterprises and state organs are regulated by economic contracts, all parties to which have equal rights.

—Differences in the level of remuneration of the work force at different enterprises depend exclusively on the quantity, quality, and organization of the work (the labor basis of differentiation of the well-being of different work collectives). This is secured by the fact that the state evaluates the economic conditions at enterprises and partially redistributes their incomes in order to make the conditions more equal.

—The enterprise is not permitted to monopolize the production and sale of a certain product on a national or regional scale. If, however, a monopolistic situation develops, the state restricts the enterprise's independence in planning and price formation and begins monitoring its activity closely.

—The enterprise bears full responsibility for its economic mistakes and omissions and makes full compensation (including lost profits) for harm inflicted on society, other enterprises, and citizens by improper fulfillment of its obligations.

The enterprise's new status must include precise and definite norms and procedures that regulate: the contractual form of transfer of public property to the economic possession of the enterprise (the possessor's rights approximate but are not identical with the owner's rights); keeping a constant check on changes in the physical composition and value of this property; conditions of use of natural resources including payment for them, the restoration of renewable resources, and ecological demands; the procedure for compensating and multiplying the value of fixed capital transferred to the enterprise (amortization withholdings pending the obsolescence of capital are probably the optimal form of such compensation. Unless the state otherwise directs, the enterprise could at its own discretion use them for the technical modernization and reconstruction of production); the procedure for forming and utilizing the production development fund; the determination of the share of the enterprise's income that goes to the state budget; the equalization of economic conditions of operation of various enterprises with the aid of rent and similar payments; the residual principle of forming the labor remuneration fund; the combination of state firm and limit prices with free contract prices (the elimination of the present "cost freedom" [zatratnaia vol'nitsa] in price formation); quality control by the consumer, inter alia in the production process; the functioning (on an exceptional basis) of normatively relatively unprofitable enterprises for the realization of social tasks; the creation of joint production facilities by enterprises on a cost-accounting basis; and the realization of cost accounting in foreign economic relations.

The fullness of cost accounting and its connection with the kind of planning regime under which the enterprise functions is of fundamental importance. It has now become fashionable to speak of full cost accounting. Whatever manner of cost accounting is under discussion, it must necessarily be full. Full cost accounting does indeed have enormous significance for the solution of such age-old and difficult problems as the problem of increasing labor productivity, improving product quality, converting to sophisticated technologies, conserving resources, and contractual and labor discipline. It cannot be generated by declarations and incantations. As we see it, the introduction of regulative planning as the leading, dominant form of planning opens the way to the effective conversion of the majority of enterprises to full cost accounting. In the case of mandatory planning and, with certain qualifications, limited mandatory planning, incomplete cost accounting is possible and useful. However, attempts to create a semblance of full cost accounting will only cause harm. Why?

Full cost accounting presupposes the fullness of not only obligations but of rights as well. *When it is characterized by the concepts "self-recoupment and self-financing," the reference is primarily to obligations, with nothing being said about rights.* We cannot be satisfied with such an abridged formula of cost accounting. The formula must at least include "self-planning, self-recoupment, and self-financing." If the enterprise is not given the right of self-planning, it cannot be charged with the full measure of obligations with regard to self-recoupment and self-financing. And if we are to be entirely precise, we should speak not of the right of self-planning but of the right of self-management (self-planning is an element, a key element but not the only element of self-management). We are speaking of self-management in a relative sense because state management of the national economy remains supreme as a unified whole. This management is expressed in state planning (in the given instance, regulative planning), in legislation, in state control, in investment, structural, resource, financial, and cadre policy, in a word, in the entire economic policy mechanism. Taking this into account, it can also be said *that cost accounting is self-management, self-recoupment, and self-financing.* And if we compress and define this formula more precisely, then *cost accounting is the economic aspect of the self-management of enterprises under the conditions of labor emulation and socialist competition.*

Under full cost accounting, the well-being of the work collective and its acquisitions and losses depend entirely on the final economic results of its socially useful activity. But the collective cannot be placed in such strict dependence (without it there is no full cost accounting) unless it is given the freedom, as a basic prerequisite to the economic effectiveness of its activity, to plan and decide the questions of what to produce, under what conditions to produce, and how to market the product. If such questions are decided by the state and if the enterprise is given merely an advisory role, it [the state] thereby assumes the responsibility for the economic consequences of its actions. That is the crux of the matter. *Full cost accounting is impossible in the case of incomplete, minimum self-management!*

The semblance of full cost accounting of enterprises functioning under the conditions of the presently weakened, largely disorganized mandatory planning [regime] must be eliminated, not legalized. This is because enterprises have learned very well how to use formal plan indicators to exaggerate their performance (the production of "advantageous," i.e., costly products, jacking up prices, "double counting," the exploitation of their monopolistic position to force large quantities of inferior products on the customer, etc.). Frankly speaking, this is the extraction of unearned income and social parasitization that demoralizes work collectives, management, and the working people. *The expansion of the independence of enterprises without basic change in these economic and organizational conditions essentially invites them to an even greater degree to be parasites on the flaws in the economic mechanism.*

Consequently, full cost accounting must be introduced, approved, and regulated where it is applicable, and the limits to incomplete cost accounting must be outlined where it is useful and where full cost accounting is impossible and threatens to disorganize production.

Continuing what has been said above regarding the status of the enterprise in the planning system, this could be expressed as follows in normative form. Full cost accounting is extended to enterprises functioning under the general (regulative) regime of state planning. The profit received by the enterprise, minus the share fixed by legislation and branch norms, is placed entirely at the enterprise's disposal and may not be taken away by higher and other state organs based on considerations of economic expedience. The enterprise is fully responsible for the wrong or improper fulfillment of the plan. Cost accounting extends to enterprises operating under temporary or special state planning regimes with the following change: responsibility for negative consequences of the erroneous planning decision of a higher organ, if it has been properly carried out, passes from the enterprise to that organ.

With the differentiation of forms of planning and degrees of cost accounting it will be necessary to closely coordinate the organization of management at enterprises and in associations (not present associations, which differ little from enterprises, but real associations of enterprises as independent economic organizations jointly forming a certain activity). Developed forms of self-management, which include the deciding power of councils of work collectives and the election of managers, and the formation of self-managing economic associations, are associated with regulative planning. Consultative rights of councils of work collectives, the appointment of managers from above (taking the collective's opinion into account), and the formation of state economic associations (directly controlled by the state) correspond to mandatory planning.

Such, it seems to us, is the basic status of the enterprise in the new economic mechanism.

As the basic link in the economic system, the enterprise is the focus of the production relations that directly or indirectly determine all other social relations. The economic might of the nation, the level of satisfaction of the material and nonmaterial needs of society in general and of each member of society and territorial communities, depend on the work of the enterprise. The real democratic organization of management at the enterprise makes it possible for the work force to create, to develop, and to freely realize its potential. The democratic organization of production activity and socialist economic democracy in general are the best guarantee and only possible basis for the all-around development of political democracy, for the eradication of bureaucratic distortions in management, for reducing the size and increasing the efficiency of management, for curbing the inclination of individual groups and persons to acquire and retain various elitist-caste privileges that are incompatible with socialism.

The resolution of most socioeconomic and political problems that urgently confront the state, the party, and the people today is in one way or another connected with the reform of enterprises' activity. State policy is now focused on bringing this activity entirely into line with the character of today's productive forces. The adoption of the Law on the State Enterprise and other recent directives is an important step in the necessary direction. But the search for effective forms of economic management must continue.

Note

1. T. I. Zaslavskaia, "Chelovecheskii faktor razvitiia ekonomiki i sotsial'naia spravedlivost"' *Kommunist,* 1986, no. 13, p. 64. [See the English translation of this article in *Problems of Economics,* vol. 30, no. 1 (May 1987), pp. 5–26.]

V. A. KOROSTELEV

The Rebirth of Small-Scale Commodity Production

The shady sides of the concentration of production

The insufficiently deep theoretical study of the place and role of small-scale commodity production under socialism is a serious impediment to increasing the effectiveness of social production. Of course, the issue of concentration is very complex. It has its strong and weak sides. Our victory in the Great Patriotic War, the conquest of space, and the raising of the population's living standard would have been impossible without concentration. Its minuses became especially apparent beginning in the early seventies. We lost sight of the fact that ". . . concentration at a certain level in its development leads to monopoly."[1] More precisely, we applied this scientific discovery by V. I. Lenin only to the capitalist mode of production on the assumption that socialism is immune to the negative aspects of concentration. Alas, numerous facts indicate that the reverse is true. Many large enterprises and associations have become real monopolists with all the attendant consequences. Lenin warned that the greatest evil of the monopoly was that it

Russian text © 1988 by "Nauka" Publishers and "Ekonomika i organizatsiia promyshlennogo proizvodstva." "Renessans melkogo tovarnogo proizvodstva," *Ekonomika i organizatsiia promyshlennogo proizvodstva,* 1988, no. 2, pp. 21-33. *EKO* is published by the Institute of the Economics and Organization of Industrial Production, Siberian Institute of the USSR Academy of Sciences.

V. A. Korostelev holds a candidate's degree in economics and is affiliated with the Scientific Research and Planning-Design Institute of Computerized Systems for Urban Economic Management in Kiev.

promoted the trend toward stagnation and putrefaction.[2] We will not characterize here all forms of stagnation of the productive forces and production relations. In the context of this article, only one of them is important to us.

The result of the concentration of production in a certain stage was that the activity of large enterprises generated by concentration ceased to cover the mixed gamut of constantly growing and continuously changing human needs. At first this was not especially noticeable and we managed in one way or another to remedy the situation, attributing the shortages arising here and there to miscalculations in planning, supply, and trade. But time passed, and the incongruity of interests of large enterprises and consumers not only did not diminish but increased to catastrophic proportions. "Zones of inattention" began to form and developed into persisting "dead zones."[3]

"Dead zones" (or "economic niches") are sectors of social production that are economically uninteresting to large enterprises. The needs that fall into these zones are also correspondingly uninteresting to industrial giants. We are primarily discussing needs that are subject to frequent and quite dramatic changes—personal human needs.

The volume of our needs has risen significantly in recent years, and their structure has become more complex. While in the past one or another need existed in relatively few forms, today there are tens and hundreds of forms, and the difficulty of satisfying them is snowballing. The mix of goods available to the customer now exceeds 660,000 items; taking varieties of products into account, over one million.[4]

Another characteristic feature is that you must offer today's consumer that which no one else has. He is not wont to lose his individuality even (or if only) in clothing. Today, it is not only grownup representatives of the fair sex that shudder and grow pale upon seeing "their" dress on other women. Even children refuse to wear the same clothes.[5] However, the existing structure of social production and the traditional branch system of management does not guarantee this "luxury" to the consumer.

Let us take the sewing industry as an example. Not so long ago we proudly proclaimed our sewing industry to be the most highly concentrated in the world. In the early seventies, the USSR Ministry of Light Industry numbered more than 700 enterprises, 48 percent of which employed more than 600 workers and 10 percent employed more than 4,000 workers. (In the United States, which has the largest sewing industry of all the developed capitalist countries, 80 percent of the sewing factories at that time had 50 workers or less, and only 2 percent had more than 500 workers.) Almost 70 percent of the branch's output was produced by large sewing factories (with a capacity of 1.2 million rubles of gross output a year) while relatively small factories (under 600,000 rubles) produced only 10 percent.[6]

Despite the fact that the first signs of oversaturation of the market with products of the sewing industry were noted as early as the beginning of the seventies (65-70 percent of the population was wearing factory-made clothing),[7] the concentration of production and the growth of capacities continued. That is, the sewing industry was to an ever-increasing degree oriented toward mass production, to the detriment of the interests of the individual consumer.

The picture was similar in other branches as well: the fact that large enterprises were interested in series and mass production meant that they ignored "small-series" needs; there was also stubborn resistance to the production of consumer goods. Despite "strong pressure throughout the entire field," half the enterprises in some branches produce no consumer goods whatsoever.[8]

However, it is unjust to blame enterprises and their managers alone for these undeveloped relations with consumer goods production. The negative attitude toward individual needs results not only from management's level of consciousness. If we allow common sense to return us from the positions of "economic idealism" to the stern prose of cost accounting [khozraschet], we will have to admit that much of our economic policy has the unpleasant aftertaste of subjectivism, stemming directly from the ignorance or nonuse of economic laws. How can it otherwise be explained that for many years there has been a persistent effort to force industrial giants to produce consumer goods outside their area of specialization? After all, an enterprise, like any independent organism, functions according to certain laws. One of them is: the larger the enterprise, the more it gravitates toward large-series and mass production; otherwise, it will inevitably sustain losses. The West German economist H. Wagenführ maintains that the automated production of a good will be profitable if it has at least 100 million potential customers.[9] This is why the heads of large associations are so reluctant to increase the production of consumer goods and to expand their mix. It is unprofitable for them to do so!

Nor does society extract any particular gain from such an approach. Judge for yourselves: we first concentrate production with the aim of raising labor productivity and profitability and then undermine both one and the other through our "tax on heavy industry" in the form of compulsory consumer goods production [*promrazverstka*].

The emergence and expansion of "dead zones" have been promoted by the excessive increase in the concentration of production and the incorrect approach to its specialization. Economic theory was for a long time dominated by the view that the expansion of production was necessarily accompanied by the specialization of production. However, practice showed that specialization in itself without proper development of cooperation in production not only was incapable of increasing the effectiveness of the economy but could also threaten many directions of economic policy (above all, the realization of a higher goal). And so, the policy of highly concentrated production and intensive, ill-conceived specialization gave rise to the emergence and increase in area of "dead zones." In our view, however, "dead zones" are not so much the consequence of subjective miscalculations in the organization and planning of production as an objective phenomenon. They are a kind of payment for the concentration of production and for the growth of labor productivity. The higher the degree of concentration of production, the larger is the share of personal needs that end up in the "dead zones."

Up until now, we have for the most part been discussing the economic nature of the "dead zones." Let us now discuss their social essence. For a long time, the following conception held sway in economic science: the growth of personal needs requires an increase in consumer goods production, and this is attainable only through higher labor productivity based on the intensified concentration and specialization of production. However, real life proved to be considerably more complex, and the results were largely contrary to the expectations. "Dead zones" are powerful generators of economic shortages. On the one hand, they are sectors of the national economy with a lower attractiveness coefficient to large enterprises, while on the other hand they increase the gap between demand and supply by the magnitude of the shortage. Shortages generate profiteering, encourage the growth of unearned income, and restrict the majority of the population's real consumption. This is the practical result of the excessive concentration of production.

Under these conditions, the content of the concept "profiteering" changes substantially. It grows from a legal category into a socioeconomic category and assumes a specific, distorted form of action of the law of proportionality. Without going into a long discussion about its formulations, we note that according to the law of proportionality a dynamic correspondence must exist between all economic processes and phenomena (including demand and supply). However, under conditions of chronic shortage, it can only be achieved by raising prices. That is to say, whether we wish it or not, there is an objective need to compensate the shortage of the supply of goods by raising their prices. If the state does not do so, we observe the unsanctioned increase in prices by private persons, or, to put it more simply, profiteering. Despite the extremely negative attitude toward profiteering, we cannot but note that it is in some degree instrumental in balancing demand and supply. Therefore, when we step up the fight against profiteering with the aid of legal means, we should not forget that the center of gravity should be shifted to economic methods of eliminating shortages. We will not put an end to shortages unless we get rid of the "dead zones."

Thus, "dead zones" are an objective economic category characterizing the excessive proliferation of areas of social production to which large enterprises pay no heed. On the one hand, they are a kind of payment for the excessive concentration of production while on the other they are a form of weakening of the economy associated with the monopolistic position of large producers.

How can this situation be changed? There are two directions: [promoting] the development of small enterprises and expanding the sphere of individual labor activity.

The large potential of small enterprises

Until recently, the productive forces in our country developed without proper regard to the role and potential of small enterprises. Unconditional preference was given to large-scale production. Economic science unfortunately did not formulate methodological principles for determining the optimal dimensions of concentration and depth of specialization of production. What is more, the authors of the few works devoted to small-scale commodity production under socialism usually directed their primary efforts toward proving its atavistic nature. Small enterprises were for the most part berated for their extremely low level of labor productivity and for the low effectiveness of their production. The sole consideration was departmental, not national economic, effectiveness.

We are now beginning to free ourselves of gigantomania. The myth of the absolute superiority of large enterprises is gradually being dispelled. Evaluating the significance of concentration in agriculture in his work "Capitalism in Agriculture," Lenin made important general methodological remarks: first, "... the law of superiority of large-scale production is by no means as absolute and as simple as is sometimes thought ..."; second, large-scale production is superior only to a certain point; third, in some branches, small-scale production can compete with large-scale production.[10]

As foreign experience shows, there is a stable symbiosis of gigantic and very small firms. For example, one of the superior features of the Japanese Toyota concern is the ramified network of its suppliers: 250 primary suppliers, supported by 15,000 sub-contractors, account for almost 70 percent of the value of an automobile, whereas the General Motors Corporation produces more than half of the necessary components in value terms.[11]

Both sides are interested in such collaboration. A ramified system of small subcontractors frees large firms of many unprofitable functions and allows them to concentrate on the most profitable and promising spheres and operations.

An interesting form of private small-scale enterprise has been found in the German Democratic Republic, which has an especially large number of private tailors, shoemakers, and car, radio, and household appliance repair shops. They are usually family enterprises, but they are also allowed to take on apprentices. Such a private sector does not threaten public ownership. It accounts for only 1-2 percent of the national product.[12] Nevertheless, this sector, which is optimally built into the socialist economy, makes it possible to resolve many problems, in particular, to satisfy the population's needs more completely, to increase real income, and to promote initiative and creativity on the part of the working people.

The Bulgarian Industrial Economic Association, which combines 1,400 small enterprises with a work force ranging between five and 200 persons, demonstrates a high degree of effectiveness. It offers consultations, makes recommendations, organizes collaboration with foreign firms, and grants loans on a competitive basis. The wages of the management apparatus (consisting of only seventy persons) depend directly on the successful performance of the association as a whole.

Among the advantages of small enterprises, we should mention the dramatic reduction in the cost of their construction and the early recoupment of capital investments. In Bulgaria, for example, small enterprises occupy old rebuilt production space, and as a result capital investments are on the average recouped in 7-8 months. Similar experience in creating relatively small enterprises (affiliates of sewing, footwear, knitwear factories) in Central Asia and the Transcaucasus shows that their construction can be shortened to 6-12 months compared with the usual period of 21-24 months.[13]

Small-scale commodity production in our economic structure should be represented not only by state and cooperative property but by individual property as well. In view of the unconventionality of such an interpretation of individual property, let us examine this question in greater detail.

Small-scale production, which is represented both as small economic units at large plants and by independent enterprises, not only does not exclude the concentration of production but is even one of the necessary conditions of its successful realization.

Overcoming prejudices against unsocialized labor— individual and collective

In recent years a heated debate has been waged in the pages of newspapers and magazines concerning the nature and place of individual labor activity in social production. It was essentially reduced to the attempt to answer the question: "Individual labor activity—the stepchild or legal offspring of the socialist economy?" The heat of the debate and the polarity of the views indicated that a large "nerve center" of social contradictions in modern society had been touched. Like a drop of water, the problem of individual labor activity reflected many socioeconomic incongruities: between large- and small-scale production, between planning and spontaneity, between social groups.

As a result of difficult reflections regarding problems of unsocialized labor and the struggle of opinions and social forces, the view that such activity is an objective process, the reaction of the economic system to the existing interests of social production, began to blaze its trail more and more boldly. It was probably largely due to these innovative conclusions that it became possible to adopt the important legal act: the Law of the USSR on Individual Labor Activity.

It should be admitted that notwithstanding the stubborn reluctance of some circles to recognize this fact, individual enterprise has been flourishing among us for a long time. We encounter it at every step. If the television set is in need of repair and we call the repair shop but can't get through, we call in a skilled craftsman from down the street. If we want to have some tailoring done but the shop is booked up for several months in advance, we get in touch with Valentin Petrovich through acquaintances and he does everything to a tee in three days' time. If we want to have a hot bed built at our vacation cottage, we call upon a third type of artisan. Each one of us could continue the list of situations.

In other words, we frequently deal in practice with unsocialized labor—individual and collective. We call the former private trades-men [*chastniki*] and the latter free-lance work teams [*shabashni-ki*].[14] But their nature does not change from the difference in their names. They are agents of individual labor.

In the press there is a lively discussion of the nature of the modern free-lance worker, of his place and role in the socialist economy. The popularity of this social figure is explained by the fact that the population is fed up with flaws and gaps in trade, in personal services, and in social production as a whole. Its very existence reflects the inflexibility of the existing system of planning and economic incentives and the lag of economic law behind practical demands.

And yet, the times when the free-lance worker was declared to be quite a shady character are still not beyond the horizon of memory. He was reputed to be a self-seeker, a slipshod worker who had a demoralizing impact on those around him, who undermined the prestige of honest labor and the ruble. The quality of his work, his health and his family all reportedly suffered. . . . In a word, the free-lance worker was considered an alien body in the economic system of socialism, and the happy moment was eagerly awaited when this anachronism that spoiled the picture of total socialization would die out.

These expectations were not destined to come true. Our rosy picture of the early, 100-percent socialization of production faded. The number of free-lance workers not only did not diminish but even increased, like the volume of work performed by them. And no matter how we feel about private tradesmen and free-lance workers, we cannot but recognize the following facts.

They performed quality work in strict accordance with the customer's wishes and at a time that was convenient to him. Therein lay their strength and their superiority over state sector enterprises that were bound by numerous restrictions.

The number of individual entrepreneurs grew continuously, since the sphere of application of their labor ("dead zones") also increased, thereby leading to rampantly, spontaneously developing rates for their services.

At the same time that individual entrepreneurs efficiently satisfy our needs on a quality basis, they have frequently used state buildings, equipment, electric power, raw materials, and supplies. Therefore, their activity was not inoffensive to the state.

And your and my position in this case was by no means above reproach. When we have paid our precious rubles to moonlighters, we have willy-nilly committed at least two unlawful acts: we have helped them obtain unlawful income, and we have contributed to the deception of the state, society, and ultimately ourselves.

Strange as it may be, while we have realized down deep the ugliness of our behavior, we have nonetheless time after time called upon these free entrepreneurs for their assistance. What is this—a deficiency in our economic education? Moral unsteadiness? Or a manifestation of an objective force that compels us to act one way and not another despite our will and consciousness? It would seem that for all the importance of economic and moral education, the last guess is closer to the truth.

Part of effective demand that does not get the attention of large-scale production becomes the booty of small-scale, individual enterprise. The vacuum of attention, supplemented by a powerful "magnetic field" generated by unsatisfied demand, acts like a gigantic pump that draws in the agents of individual labor and our precious rubles.

The following figures give some idea of the power of this pump. Specialists estimate that providers of private services alone earn 5-6 billion rubles a year. This is comparable with the earnings of the service sphere, which has a work force of up to 20 million workers. In the overall volume of personal services enjoyed by the urban population, the "handicraftmen's shop" [*tsekh kustarei*] performs 50 percent of all footwear repair work, 45 percent of all apartment repair work, and 40 percent of all repairs on private automobiles.[15] But it is unable to cover the "dead zones" entirely. The population's current unsatisfied demand for services alone is estimated to be 5.5 billion rubles. The overall size of the "dead zones" can be roughly determined through deferred demand, one form of which is the total cash on deposit in savings banks. This sum is growing from year to year: 1983—by 12 billion rubles; 1984—by 15 billion rubles; 1985—by 18.7 billion rubles. For the sake of comparison, we note that deposits in 1965 totaled 18.7 billion rubles, while they now total more than 220 billion rubles.[16]

But since there are needs and very substantial uncommitted monetary resources, no manner of prohibitions will eliminate the problem of "moonlight work." And demand that is not lawfully satisfied will ultimately be satisfied in one way or another in contravention of the law. That is how it has been until recently. There has been no actual, clearly defined legal regulation of labor activity by individuals (private tradesmen) and collectives (free-lance work crews). However, there has been a need to bring the legal mechanism into line with objective reality, ridding the individual producer, you, and me of the necessity of concealing something, of deceiving someone. There is a need to return the feeling of social worth to the honest worker and to shrive the consumer's sins. It is specifically this gap in the economic mechanism that the extremely important state acts adopted in 1986 were called upon to eliminate. The reference is to the Edict of the Presidium of the USSR Supreme Soviet "On Intensifying the Struggle Against the Extraction of Unearned Income," to the decree of the USSR Council of Ministers "On the Regularization of the Organization and Remuneration of the Labor of Temporary Construction Brigades," and to the Law of the USSR on Individual Labor Activity.

The great significance of these legal acts consists in the fact that while they are "load-bearing components" of the mechanism for legalizing individual labor activity, they determine its worthy place in aggregate labor and promote the more complete manifestation of socialist enterprise; quite strictly define the "corridor of freedom" of the unsocialized entrepreneur, preventing the transformation of individual labor activity into private entrepreneurial activity; promote the prevention of illegal activity, the regularization of individual labor activity, and the normalization of the moral climate in society. The framework of the law protects us from the tyranny of the "private tradesman" and the latter from the petty interference of oversight agencies. The state, on the other hand, will receive the money that is due it for building leases, for the depreciation of machinery and equipment, for the use of electric power, heat, and water. Taxes on individual workers will comprise no small share of budget revenues.

Naturally, a large effort to implement adopted legislative acts lies ahead of us. We cannot fail to foresee the considerable opposition of certain strata of society to new approaches to individual labor activity who do their utmost to brake the realization of promising initiatives. At the same time, they put into play such tested means as compromise (we recall the incidents surrounding the edict "On Intensifying the Struggle against the Extraction of Unearned Income") and emasculation (which has frequently been observed vis-à-vis the Law on Individual Labor Activity).

What is the nature of the forces that do not favor the incipient restructuring of economic law?

I think that the largest share in the opposition is made up of people who are directly damaged by the new order. They are moonlighters, *kalymshchiki* [people who make extra money on the side], pilferers, and profiteers. One can imagine the depth of their dissatisfaction: after all, the legal wages of many of them were only a "makeweight" to "moonlighting" income.

The next group of "oppositionists" are bureaucrats and people who play it safe, i.e., people who do not take a single step without having the proper instructions and statutes. To those who play it safe, every enterprising person is an adventurist and a political opponent. Because he frequently works not only without instructive materials, but even contrary to them. It is the formalists who are interested in preserving the status quo when a healthy initiative is morally, materially, and legally punishable.

Loafers and klutzes fear the individual enterprising worker. Behind a screen of bombastic words about social justice, they are doing their utmost to put leveling into practice. They personally are unable to hold anything but a spoon, but they try to see to it that it is equal in size to that of those who really know how to work.

And many of us are probably not above reproach in every respect. We should ask ourselves: do we always properly relate to people who, putting an enormous amount of labor into the construction of houses and roads, into raising fruits and vegetables, receive money several times greater than our wages? Are we often not like O. Henry's hero who considered an extra dollar in someone else's pocket a personal insult? Are we not hypnotized by modern philistinism which interprets universal equality under socialism primarily as equality of personal incomes? But after all, the first phase of communism still cannot secure the full equality of all members of society. We must abandon that harmful illusion. In the sphere of personal incomes, we must observe only one equality: their correspondence to the labor contribution.

It is very regrettable that a considerable percentage of the personnel of law-enforcement agencies must be also classified among the opponents of individual labor activity. The paradox of legal regulation that existed until recently was that on the one hand it did not avert crimes associated with unearned income, while on the other it did not hinder business initiative but frequently punished people for income earned by honest labor.

For example, several years ago criminal proceedings were instituted in Chernigov Oblast' against four members of a free contract brigade that built a road to a collective farm in record time and received a large sum of money for the great amount of labor involved. The collective farm chairman who paid out this money spent about a year in an investigatory isolation cell.[17] But not even this is the worst of it. The road construction costs were recouped during the first year of operation. Nevertheless, from the standpoint of economic law of that time, society had suffered an injury. This will help to understand the attitude of a considerable percentage of law enforcement personnel toward persons engaged in individual labor. It was clearly formulated by A. Didenko, a lieutenant colonel of the militia: "The socialist production collective has no need for a free-lance worker whatsoever. He is not needed by our management principle. He is not needed by our morality. What is more, he is socially harmful."[18]

The reason for the condemnation of honest workers also becomes clear: they are approached from the standpoint of the presumption of guilt. "If one is a free-lance worker he is automatically guilty!" This position is an echo of those distant times when all trades were required to pay such heavy taxes that the tradesmen went underground. In the postwar period, the pressure on individual labor activity was most heavy in the fifties. In 1951-52, the tax rates were raised substantially on cooperative crafts "with the aim of promoting the development of cooperative crafts by encouraging craftsmen who were not members of a cooperative to joint the cooperative craft system,"[19] which was abolished in 1959.

In light of this, the great significance of new documents legalizing and regularizing individual labor activity becomes even more obvious. ". . . While suppressing unearned income," it was stated at the Twenty-seventh CPSU Congress, "we must not allow the shadow to fall on those who realize additional earnings through honest labor. . . ."

Notes

1. V. I. Lenin, *Polnoe sobranie sochinenii*, vol. 27, p. 315.

2. Ibid., p. 397.

3. The term is borrowed from military terminology, where "dead zone" refers to a sector that is not fired upon because of the technological design potential.

4. Ia. Orlov, "Interesy pokupatelei—v tsentr vnimaniia rabotnikov promyshlennosti i torgovli," *Politicheskoe samoobrazovanie*, 1986, no. 2.

5. See, for example: M. Lebedeva, "Detki v kletku," *Izvestiia*, October 6, 1985.

6. M. V. Udalov, *Kontsentratsiia proizvodstva v shveinoi promyshlennosti*, Moscow: TsNIITEI, 1971, pp. 4-11.

7. Ibid., p. 3.

8. V. Romaniuk, "Dlia kazhdoi sem'i," *Izvestiia*, October 3, 1985.

9. H. Wagenführ, *Zukunft in Wort und Zahl*, Tübingen, 1972, p. 170.

10. Lenin, vol. 4, pp. 110-11.

11. *Upravlenie protsessom kontsentratsii i spetsializatsii proizvodstva*, Moscow: "Nauka" Publishers, 1981, p. 118.

12. E. Ambartsumov, "GDR. Nachalo 80-kh," *Literaturnaia gazeta*, November 3, 1983.

13. I. Golovin and A. Pevzner, "Nebol'shie predpriiatiia v sisteme upravleniia obshchestvennym proizvodstvom," *Planovoe khoziaistvo*, 1986, no. 11, p. 82.

14. In literature and in conversational speech, the synonymic series of names of this category of people is much broader: from colloquial—*shabashnik, otkhodnik* [peasant migratory worker in towns], *sezonnik* [seasonal worker], *kustar'* [home worker], *chastnik, levak* [person illicitly working on the side], *kalymshchik* to the entirely respectable: member of a hired brigade, member of a free contract brigade, representative of private service.

15. G. Gusakov and V. Tolstov, ". . . I drugie zainteresovannye litsa," *Izvestiia*, August 19, 1985.

16. *Pravda*, January 29, 1984; January 27, 1985; January 26, 1986; *Narodnoe khoziaistvo SSSR v 1985 godu*, Moscow: "Finansy i statistika" Publishers, 1986, p. 517.

17. I. Kruglianskaia, "Doroga," *Izvestiia*, April 18, 1985.

18. "Esli govorit' otkrovenno," *Izvestiia*, June 16, 1985.

19. *Istoriia sotsialisticheskoi ekonomiki SSSR*, vol. 6, Moscow: "Nauka" Publishers, 1980, p. 509.

D. PALTEROVICH

Competition and Democratization

The need for the purposeful development of those elements of new production relations and the economic mechanism that are integrally inherent in democratization and that actively promote the process stems from the mutual causality of the two main aspects of restructuring [*perestroika*]—democratization of society and radical economic reform. In our opinion, one of the first places among these elements belongs to the broad development of competition.

Only under competitive conditions can such important elements of democratic rights and freedoms as the right to choose the best manager, the optimal variant of a plan, a project or economic decision that is advantageous to the supplier or performer, be realized not on paper but in substance. Consequently, it is competition that creates the conditions for the working people to demonstrate real activism and initiative and to participate directly in management, the quintessence of socialist democracy.

The economic competition of enterprises envisaged in the USSR Law on the State Enterprise (Association) must become an important step in the development of competition. But, as will be shown below, conditions for such competition have yet to be created. Competition as a prerequisite to democratization means more than the economic competition of enterprises. It must also embrace: (a) the formulation and adoption of programs, plans, projects, and other decisions of a socioeconomic, scientific-technological, and organizational nature; (b) interrelations of not only state but also cooperative enterprises, scientific research and

Russian text © 1988 by "Pravda" Publishers and *Voprosy ekonomiki*.

"Sostiazatel'nost' i demokratizatsiia," *Voprosy ekonomiki*, 1988, no. 6, pp. 22-32.

The author holds a doctor's degree in economic sciences and is leading research associate at the Institute of Economics, USSR Academy of Sciences.

planning organizations, and persons engaged in individual labor activity; (c) the economic competition of shops, brigades, departments, and other subdivisions, and individual workers, which does not exclude their close interaction in attaining the final goals of enterprises or organizations; and (d) the formation of the management apparatus of enterprises, organizations, and their subdivisions on the basis of election and competition.

From what has been said, it is clear that the mere adoption of the Law on the Enterprise is not sufficient to make competition an integral, component part of the economic mechanism. It is therefore necessary to reexamine a number of principles of economic theory, to form multiple variants of economic thought, to make changes in the organizational structure of the economy, to create a tangible legal and material base for competition, and to substantially alter the procedure for formulating programs, plans, and other decisions to this end.

Let us examine the principal direction of competition today—the economic competition of enterprises. The "Guidelines for the Radical Restructuring of Economic Management" adopted by the June 1987 Plenum of the CPSU Central Committee, note the need to create conditions for economic competition. One such condition is the elimination of our political economy's view that the relations of economic competition under socialism are negative or insignificant.

We must understand the relations of economic competition as a special category of socialist production relations that must become a key factor of intensification. The following must be classified among the basic characteristic features of these relations. First, the diversity of forms and the broad spectrum of the subjects of the indicated relations. Brigades or families working under contract and citizens engaged in individual labor activity may, in addition to state and cooperative enterprises, organizations and work collectives in social production, also be the subjects of economic competition relations. In our view, the former may not only be an adjunct to the primary job, but in a number of cases may also be the principal employment of individual persons if this activity satisfies social needs. Second, economic criteria (unlike competition in sports and competitive entrance examinations for higher education institutions) occupy first place in economic competition relations. Every subject tries to win the customer's confidence, to guarantee himself demand, and on this basis to receive the maximum amount of net income. Third, success or failure in economic competition entails substantial material and moral consequences for enterprises, work collectives, and individual workers. Fourth, methods of economic competition in a socialist economy must exclude the infliction of harm on society.

Economic competition relations were developed to a certain degree in our country during NEP [New Economic Policy]. However, those elements of the economic mechanism that promoted the development of competition were gradually eliminated with the transition from NEP to predominantly administrative methods of economic management. The abolition of commercial credit; the ever tighter regulation of all economic activity, including the distribution and use of profits and depreciation allowances; the excessively centralized character of price formation, finance-credit relations, and the distribution of all types of products; the separation of foreign trade functions from the direct producer; the disappearance of the patent system; the establishment of a factual monopoly of head enterprises and scientific research institutes and basic scientific-technological areas; the transfer of most technical innovations from one enterprise to another free of charge—all this taken together formed a type of production relations in which there was no place left for genuine competition. Antidemocratic management techniques deprived man of the freedom of choice in all spheres of his activity.

Economic theory played no small part in this process. While recognizing the limited scope of action of the law of value and such value categories as price, profits, and profitability under socialism, our political economy occupied a negative position vis-à-vis not only negative competitive properties but also those manifestations of it that promote the acceleration of the development and intensification of the economy. It seems to me that the theoretical roots of the conception, which essentially excluded competition, were most closely connected with the rejection of the regulatory role of the law of value in most spheres of the socialist economy. However, there are still gnoseological reasons why political economy ignores the role of competition as an important element of socialist production relations. In our view, this is responsible for the limited approach taken toward man as merely a production worker and the insufficient attention to his specific needs, interests, aspirations, and to psychological assessments of moral and material values. In particular, no consideration has been given to the striving for success, to winning in the competition with other members of society or collectives—one of the most important properties of the human personality and the motivation behind the production and social activity of the majority of people. Having excluded this objective feature of the human personality from its field of vision, political economy—even in the process of constructing the theoretical foundations of socialist competition—essentially ignored competition, reducing it to fulfillment of the obligation of bringing laggards up to the mark. In our opinion, this is a manifestation of one of the shortcomings in the organization of socialist competition and the lack of real interest in it on the part of many participants. Economic competition, which has become the most important form of socialist competition, enriches it and strengthens the impact of competition on the production intensification process.

Naturally, bringing laggards up to the mark is an important principle of socialist competition. However, it should not be counterposed to competition to get ahead. What is more, the mutual aid mechanism proper should be constructed in such a way that it is economically advantageous to both the receiver and the giver. For example, according to Article 4 of the Law on the Enterprise, when an enterprise transfers material resources, equipment, or monies from economic incentive funds to cooperating enterprises, it assists them and at the same time improves the conditions of its own production activity.

As a result of the lack of development of economic competition relations, our national economy lost powerful levers and stimuli for conserving resources, for raising product quality, and for accelerating scientific-technological progress. There developed a dictatorship of producers of goods, services, and scientific-technological innovations over their customers. Thus, the underestimation of the role of economic competition relations should be viewed as a factor that impedes the acceleration of economic development, its intensification, and the formation of an anticost economic mechanism. However, competition is not merely competition for the best product delivery terms, for product quality, for diversity, for correspondence to the customers' interests, for lower costs and prices. This is also a basis for instilling multivariant economic thinking in which the product mix, the best supplier, the best technique, technology, and organization of production are determined through the analysis of a number of possible alternatives and the selection of an optimal variant.

The possibility of a rational choice of variants presupposes different external conditions of their realization, the elimination of economic, administrative, or legal restrictions on various subjects of competition. At the present time, this equality is systematically violated. Thus, enterprises belonging to the same branch have different norms governing the formation of the wage fund, the distribution of profits, etc., and moreover these differences frequently do not correspond to an objectively conditioned difference in the composition and technical level of the production apparatus. Obviously, enterprises that have less advantageous norms, that have marginal supply and financing, that do not have the right to trade in the external market, etc., operate under marginal conditions of economic competition. Inequality is manifested still more sharply in the different conditions of supply of state and cooperative enterprises with premises, scarce equipment, and materials; in constraints on the possible sphere of activity of cooperatives and on the taking on of persons who are not working at state enterprises, etc. In our opinion, one of the central tasks in the transition from command-administrative methods to economic methods of management is to repudiate such inequality and prohibitions. Such repudiation is the prerequisite not only to the development of competition but also to ensuring a high level of economic activity of society, to the formation of genuine economic democracy. The new Law on Cooperation will be a fundamental step in this direction.

The removal of restrictions hindering the development of cooperative activity can promote the more complete satisfaction of the demand for consumer goods and services. It would also be expedient to develop these cooperatives so that they, playing a considerable role in the satisfaction of the population's demand, in the next few years could become worthy competitors of state enterprises and could influence the level of their prices and the quality of their products.

At the same time, the Law on Cooperation opens up the possibility of making the transition to the new stage in the development of cooperation for the purpose of satisfying the demand not only for consumer goods and services but also for producers' goods. This may pertain in particular to the fabrication of a number of interbranch products, spare parts, riggings, nonstandard equipment, the performance of repair work, and the performance of scientific-technological and start-up services. For example, the solution of the spare parts problem or specialization of the production of general machine-building parts and assemblies can be greatly simplified if large state enterprises promote the creation of cooperatives for the production of the indicated products to order. This may cause some workers to migrate from state enterprises that will be compelled to offer labor organization and wages at least on a par with cooperatives.

In our opinion, economic competition relations must be formed in all spheres of economic activity. While not claiming the list to be comprehensive, the following spheres can be singled out: the production and distribution of most producers' and consumer goods; trade and public catering; the performance of personal and a considerable part of social services; the distribution of capital investments; the design and construction of various projects; the creation and introduction of new technology; filling a wide range of positions; and material incentives. Naturally, the character, rate, and degree to which every sphere is embraced by economic competition relations will be different.

The most important lever in developing economic competition relations in the spheres of production and distribution of the means of production must obviously be the transition to wholesale trade in these means coupled with customers' enjoyment of the right and real possibility of choosing a supplier. But the first steps in this direction, which were associated with the conversion of the Ministry of Construction, Road, and Municipal Machine Building and certain other ministries and departments to wholesale trade exclusively through territorial organs of management of Gossnab [State Committee for Material-Technical Supply] starting in 1987, still did not provide the conditions for competition. Such conditions will take shape with the development of wholesale trade in the means of production in the form of unrestricted buying and selling under contracts between producers and customers or intermediaries as well as through factory stores. The transition to trade as envisaged in the "Guidelines for the Radical Restructuring of Economic Management" must be completed in four or five years.

This schedule is evidently designed for the purpose of eliminating scarcity. However, with the continued existence of ceilings, it will not be possible to eliminate scarcity for a long time. At the same time, as shown by the experience of a number of enterprises and organizations, particularly in Estonia, the transition to wholesale trade in itself leads to the substantial reduction of demand for materials and products that were until recently considered scarce. It seems to us that the transition to wholesale trade must be made not by branch or region but by types of products, and moreover that a considerable part of them should be removed from the centrally allocated system of distribution in one or two years.

The gradual transition to unlimited wholesale trade will promote the reduction of commodity inventories and the demand for many types of products, which will allow the respecialization of capacities to produce other types of products. In order to obtain orders when demand slackens, suppliers will be forced to expand the product mix, to improve quality, to lower prices, and to adapt the terms of delivery to the customer's demands. Unlimited wholesale trade in the means of production will thus prove a powerful lever for developing competition in the economy and for transferring the leading role from the supplier to the customer.

The insufficient efficacy of the economic mechanism in which competitive relations are not used has been clearly manifested in the complex task of improving product quality. The quality situation was supposed to have been radically improved with the introduction of product certification into quality categories, the introduction of planning of the share of products in the highest quality category, and the introduction of price markups. However, the economic system quickly adapted to the new indicators: enterprises tried to get the certification demands lowered, to get various products exempted from the certification process, etc. In a competitive situation, it would obviously be impossible to get quality requirements waived on products that are of inferior quality or that do not correspond to demand.

Competitive relations must also play a substantial role in bringing order to price formation. We know, for example, that the growth of prices on many types of machinery and equipment is significantly higher than the increase in their productivity, power, capacity, and other consumer properties. The USSR State Committee for Prices oversees draft prices submitted for approval by manufacturers of all types of series-produced machine-building products. But this oversight is not sufficiently effective.

The problem here is not only that it is impossible reliably to verify the correctness of the calculation of prices on hundreds and thousands of machines, apparatuses, and instruments from a single center, but also that the same machine offers a different effect to different customers. With the transition to self-financing and full cost accounting in the future, the indifferent attitude of customers toward the coordination of prices and the magnitude of the economic effect of new machinery will be replaced by a thrifty, commercial approach. However, such an approach can be manifested in full measure only if the customer for equipment receives it not on a mandatory distribution basis (on the basis of warrants [*nariady*] that are often issued by higher organizations without the consent of the customer), but as a result of the study of the market in the means of production, the choice of supplier, and the coordination of the parameters of a given machine, prices, and terms of delivery with the supplier. Customers will carefully monitor the prices and select the equipment they really need with parameters corresponding to their production requirements. Suppliers entering into cooperative relations with one another will strive to reduce production costs and prices, to improve product quality, to diversify product models and modifications, to improve the terms of delivery, service under warranty, and repair.

Competition must also play a large part in raising the effectiveness of financial and credit relations. The finance-credit mechanism must actively promote the fulfillment of the function of balancing needs and resources, in particular, in the sphere of capital construction. Capital investments, as a scarce resource, must be allocated first of all to enterprises that can with their aid secure the optimal satisfaction of social needs and the maximum cost-accounting effect. The use of the cost-accounting principle in distributing capital investments under the conditions of a socialist economy must have a limited framework: means for realizing strategic tasks, in particular for the development of fundamentally new scientific-technological directions, must be allocated without regard to this principle. However, when capital investments are distributed for the purpose of expanding the production of non-strategic goods, of providing credits for the technical retooling of production, etc., competition between enterprises should be organized on the basis of competitive bidding. The total requests for capital investments will usually substantially exceed the allocated resources of a given branch, for example, and after all requests have been submitted (naturally, together with quite detailed socioeconomic substantiations), a competent commission of experts will determine the necessity for and the sequence of allocation of capital investments. In the process of distributing credits, the role of arbiter could be played by the loan-issuing banks that take into account the conclusions of experts and the evaluation of the solvency of enterprises.

Competitive relations should be developed most widely in the area of scientific-technological progress. These relations must embrace: (a) the formulation and selection of plans for new enterprises, production facilities, reconstruction, and technical retooling; (b) the formulation and selection of variants of new equipment, technology, and organization of production; (c) the distribution of orders between suppliers of new equipment; (d) the distribution of orders between suppliers of science and engineering services, including services relating to the program and technology for the introduction, assimilation, maintenance, and repair of new machinery; and (e) the use of inventions and other technical innovations. In most general form, the development of competitive relations must lead to a situation in which every customer for new machinery will have a real opportunity to choose its developer, designer, and manufacturer, and they in turn will be compelled to compete for the most advantageous orders and to offer the best terms for filling them, for deliveries, or for the performance of services.

In actual practice, competitions for the design of enterprises, new equipment, or new technology are announced only in exceptional cases even though according to specialists, the submission of variant designs makes it possible to reduce the estimated cost of construction by up to 24 percent.[1]

How can it be explained that even orders contained in party and government decrees on the competitive selection of designs and technical solutions are not even being carried out? In our view, the following are the main reasons. First, the resistance of head ministries, departments, scientific research institutes, design offices, and science-production associations (for a given type of project or technical direction) that do not want to allow "strangers" into their sphere of activity. Second, the lack of wholesale trade in the means of production, the too unwieldy and strictly limited system of their distribution, which not only does not permit competition for orders, but even precludes the acquisition of already produced equipment or materials necessary for the realization of technical innovations. Third, the lack of an "antimonopolistic mechanism" in our economy and the existence of a system of head organizations that occupy (regardless of their merits and real potential) a monopolistic position in resolving the basic problems in the development of a given area of technology. Fourth, the lack of development of a science and engineering-services industry—start-up, consulting, and other organizations—especially interbranch or nondepartmental organizations. Fifth, the quite common opinion (even among economic scientists), that the parallel development and design work required for the organization of competitive bidding will require larger superfluous expenditures or will be impossible due to the lack of capacities of science-engineering and design organizations.

In actuality, in many cases additional expenditures will not be required because in almost all head scientific research institutes or design offices and outside their walls (at enterprises, at institutions of higher learning, in research and design organizations of consumer goods ministries), there will be collectives of creative workers who use different methods of resolution and who are prepared to submit their designs to competition (which is naturally open and objective). But even if additional expenditures are required, they will be recouped many times over not only on the basis of the selection of the most effective designs and solutions but also on the basis of the overall improvement in the quality of development and design efforts. What is more, after selecting the most rational design, the customer will also be able to use some of the best features from other designs, which will significantly increase overall effectiveness.

The mere reference to the expedience of competitive design or even its declaration as a general rule for the most important products from a national economic standpoint, as provided in the USSR Law on the Enterprise, is obviously insufficient to overcome the above-enumerated antistimuli to the development of competition. There is also a need for such guarantees as the invariable allocation of funds for financing alternative projects; the mandatory publication of conditions for open competition in a special bulletin; oversight by a higher organization and the bank up to and including the prohibition of financing of projects without the observance of the competitive selection procedure.

In our view, there is one more factor that hinders the development of competition in the sphere of creation and introduction of new technology: the existing procedure for using inventions that permits practically any organization to use almost free of charge any invention, which becomes "ownerless" as a result. Organizations or enterprises that create effective technical innovations are less interested in their broad diffusion, since costs and not the potential effect derived by customers become the decisive factor underlying the formation of their value. All this excludes the very basis of competition in the use of inventions and other technical attainments. In our view, a large role could be played by the transition to a modified patent system that promotes the transformation of the results of scientific-technological activity into a special type of commodity output, raises the interests of the creators of technical innovations in seeing to it that they are of a high technical level and quality and that they are widely diffused. On the other hand, organizations or enterprises that acquire licenses will contest this result in competition with other enterprises, which will raise their responsibility and ensure the more effective use of inventions.

The development of competition in the spheres of trade, public catering, personal and other services is of special significance for the satisfaction of man's urgent needs. The lag of these spheres behind modern demands and the needs of millions of people is in large measure connected with their monopolization by one organization or one department that has no competitors. For example, manufactured goods stores in the consumer cooperative system exist only in rural areas and raion centers. In cities, on the other hand, there is for the most part a uniform network of state stores: department stores, clothing stores, fabrics stores, household goods stores, etc. At the same time, most specialty stores in the city usually have the same departments, a very similar product mix (because they receive their products from the same base), and perform the same services. However, some socialist countries have established a wide network of urban cooperative department stores, factory stores, and specialty stores that in the interest of attracting customers offer a broad spectrum of services, apply various trade forms and methods and modern market research techniques, and exert a serious influence on the producers of consumer goods, and state trade enterprises have to improve their work as a result.

It is essential to bring about a radical change in the service sphere, where as a rule every person can go to only one personal service combine, to one apartment repair office, to one dry cleaning plant, to one household appliance repair shop, etc.

If the possibility of choosing a supplier or a performer of production services plays the decisive role in increasing the effectiveness of production, the effectiveness of labor in the social sphere can be substantially raised by granting the real opportunity of choosing a physician, teacher, a supplementary television program, etc. In every sphere, the task of expanding the possibility of choice has its own specific methods of realization. For example, the choice of a physician may become a reality if the network of cost-accounting polyclinics is expanded and if the rigid policy of assigning patients to sector physicians is discontinued. Naturally, a large number of patients will try to become patients of the more highly skilled specialists whose earnings should be higher.

The development of competition in the economy is directly connected to the restructuring of the economic mechanism. Such key directions in its reform as the expanded independence of the enterprise, its increased responsibility for its performance, self-financing and full cost accounting can be realized best under the conditions of competitive economic relations. This is because these relations confront the leadership of associations and enterprises with the need to show independence in all manner of economic situations, to bear responsibility for decisions made not only before higher organs but also before work collectives, since the possibility for the further development of production, for stimulating workers, and for realizing other socioeconomic tasks depends on success in economic competition. In other words, the principles of independence and responsibility of enterprises cannot be realized in full measure outside of competitive relations.

Naturally, there is need for certain guarantees against the consequences that can result from competition under the conditions of a capitalist market. The ruination of an enterprise entails such phenomena as its declaration of bankruptcy, the sale of its property at an auction, and the wholesale dismissal of its work force. In a socialist economy, the arsenal of means used by the state to influence an enterprise is fundamentally different: financial aid from special funds for the assimilation of new technology and technical retooling; the granting of credit; modification of the product mix up to and including the total respecialization of the enterprise; change of management; reduction of workers' wages; the transfer of the enterprise to another association; and, only as a last resort, the closing down of the enterprise. The selection of these measures and the rate and sequence of their application must be determined in such a way as to bring sufficient pressure to bear on enterprises failing to withstand competition, to ensure their profitability and self-recoupment. The Law on the State Enterprise provides substantial guarantees for the work force in the event an enterprise is closed down.

The question of forms of competitive relations requires special study, and therefore we shall confine ourselves only to certain considerations. From the foregoing it is clear that competition in a socialist economy can be manifested in the form of market relations under the influence of the systematic regulation of national economic proportions and strategic socioeconomic goals. The market form of competition is already developing and must be still more widely developed primarily in the production and distribution of consumer goods and services—not only personal services but also technical production, repair services, etc. With the advent of a number of alternative possibilities there will be development of the service market, which will play a large role both in the improvement of the quality of services and in eliminating "blank spots" from this sphere: organizations and enterprises whose services are not in demand will try to respecialize or diversify their activity, begin rendering services that are in particular demand, develop new types of services, and acquire high prestige in their area.

A special form of competitive relations is the competition of our enterprises in foreign markets. For a long time the state monopoly on foreign trade was regarded as the monopoly of organizations belonging to the USSR Ministry of Foreign Trade, which frequently hindered the initiative of associations and enterprises. At the same time, the practice of individual production associations shows that the direct participation of their managers in negotiations with foreign trading partners, in the organization of the advertising of their products, in the coordination of demand with the potential of their association, etc., produces better results than trade through intermediaries. Unlike the monopoly of foreign trade, which can by various methods secure the implementation of state policy and the observance of state interests in foreign trade activity, the monopoly of foreign trade associations frequently lowers the positive results of our enterprises' participation in competition on the world market.

After the adoption of the decrees of the CPSU Central Committee and USSR Council of Ministers, "On Measures to Improve the Management of Foreign Economic Relations" and "On Measures to Improve the Management of Economic and Scientific-Technological Cooperation with Socialist Countries," in 1986, the situation was supposed to change dramatically. Participation in competition in foreign markets confronts enterprises and associations with complex new problems. It is not only necessary to improve product quality and make it competitive, it is also necessary to master the methods of foreign trade activity. Leading associations are already creating special foreign trade services for the purpose of studying business conditions and the movement of products to the markets of foreign countries. However, in many cases financial and other conditions still do not promote the development of foreign trade activity and the creation of joint enterprises with firms from capitalist countries.

With the scarcity of skilled cadres, especially creative scientific and engineering-technical personnel, that developed under the influence of disproportions in pay and a number of other factors, the competition of enterprises and organizations to attract them becomes an important form. At the same time, with the expansion of the rights of the primary unit in the establishment of wage supplements, the strengthening of the relationship between pay and its final results, the higher demands on workers capable of making their contribution to the acceleration of scientific-technological progress, the significance of this form of competition will grow. On the other hand, the number of people desiring to work at enterprises that give their workers a higher level of pay and social services and payment for bonds issued,[2] may exceed the requirement of these enterprises. In such cases, job vacancies should be filled on a competitive basis.

As already noted, competitive bidding should become one of the most important forms of competition. However, the sphere of their action is not limited to the selection of technical designs and decisions. It would be expedient to create, as has been done in many countries, capital investment funds for the realization of designs and inventions that have not found demand. Customers may organize such competitive bidding for performer enterprises that propose to assimilate one or another type of product or fill another order.

Various forms of competition must also find their place in the formulation of draft plans; socioeconomic, scientific-technological, and regional programs; variants of restructuring of individual aspects of the economic mechanism; plans for the development of natural resources, for the transformation of nature, etc. In the past, many important plans and decisions adopted at the branch, regional, and national economic levels proved to be erroneous or unfulfillable due to the absence of a truly democratic procedure for drafting and approving them. Competition presupposes the real possibility of choice: the preparation of not one but two or several variants of a decision by collectives that are independent of one another; engaging specialists subscribing to different points of view in the discussion; raising the role of competent and independent expertise; secret voting; holding of referenda, etc. Only the democratic procedure for summing up the results of competition guarantees its objectivity.

In order to secure the development of competitive economic relations, it is important to expand substantially the diversity of forms of the organizational structure of production, to eliminate such errors of the past in the given area as the creation of monopolistic enterprises in the production of individual types of products, and the endowment of many head scientific research institutes and design offices with functions and rights that remove their developmental efforts from competition and enable them to avoid *glasnost'* and the open competition of plans and ideas.

It is necessary to formulate a kind of "antimonopolistic mechanism," which demands a certain reconfiguration of the management structure. The point is that we must rid ourselves of the idea that the existence of one head organization, one association or enterprise that is responsible for a given type of equipment, technology, or materials, ensures the unity of technology policy and therefore leads to progress. On the contrary, this leads to stagnation. Planning agencies, ministries, and departments must therefore ensure conditions for competition in the process of forming the structure of enterprises and scientific and planning organizations and in the process of determining their functions and responsibility. Naturally, the existence of one or two producers of one and the same product in the nation practically places them outside competition in the internal market, and this situation cannot be changed in a short period of time. However, such producers are relatively few and they may have competitors in the external market. The great majority of products are produced or should be produced by a number of enterprises, and the task of management agencies consists in such a determination of the specialty of existing and new production facilities that would secure the development of economic competition between them.

As regards the sphere of technological progress, in many cases competition may take place when there is duplication of topics within the framework of not two or three but one scientific research or planning and design organization—through the creation of competing departments or temporary collectives that independently work on the same problem from different angles. The head organization here must be not that which is designated by a higher agency but the organization that has through its activity won the authority of a head organization and that is better than others at solving problems in the given area. But even if the head organization is designated "from above," it must submit its competitive plans on a par with others.

The diverse forms of competition must be integrally combined with elements of intraproduction democracy. Elections of production managers and work collective councils; discussions in the process of preparing and defending the best solutions; the distribution of earnings with due regard to the coefficient of labor participation; the considerable growth of the activity of workers who try to prove their usefulness to production at a time when superfluous workers are being released, not only through their labor but also through proposals for cutting costs, for improving product quality, etc.—all these forms of competition in the work collective must simultaneously become forms of the manifestation of democracy.

To conclude, it must be emphasized that the formation of competitive relations in highly diverse spheres of the socialist economy is a large-scale and multifaceted problem. Its theoretical and practical solution will enrich the production relations of socialism with new elements that promote the acceleration and intensification of economic development. At the same time, competition is the opposite of command-administrative methods of management and is a powerful factor in developing the initiative of the working people, in the democratization of social relations.

Notes

1. See *Proektirovanie i inzhenernye izyskaniia*, 1983, no. 5, p. 15.
2. In our view, the current practice of a few enterprises to issue bonds or stocks to their personnel in order to attract their resources for the development of the enterprise or to increase their interest in its performance should become more and more widespread with the growth of profits.

E. Torkanovskii

The Participation of Working People in the Management of Production as a Factor in Heightening Labor Activism

The decisions of the Twenty-seventh CPSU Congress defined the character and rate of movement toward the qualitatively new state of Soviet society: the intensification of the economy based on the sharp acceleration of the rate of scientific-technological progress, and the radical restructuring of the economic mechanism and the system of management in general. The Soviet state has entered a critical period in the development of the economy. The human factor becomes more important in every critical period of social development, especially when socialist development is the point at issue. Ideological and educational measures plus economic reforms (especially the restructuring of the economic mechanism) are instrumental in activating this factor, in restructuring people's thinking, in orienting them toward the acceleration of scientific-technological progress, in improving product quality, and in increasing responsibility for performance. The main direction in the concept of this restructuring is known: the improvement of centralized management in the solution of strategic problems combined with broader rights and increased autonomy of enterprises and associations.

The question of increasing the labor activism of the individual worker and of the work collective exists today as well in the given context of strengthening and deepening democratic centralism. Such activism characterizes the degree of direct participation in social production and reveals the potential and attitude toward labor of an individual who

Russian text © 1986 by "Vysshaia shkola" Publishers. "Uchastie trudiashchikhsia v upravlenii proizvodstvom v sisteme faktorov povysheniia trudovoi aktivnosti," *Ekonomicheskie nauki*, 1986, no. 10, pp. 53–59.

The author holds a doctor's degree in economics.

lives under certain socioeconomic conditions, and it is determined by people's motivations.

Labor activism may stem from both external and internal motivations. The former is the result of an imperious command or of material incentives. The latter is the result of the interest of workers in the content of labor, of relations within the collective, and in all cases, awareness of the meaning of their activity. The labor activism of a person is determined not by some one motivation, but by an entire complex of motivations, the structure of which is not constant. Each mode of production generates its own characteristic motivations and stimulation for labor activism. Under capitalism, this is the quest for profit on the part of some and the threat of unemployment for others. The latter is a whip that is used by the owner of the means of production to compel workers to work productively and with a sense of discipline. Under socialism, the labor process becomes the form for expressing all the powers of the individual—the master of social production. Participation in the latter acquires social significance not only through the substantive result, *but also directly because it is the mode of the individual's self-expression.*

The structure of the motivational complex undergoes certain changes as socialist society develops. In its early stages, when the level of economic development was relatively low and the standard of living was correspondingly lower, an external influence—material rewards as well as punishments—occupied a decisive place in this complex. For example, even a minor increase in material incentives produced a very appreciable effect. However, with the general rise in the standard of living for all members of society, material incentives alone are not sufficient to stimulate the labor activism of the individual. In addition to external factors, internal motivation—satisfaction with work, with its content, and with the social significance of its results—takes on greater importance.

With the introduction of the Shchekino method, the decisive stimulating factors are not so much additional payments as the new working conditions and the expanded functions of workers. At many enterprises where the Shchekino method was introduced, the workers actively supported it even before the additional payments became a practice, because the work had become more interesting and challenging.[1] The same also applies to the diffusion of the team form of labor organization and incentives. Even with the team organization of labor, material incentives are not the key factor. The working people in teams actually participate in the management of production; the teams advocate variants of development of production that do not always coincide with the administration's opinion, and thus they feel that they are the full-fledged masters of production. The motivations created here for labor activism by participation in management have proven to be no less important than material incentives.

Naturally, this does not mean that job satisfaction as a motivation for labor activism must be counterposed with material interest. On the contrary, the more completely active participation in the management of production is reinforced by material incentives, the firmer is the basis for the success of the work colllective. Material incentives retain their significance all during the socialist phase of the communist mode of production. The securing of normal conditions for the reproduction of labor resources and the satisfaction of the population's consumer needs through the improvement of forms of wages, the organization of the supply of consumer goods, the construction of housing, childcare institutions, etc., is a necessary condition to raising the creative activism of the masses. But the fact of the matter is that this is no longer sufficient to arouse the level of interest that is required to attain the planned acceleration of the country's socioceconomic development. We cannot be oriented toward the power of material incentives to the same degree as in earlier stages of our society's development. At a meeting with veterans of the Stakhanovite movement, leading production workers and innovators at the CPSU Central Committee, M. S. Gorbachev noted: ". . . all motivations for highly productive labor cannot be reduced to the ruble. For the working person and especially for front-rank workers and innovators, moral incentives and the recognition of their services by society is no less important and indeed is often more important."[2]

Changes occurring in the complex of motivations underlying labor activism are the consequence of the rapid growth of the productive forces and of the improvement in production relations. The increasing complexity of the technical base of production requires that a worker take a creative approach. Performance alone, no matter how perfect, is no longer sufficient. The scientific-technological revolution requires maximum use of human ability, knowledge, and enthusiasm. There is need first of all for voluntary creative effort based on the performer's inner motivation. This does not diminish the significance of other motivations behind human activity based on external influences, be they material rewards or punishment. Such impulses should and are presently being implemented and practiced widely, and they are producing positive results when skillfully applied. However, the latter in the given instance do not go beyond performance and the precise execution of the given orders. This cannot be confined to the functioning of the productive forces during the scientific-technological revolution. It objectively requires a creative attitude toward labor and the ability not merely to carry out orders, but also to get one's bearings quickly in a situation and to make correct decisions in the event of deviations from the normal course of the production process.[3]

It is no less important to effect changes in the structure of needs, and especially to raise in labor the role of need, which is particularly dynamic in its development and which is filled with new content in proportion to the progress of the entire system of production relations in the communist formation. As a product of material and social living conditions, needs in general and the need to work in particular are at once a recognized goal and an "ideal, internal motivation for production. . . ."[4] With the improvement of socialism, the role and significance of the need for labor substantially intensify under the influence of the action of the general historical law of increasing needs.

The level of well-being attained under the conditions of mature socialism allows for the more complete satisfaction of the material needs of every member of society. Under concrete historical conditions, the latter have a saturation point that should not be exceeded for fear that the individual's development will be devoid of spirit.[5] As is known, the task of fully satisfying rational material needs is realized in practice through the elaboration of scientific norms governing the consumption of foodstuffs and the ownership of consumer goods and the determination of the population's saturation point for one or another good.

As material needs are satisfied, there arises the task of satisfying higher social and cultural needs, which include, for example, the striving for creative activity, for personal contacts, for self-affirmation, for a broader understanding of the world, for new knowledge. Such needs cannot be satisfied by things but by creative activity, and they have no saturation point. Therefore, even now and especially in the future, the satisfaction of non-material needs will become a more and more pressing and complex problem of social development. The need for labor, for creative activity is not only one of the noblest, but is also one of the most basic, deepest, and ineradicable sociocultural needs of man.

Under socialism, labor for every person continues to be first and foremost a means of livelihood. However, even in the lowest phase of the communist formation, man (and this is confirmed by all sociological research without exception) seeks in labor not only the source of satisfaction of other needs but also satisfaction with labor itself—its content, conditions, and influence on the attainment of socially significant goals. Under socialism, labor is a means of livelihood and at the same time serves the development of the producer's creative potential. Under these conditions, man cannot reveal his full potential as an individual unless he is satisfied with his work. The development of such satisfaction conditions a qualitatively new character of the entire system of the individual's needs, in which the need to work gradually comes to occupy the dominant position.

What conditions are necessary (do they exist and are they already developing?) for the transformation of labor into a primary vital need? In answer to this question, Karl Marx wrote: "Labor in material production can acquire such character only if (1) it has been given a social character and (2) this labor has a scientific character. . . ."[6] It follows from this that the development of a need to work is determined by its social character and by its heightened challenge ("scientific character"). The latter is associated with the growth of elements of creativity in the work. The increase in creative content makes work an enjoyment that can fire a worker's enthusiasm. Such labor reduces physical and nervous tension and delays the onset of fatigue. However, labor may also be mechanical and monotonous and incapable of arousing the worker's interest. In such a case, Marx notes "all during work time, there must be a purposeful will that is expressed in attention. The less inviting labor is to the worker by virtue of its challenge and mode of performance, and hence, the less the worker enjoys labor as the play of physical and mental forces, the more will is required."[7]

The increase in elements of creativity in labor as a general trend is associated with the mounting positive changes in the productive forces and with the gradual creation of the material-technological base of the highest phase of the communist formation. The unmechanized, strenuous, monotonous, purely perfunctory labor that predominated in earlier stages of development of socialist society was the result of the insufficiently high level of development of the productive forces. Such labor is also a reality in the present stage of development of socialism (albeit on an incomparably smaller scale). Since there are multiple variants of the development of the productive forces, socialist society can and should influence it through the purposeful choice of such variants of technological progress that are the most favorable from the standpoint of the saturation of labor with creative elements. In other words, scientific-technological progress under socialism must develop overall in accordance with the demands of socioeconomic policy and, in particular, must satisfy the "social mandate" for labor that is more challenging. The fulfillment of this "mandate" and the demand to increase the creative challenge of labor are directly included in the content of the objective of the development of our production. "Qualitative changes in the social sphere," M. S. Gorbachev noted in the Political Report to the Twenty-seventh Party Congress, "are impossible without *deep-seated change in the challenge of labor*. A special part here must be played by the technical reconstruction of the national economy—mechanization, automation, computerization, robotization—which, I particularly wish to emphasize, must have a clear social orientation."[8]

Radical changes not only in equipment and technology but also in the organization of production transform the content and character of labor, enrich its functions with creative content, intensify the intellectualization process, and increase the significance of mental work in all of society's aggregate labor.

Concrete organizational forms directed toward the enrichment of the functional content of the labor of each agent of production have been developed and successfully applied at several enterprises. They may include, first, the *rotation of works and their expansion* (the increase in the labor cycle). The essence of the rotation is that the worker changes his place of work in a certain sequence but "in a circle." Upon being expanded, fragmented operations are combined, and the cycle of projects takes not 2–3 minutes but 5–10 minutes or more. As a result, the work becomes more challenging and less monotonous, and differences in wages are to some degree diminished (the same worker performs operations that are more and less complex, and hence, operations that qualify for higher and lower pay). Second, the *enrichment of operations* is involved here. It is closely associated with scientific-technological progress. The consequences of the fragmentation of labor are not only attenuated, but the very nature of the operations also change: the worker must adjust the equipment, perform minor repairs and maintenance, etc.

At the same time, the possibility of raising the level and increasing the challenge of labor, and consequently of providing greater satisfaction with the labor process, is limited by the existing level of development of the productive forces. It will hardly be possible to eliminate unchallenging, monotonous labor in the foreseeable future. Does this mean that our society's members will be unable to attain the proper level of labor activism until we attain such a level of the productive forces that will make all labor highly challenging? No, it does not.

While the challenge in labor plays a significant part in making labor a primary, vital need, the social character of labor is a no less, if not more important, factor. The social significance of the process and results of labor is an indispensable condition to the formation of the need to work, and thereby to increasing the labor activism of agents of production. A proprietary attitude toward one's work—realized through participation in the management of production—is a powerful factor in increasing labor activism, which is inherent only in socialist society and which is eminently capable of serving as an internal motivation for labor activism that not only compensates the insufficiently high challenge of the labor process in individual operations, but that also becomes the basic internal motivation behind its manifestation. All historical experience confirms the fact that even the most sophisticated systems of incentives for the non-owner cannot compare in their positive impact on labor activism or in their creative approach with the force of the proprietary attitude of the owner who views the conditions of production as his own, which makes him interested both in the actual appropriation of material goods, in their preservation, in their constant expansion, and in their most effective use.

From this it follows that under the conditions of socialism, the requirement for creative labor cannot be realized without simultaneous satisfaction of the requirement for participation in managing the affairs of society in general, and in particular of the production sector where labor is applied. It must be considered that labor as such, labor that is purely perfunctory, and labor activity without any understanding of its future social results cannot become a primary, vital need.

Labor becomes a primary, vital need only when it has social meaning, when every working person is aware of his place and role in the production process, when the working person uses his abilities not only for the performance of production targets, but also for the formation of the actual labor process, for the establishment of its goals and the means of attaining them. In other words, the satisfaction of the need for labor and the saturation of the latter with elements of creativity depend not only on the functional content but also on the social character of labor. Unless the individual takes an active social stance, unless the individual participates in the management of production, it will be impossible to satisfy his need for labor as creative activity.

From the above it follows that satisfaction of the need for creative labor, which includes the need to manage production affairs, *acquires priority significance* and becomes an urgent necessity because the effect of an unsatisfied need to manage is extremely negative: it not only hinders the improvement of the system of production management, but also reduces labor activism and generates indifference to the results of labor.

Nevertheless, merely establishing the fact that the objective conditions of functioning of ownership relations create all the necessary conditions for the origination and development in every agent of production of the need to manage cannot lead to the strengthening of labor activism. As practice has shown, it is not enough to give agents of production the opportunity to participate in management. It is also essential that they have the desire to manage, that each of them actually develops the need to manage. And it follows from this that in the given instance as in others, society cannot be the passive recorder of the spontaneously arising need of its citizens. Society has the obligation to shape this need actively, based on the possibilities created by the system of socialist production relations.

The formation of the need to manage production as a function of the proprietor of society's property is one of the basic directions of ideological work. But this work will be sufficiently effective only with the creation of corresponding economic and organizational conditions such that the personal and social interests of producers coincide to the maximum possible degree. Such a coincidence is attainable when the economic mechanism is converted to a qualitatively new level, when it is deeply restructured in the direction of democratization of production management.

In the [ongoing] large-scale [economic] experiment, not enough attention has been devoted to the realization of this task. Even the introduction of collective forms of labor organization, which are a concrete form of socialist self-management of production, has not been sufficiently associated with experimental innovations. This can be explained to a certain degree. The traditionality of the approach to the improvement of the economic mechanism has been expressed first and foremost in the greater efficacy of centralized levers of management. This is, of course, the most important direction of improvement of the economic mechanism. However, the time has come to devote considerably more attention to the activation of work collectives. Otherwise, the traditional problems—indicators, norms, balances, material-technical supply, and others—can overshadow the essence of the restructuring, which lies in the mobilization of the socioeconomic activism of work collectives, in upgrading their responsibility for performance, in the development of the initiative and creative activism of the working people.

Participation of the working people in the management of production as a factor in increasing labor activism will become a reality if in the restructuring of the economic mechanism a twofold demand is observed: on the one hand, that the content and methods of production management ensure the most complete development of the management activism of the working people, and on the other hand, that the forms of the working people's participation in management make it possible to secure the maximum effectiveness of the latter. The entire mechanism of management of socialist production must be "x-rayed" from this standpoint, starting with the participation of the working people in planning and ending with individual and collective forms of material incentives and with the system of expending social consumption funds.

Consequently, the point is that changes in the content and methods of economic management must be viewed as one of the factors in the development of democracy in production: organizational structures, the principles and methods of management, its content, management procedures, and other attributes of state economic management must accord with the possibility of developing the managerial activism of the working people and must ensure the constant collective search for reserves.

At the same time, it is essential to elaborate a system of "intracollective" measures of a primarily economic character to interest every member of the work collective in participating actively in management. This refers to the necessity of creating an economic mechanism that would ensure the real motivation of every worker to make social production more effective. The other side of such motivation is the upgrading of the economic responsibility not only of economic managers but also of the entire work collective for irrational management, for the breach of contracts concluded by enterprises, for the deficient technical level of production, for flaws of management, etc. This responsibility must be weighty and inevitable. In other words, the economic mechanism underlying the involvement of the working people in the management of production must be built according to the principle: the dependence of performance on every agent of production and the dependence of the receipt of goods by everyone on the performance of the collective.

It is on this principle that the collective forms of the organization of labor and wages are built. The creation of self-managing work collectives leads to the greater functional challenge of labor on the one hand (as a result of the mastery of several specialties by members of the group), and on the other hand (and this is most important) the self-managing group bears collective responsibility for the end results of labor and has the right to make managerial decisions on such questions as the determination of the mode of target fulfillment, the distribution of rewards and the application of punishment, the admission of new members, etc. This organizational structure makes it possible (if correctly used) to satisfy the need for creative labor not only as a result of the higher challenge of the latter or the increased effectiveness of material incentives, but chiefly as a result of the satisfaction of the need to manage. The advantages of the team form of labor organization and incentives are based primarily on the use of this factor.

Thus, the more complete, deeper, and responsibile participation of all agents of production in the management of the affairs of enterprises and the state becomes one of the important factors in increasing labor activism, and thereby a necessary prerequisite to solving the problem of accelerating the nation's socioeconomic development.

Notes

1. Concerning this, see: L. Gol'din, "Stimuly novatorstva," *Kommunist*, 1983, no. 16, p. 50.

2. *Kommunist*, 1985, no. 14, pp. 39–40.

3. In the age of the scientific-technological revolution, the productivity of the work force depends to an ever greater measure on the degree to which the intellectual potential of the direct producer is used. Even with the high level of contemporary capitalist exploitation, the reserve labor productivity of workers based on their creative attitude toward labor is estimated at roughly 30% (see E. Lenk, *Die qualifizierte Mitbestimmung der Arbeitnehmer und ihre Wirtschaftliche Problematik*, Cologne, 1961, p. 10).

4. Karl Marx and Friedrich Engels, *Sochineniia*, second ed., vol. 12, p. 717.

5. We consider it appropriate to cite the appropriate remark by E. Aleksandrova and E. Fedorovskaia: "Even though socialist society has not yet reached the threshold of saturation of all basic needs, even now it is necessary to remember that these needs are limited in their development by certain functional characteristics of the human organism (the need for food, housing, clothing, etc.), the excess of which is accompanied by a substantial decline of the socioeconomic effectiveness of their satisfaction"

(E. Aleksandrova and E. Fedorovskaia, "Mekhanizm formirovaniia i vozvysheniia potrebnostei," *Voprosy ekonomiki*, 1984, no. 1, p. 16). This is especially important to consider because the high standard of living of all strata of the population in the socialist countries creates a real threat that some people will develop a penchant for "things," i.e., the striving to acquire things as virtually the most important aim in life. The increased possibility of satisfying material needs must invariably be combined with the relatively more rapid rise of people's ideological-moral and cultural level. If this is not the case, there will inevitably be manifestations and recurrences of philistine petty bourgeois psychology. On the other hand, it would be wrong to reduce the law of rising needs under modern conditions of development of socialism to the non-material sphere. The relatively more rapid growth of non-material needs is possible only if a certain rational level of satisfaction of material needs is attained.

6. Marx and Engels, vol. 46, Part II, p. 110.

7. Ibid., vol. 23, p. 189.

8. *Materialy XXVII s"ezda Kommunisticheskoi partii Sovetskogo Soiuza*, p. 48.

Plan and
Market

LEONID ABALKIN

A New Conception
of Centralism

The Soviet economy is on the threshold of major change. The Law of
the USSR on the State Enterprise (Association) will take effect at the
beginning of the new year. Most of the basic links of industry, all of
transport, and many participants in the agro-industrial complex are
being converted to full cost accounting and self-financing.

Naturally, high results from the conversion of enterprises and associations to the new conditions can be realized only with the corresponding, quite radical restructuring of the systems and methods of centralized management. Essentially, as stated at the June 1987 Plenum of the
CPSU Central Committee, the point at issue is the introduction of a
new conception of centralism. This conception is not the fruit of impro-
visation or armchair conjecture. It is born of life and is based on deep
political and economic generalizations and a critical assessment of
historical experience.

Functions of the center

The point of departure for this new conception is a more precise
definition of the content and functions of centralized management. And
this is only possible on the basis of a comprehensive and realistic
analysis of the socialization process and the complex, dialectically
contradictory structure of the socialist economic system.

Today it is clear that the socialist socialization of production does
not by any means lead to the creation of an economy with one "common kettle" or "one large purse." Management that is based on such

Russian text © 1987 by "Pravda" Publishers. "Novaia kontseptsiia tsentraliz-
ma," *Ekonomicheskaia gazeta*, no. 50, December 1987, p. 2.

The author is a correspondent member of the USSR Academy of Sciences and
director of the Institute of Economics of the USSR Academy of Sciences.

"theoretical" premises inevitably generates dependency on the one hand, and totally unlimited, purely administrative intervention in economic life on the other. The consequences of such a practice are well known.

The socialist socialization of production has produced a complex, multilevel economy, the basic links of which are production enterprises and associations. They act as socialist commodity producers operating on the basis of total self-recoupment, cost accounting, and self-management. Only by creating a "most favored environment" for their activity is it possible to count on a radical increase in the effectiveness of production, on its reorientation toward the consumer, on the formation of a truly proprietary attitude toward labor and its fruits. The realization of all this means activating the mighty potential of public property in full force.

At the same time, the socialist economic system is not the mechanical sum of enterprises and other economic links. Originating and acquiring strength in the process of the socialization of production, it possesses the property of wholeness. Correspondingly, the public interest cannot by any means be reduced to the sum of collective and personal interests—after breaking down into them there is left a remainder.

The functions of centralized management must be determined with due regard to the complex, contradictory unity of the wholeness of the economy and the relative separateness of its primary links. Strictly speaking, there are only two of these functions. The first of them consists in the management of the national economy as a unitary whole. This includes those questions (and only those questions) that cannot be successfully resolved by the independent action of lower-level economic links. Among them are development of the strategy of economic growth, determination of the goals and priorities in the development of the national economy, and implementation of a unified scientific-technological, structural, and investment policy.

The resolution of these problems, by their essence, by their very nature, is the prerogative of the center. And naturally it must possess the necessary authority and financial resources and levers.

The second function of centralized management consists in the creation of conditions for the effective, independent, and responsible action of the basic links of the national economy. The realization of general, universal balance in the economy, the elimination of the monopolistic position of individual producers, and the creation of prerequisites for the broad development of effective economic competition are of decisive importance among these conditions. The exercise of this function is integrally connected with the incorporation in the management mechanism of the socialist market and the methods intrinsic to it.

Analysis of the existing system shows that both functions of centralized management are substantially deformed. Many decisions, including integrated programs for the development of individual branches and regions, are made without critiquing the development of the national economy as a whole: short-term, tactical problems take precedence over strategic problems. There are still restrictions on the initiative and independence of enterprises and associations.

As a result, the existing system of centralized management is a serious obstacle on the road to economic and social progress and has been the subject of entirely valid and just criticism. Management techniques require radical modernization, and this must be attained with the recently undertaken radical reform of economic management.

The transition to economic methods

The question of methods is the question of the means to be employed in attaining the stated goals and strategic objectives. One of the significant features of the new conception of centralism is connected with the understanding of the necessity and the avenues of eliminating obsolete methods.

For a number of decades, the economy was managed with the aid of predominantly administrative methods, which came to amount to commands and orders. The ranks of their advocates have grown significantly thinner. The majority now realizes that methods based on commands and orders are hopelessly obsolete and historically out of date. However, it is not entirely realized that such methods are justified and are effective only under special, extreme conditions and that they are in principle alien to the socialist economic system.

The socialist economy must be guided by its inherent economic methods. Their essence is the management of interests through interests. Only on their basis is it possible to find an answer to the most important and difficult question in the theory and practice of management, and specifically, the question of the most effective combination of planned management with the interests of the worker and the work collective.

When methods are based on commands and orders, enterprises and their personnel are the objects; when they are based on economic methods, they become the subjects of this process. Therefore, the transition to economic methods is inseparably connected to the democratization of management and the creation of an effective mechanism of functioning of public property and the use of its historical advantages.

This is not the first time the issue of economic methods has been posed. But the present understanding of them is deeper, richer, and more substantive than in the sixties. Then, the discussion was of the introduction of a new system of planning and economic incentives. Given such a formulation of the question, economic methods were viewed as a supplement to centralized planning, a kind of adjective in this system, not a noun. The Basic Principles on the Radical Restructuring of Economic Management, drafted and approved by the June 1987 Plenum of the CPSU Central Committee, contain a fundamentally different interpretation of the question. Economic methods—prices and credit, taxes and payments for resources, wholesale trade in the means of production—are regarded as key elements and component parts of centralized economic management.

Economic norms occupy a key place in this system. They are at the same time planning instruments that make it possible to regulate the most important national economic proportions, and the basis for converting enterprises to full cost accounting and self-financing. Economic norms make it possible to effectively coordinate the interests of society and the work collective in order to ensure their interest in high end results.

This is promoted to the maximum degree by unified norms governing the distribution of profit, the formation of the wage fund, and economic incentive funds. The individualization of norms for enterprises and individual years contains the danger that they will degenerate into the previous, purely administrative methods.

Naturally, the transition to uniform norms cannot be viewed as a one-time act and without regard to overcoming existing disproportions and price reforms. But it is necessary to see clearly both the final goal and the dangers presented by the use of individual economic norms.

The uniqueness of "restructuring on the march" consists in the fact that many new methods must be superimposed on Twelfth Five-Year Plan targets that have already been approved and scheduled for individual years. A contradiction arises between the need for uniform norms and the impossibility of introducing them under the given conditions.

This contradiction cannot be ignored—a way of resolving it must be found.

One such way could be to develop a scale of norms that takes into account the difference in basic conditions, for example, the level of technical equipment and profitability. In such a case, for enterprises that differ substantially in the level of profitability, normative deductions from profits to the budget will be different, but they will be uniform for enterprises with approximately the same level [of profitability]. The differentiation of other conditions of management can be taken into account in similar fashion. The construction of a scale of norms along the lines of progressive taxation is of no little merit.

Transition to economic methods of management does not mean the modernization of the existing system, but the assimilation of a qualitatively new model of the economic mechanism. Here there is much that is unusual and nontraditional. There will be a complex process of teaching the art of management based on the driving force of interests. While it is impossible to learn this art from books, without good books it will be difficult.

The philosophy of the state order

A basic distinction of the new conception of centralism is associated with the rejection of attempts to plan everything from the top. The face of socialist production must be turned toward the consumer. The consumer's order must become the point of departure in the formulation of the production program. In such a case, it is in principle entirely possible to abandon the centralized approval of the production volume and product mix.

But there are customers, and then there are customers, as they say. Among their many-faced throng, there is one priority customer: the state. Its special place is determined by the fact that it is the direct exponent of general needs. The development of a modern philosophy of the state order is contingent upon an understanding of this circumstance. These are not merely new words to designate the outmoded detailed list of centrally planned product targets, but an expression of a fundamentally different approach to the centralized management model.

The state order is by its nature limited, since it encompasses only the most strategically important and socially significant targets. Expansion of the circle of targets inevitably leads to the erosion of this principle.

The narrower the priority targets, the more strictly are they observed and vice versa.

In order that priorities be not merely an administrative form or slogan but that they acquire economic reality, they must ensure advantageousness. The state order must become the most advantageous way for an enterprise to use its production and labor potential. This advantageousness is realized by means of guaranteed sales with the aid of prices and tax benefits, and in the event of necessity, by priority in the acquisition of scarce resources. Any attempt to force enterprises to manufacture products disadvantageous to them under the guise of a state order in departmental interests means repudiating the principles of the new system of management.

The priority nature and advantageousness of the state order make it possible to place it on a competitive basis. Conditions are thereby created for including the mighty force of economic competition in such an important sphere of centralized management. It is precisely the advantageousness of the state order and its awarding on a competitive basis that make it an economic method of management. In the absence of these features, the state order degenerates into the usual, ineffective system of purely administrative pressures on economic processes.

Control figures also take on a fundamentally different role. They are conveyed to the enterprises in the preplanning stage and are not of a mandatory and obligatory nature. The attempt to force targets established in the control figures on enterprises is a throwback to the old methods and a graphic manifestation of the urge to administer by command.

The question naturally arises: Why do we have control figures if they do not have binding force? In the new conception of centralism, the control figures serve as guideposts that planning agencies use to inform enterprises on future changes, and on the expansion or reduction of demand for the output of the relevant branches and production facilities. They perform a special, previously little known, specifically informational and orientational function of centralized management. The conditions are thereby created for increasing the flexibility of demand and for its effective combination with the expansion of the independence and initiative of enterprises, with the increase in their responsibility for the quality of their economic activity.

The restructuring of the entire model of centralized economic management cannot fail to affect the structure of its organs. By no means have all questions been resolved here. The creative interpretation of approaches to the structuring of organs of economic management is all the more urgent here.

Organs of economic management

Unlike political organs of state, organs of economic management are a product of the socialization of production. The creation and reorganization of these organs by the state make it difficult to understand this truth but do not in any way abrogate the objective logic of formation and development of the structure of economic management.

The essence of this logic is that the socialization of production naturally generates certain general functions. Their implementation becomes more effective not when it is carried out by the enterprises themselves but by the special organs created for this purpose. Enterprises transfer part of their rights and powers to these organs in the hope—not without foundation—that they will be exercised more successfully. There is a kind of ''delegation of powers'' from below to the higher echelons, and not vice versa as is frequently depicted.

Thus, the organs of economic management play an auxiliary role vis-à-vis the basic, primary links in the economy. As is known, the state and its organs in equal measure play an auxiliary role vis-à-vis socialist society.

One of the contradictions in the socialization process is that the organs of management created in the course of its development have a tendency to become separate entities, to acquire special interests of their own, and to rise above those who gave them their powers. The gradual development of these trends if they go unchecked inevitably leads to the bureaucratization of management and generates a command-administrative style. In order to prevent such phenomena, there must be powerful counterweights—the development of democratic principles in management, *glasnost'*, the accountability of economic management organs. It must always be remembered that it is not enterprises that exist for ministries but ministries that exist for enterprises, for the creation of conditions for effective management. This also applies to other economic management organs.

Taking what has been said above into account, the restructuring of economic management will evidently proceed in two directions. First, the voluntary creation by enterprises themselves of organs subordinate to them (and only to them) for carrying out common functions—in the area of supply and marketing, for the creation of facilities in the production infrastructure, etc. Second, in regard to the reorganization of existing economic management organs—their reduction and streamlining, and the more effective fulfillment of functions generated by the socialization of production.

It can be assumed with sufficient certainty that in time the development of these processes will lead to the formation of a qualitatively different structure of economic management that is distinct from the present one. It is as yet very difficult to paint its picture in specific terms. But it is important to sharply intensify the politico-economic critiquing of the question and analysis of the objective logic in the formation of organizational structures of economic management.

The practical implementation of the new conception of centralism requires the in-depth understanding of its essence and the repudiation of many dogmas inherited from the past. There must also be substantial forward progress and a real breakthrough in the theory of socialist management. Only in this case can one count on serious economic success and on the fundamental improvement of economic effectiveness.

L. POPKOVA

Where Are the *Pirogi* Meatier?

Articles on economics today are replete with references to V. I. Lenin, who is invoked as the supreme authority on the protection of "socialist" market ideals. Lenin was indeed immeasurably more flexible and daring than subsequent figures who in both theory and practice brought socialist principles to the absurdity that he fought against at the end of his life. Words in defense of "commercial," or "profit-and-loss" socialism, to use the current expression, are indeed found in his articles and pronouncements. But anyone desiring to do so can take quotations from these works and speeches and assemble them any way they choose, which is what commodityists [*tovarniki*] and noncommodityists [*netovarniki*] (the "merchants" and "cavaliers") are doing in their polemic. . . .

I have long asked myself: Is it responsible to say that Vladimir Il'ich Lenin, for whom "liberal" (liberalism, freedom in the Western sense, competition) was a swearword, was fundamentally in favor of market relationships? Can one disregard all subsequent practice and socialist theory, in which there has never been and in my opinion never will be any room for a market economy, economic liberalism, and competition? Never, because socialism—and this is my deep conviction—is by virtue of the design of its creators, by virtue of the *instinct* of those who have consciously embodied and continue to embody the corresponding principles and customs, incompatible with the market. In all the differ-

Russian text © 1987 by "Izvestiia" Publishers. "Gde pyshnee pirogi?" *Novyi mir*, 1987, no. 5, pp. 239–41.

The author holds a candidate's degree in economics.

ent periods of Soviet history, all manner of politicians and theorists have tried to steer the country onto the market path, but it has not taken a single step in this direction. Is this by chance?

I have a certain amount of experience studying the "third path" along which West European social democrats have tried to lead their countries in the postwar decades. The "social democratic decade" has most graphically confirmed the correctness of Lenin's conviction that there is no third path. One cannot be a little pregnant. Either the plan or the market, either the directive or competition. One can seek and apply something in between, but the chance of success is no greater than the possibility of sitting on two chairs. Either there is the market economy, which operates according to precise, rigid and uniform laws for one and all, together with all its pluses (efficiency, for example) and minuses (vast inequality of incomes, unemployment . . .), or a planned socialized economy, also with all its pluses (for example, man's certainty about the future) and minuses (shortages, mismanagement).

Upon acquiring power, the social democrats immediately undertook to redistribute the wealth and to establish social justice, whereupon the economic situation in Western Europe began to deteriorate rapidly. Slogans such as "just distribution," "equality in distribution," and "social welfare" had a sweet ring to them, but their fruits proved to be very bitter. As foreign economic pressure on owners intensified, as market accumulation mechanisms were undermined, as taxes increased in the name of "public welfare," and with the expansion of "full employment" programs in the attempt to preserve jobs in branches that had lost their ability to compete and to slow down technological restructuring—with all this, the economic situation deteriorated, with growth rates declining and inflation becoming rampant (reaching the double-digit level!).

Social democratic governments have generously printed money, using this simple device to raise pay and social payments, they have applied protectionist measures to protect domestic industry from competition in foreign markets, . . . and they have been injured by what they fought for.

But analyze "third paths" ("competition to the extent that is possible, planning to the extent that is necessary") on other continents, take a look at the practice of "indicative planning," look into the kitchen of the developing countries from the standpoint of "plan or market" and you will see how rapidly we are being overtaken by those who have chosen the market, and you will also see how hungry people are where they look at the market suspiciously and menacingly, where they do not stand on ceremony in dealing with the market (naturally in the interests of some hungry faction—there is always an abundance of good intentions). Finally, take a look at the socialist countries: where there is more market, the pies are meatier.

I recall how delighted I was with G. Lisichkin's little book *Plan and Market* [*Plan i rynok*] when I was a student at the Plekhanov Institute, and how diligently I prepared for my state examination on economic reform (the teaching at the time was that it was a reality). Now, however, while cursing the noncommodityist-"cavalier" with my previous fervor, I am also skeptical of the commodityist-"merchants" who are developing illusory ideas about "market socialism." To me, this is an absurd term. I repeat: where there is socialism, there is no room for the market and the spirit of liberalism. I also extend this certainty of mine to current attempts to orient the national economy toward consumerism. In a planned economy, the law of value cannot operate advantageously; socialism is incompatible with the market. Neither Marx nor Lenin was in error in this regard. Socialism is a planned economic system. The fact that the economic effectiveness of this system and its potential for securing the rapid and stable improvement of [the people's] well-being was evidently slightly exaggerated is another matter.

On the first day of 1987, I read [an article by] D. S. Likhachev in *"Literaturka"* [*Literaturnaia gazeta*] which stated that "a 'half-truth' is the worst type of lie." While it is difficult for me to agree with these words entirely, because life has taught me that the half-lie also occasionally has merit, the academician in the given instance appears to have precisely defined one of the unique features of our time. There are those who truly proceed from the outright lie to the half-truth. They reread Marx, for example, to be able to say that in his early works he indicated the possibility of making the evolutionary, peaceful transition from capitalism to communism and that only out of ignorance and inattention to the "whole Marx" has the world read into the *Communist Manifesto* that socialism should be built through revolutionary intervention in property relations and by destroying everything in the old, rotten, exploitative society. They would persuade us that Marx was not such a militant, that the idea of the "expropriation of the exploiters" was not the most important feature of Marx's genius, that somewhere between the lines, in the footnotes, in his letters, in the notebooks of his youth, he also countenanced the peaceful avenue of development and that we today should take these *footnotes* and use them and Marx to substantiate our "new peaceful path," our efforts to finally make "plan" and "market" compatible, our attempts at becoming a little bit pregnant.

Some new little quotations for the next case. . . .

We reread Lenin in order to show that in the struggle against the "cavaliers," he also uttered certain kind words about "merchant" methods of management, but someone did not quite hear these words and as a result this socialism that was built was not entirely the socialism that was bequeathed to us. This socialism! Hear me right—this socialism! Precisely this one, because the other, "merchant" socialism is not socialism at all. Not one of the opponents of the market's spontaneity, private property, money grubbing, and exploitation—from the most primitive to the most serious—admits to the possibility of the existence of a mechanism for generating and selecting innovations and discoveries, of the best ways of interaction between man and nature, between man and society that is independent of ideology, of a political and ideological center. The utopian phalanxes and their phalansteries require a space that is cleansed and free of all traces of the old life. Look at the blueprints of cities of the future left to us by Thomas More, Campanella, and other precursors of scientific communism; take note of the regularity and correctness of all the structures and the absence of room for the slightest randomness, play, fantasy, and inexplicability. The brilliant dreamers, unlike some of the scientists' contemporary followers, were unequivocally dedicated to the idea of the rational organization of life and were proud of this fact.

Thus, the principle of "a little bit of a good plan, and a little bit of a good market" is just as alien to me as it has been to all the convinced collectivists of all times. Socialism of all hues, ranging from academic socialism to "democratic reformist" socialism, has rejected the liberal market scheme with contempt. In no socialist teaching has the market ever found a proper place, and the niche that Western social democrats have erected for it has satisfied only them and has yielded nothing worthwhile.

These are lessons that we should learn from. But why is the highest mark our political economists score always a 'C'?

. . . Two comments in conclusion. Both Western socialists and our commodityists believe that the age of the purely market economy irrevocably belongs to the past. But I sometimes think that the Western world is still merely on its threshold, at the very beginning of the road. Free enterprise was for a long time stifled by the vestiges of feudalism and the activity of utopians of every ilk, as a result of which the twentieth century proved to be so bloody. It was stifled, but it seems to me that it was not smothered, and that it has a serious future whether we like it or not. We must look the realities straight in the eye.

The second comment concerns the possible question as to where the ideological sympathies of the author predominantly lie: on the side of the plan or the side of the market. For the benefit of those interested in this question, I would like to recall Engels's famous words to the effect that a person of science should not have ideals, because having ideals means being prejudiced and makes it difficult to see reality as it actually is.

E. POZDNIAKOV

Is It Possible to Be "A Little Pregnant"?

A Dilettante's Opinion

No matter what you say, L. Popkova's short note "Where Are the *Pirogi* Meatier?" in issue five of *Novyi mir* has clearly caused a sensation. The author is to be congratulated: the ideas expressed by her have agitated people's minds for a certain time, have generated disputes, sometime even very fierce, have caused opinions to clash, and have inflamed emotions. . . .

While all this is true, nevertheless one is still left with the feeling of dissatisfaction that the author did not say all that was on her mind. . . .

"How can you say that anything was left unsaid," the correct rejoinder will be, "when the note explicitly and unequivocally states that the plan and the market cannot coalesce, and if they do coalesce, then, in the author's deep conviction, this is already capitalism more than socialism."

O, sancta simplicitas!—it must then be said that we have already drawn very close to it [capitalism]!

Was it specifically about this that L. Popkova wanted to warn us, was it this that she wished to call to our attention so as to lead us out of our confusion; to lead us, so to speak, out of the state of "restructuring euphoria" before it is too late and to steer us onto the path of true, genuine socialism, from which we appear to be straying if we have not already strayed?

Russian text © 1987 by "Pravda" Publishers. "Mozhno li vse-taki 'nemnozhko zaberemenet'"? (Mnenie diletanta)," *Mezhdunarodnaia ekonomika i mezhdunarodnye otnosheniia*, 1987, pp. 113–17.

However, in order to dispel any doubts on this score, let us turn to the note itself. Here is the author's textual credo: ". . . socialism—and this is my deep conviction—is by virtue of the design of its creators . . . incompatible with the market. . . . To me, this ['market socialism'] is an absurd term. I repeat: where there is socialism, there is no room for the market and the spirit of liberalism. I also extend this certainty of mine to current attempts to orient the national economy toward consumerism. . . . Attempts to combine the 'plan' and the 'market' are attempts to be a little pregnant'. . . . The principle of 'a little bit of a good plan and a little bit of a good market' is just as alien to me as it has been to all convinced collectivists of all times. . . ,'' and so forth in the same spirit.

The demand could not be more explicit: the words do not so much speak as shout, and it might seem that no commentary is needed. But we have taken up the pen not to quote the author, but to express our criticism. As we understand it, the reviewer's criticism is not merely to praise or censure or to present an evaluation that evokes no thought whatsoever. There is no need to weary the reader with a discourse on political economy (on which entire tomes could be written). We will be just as brief as the note's author.

We will begin with the most obvious point, specifically, the author's lack of a dialectical and historical approach to the problems under review. Is it perhaps that the author also assigns dialectics and historical method to ''market'' categories, which are unacceptable under socialism? We then ask forgiveness, but we have grown so accustomed to them that it is too late to unlearn them and it is for this reason that we cannot but be shocked by Popkova's frozen, unflexible, impenitent schemas or by her openly metaphysical logic: anything that goes beyond a simple yes or no smacks of evil. We must admit that there is even something appealing about the primordial simplicity and philosophical patriarchalness. . . . She paints social pictures with only two colors—black and white, without any unnecessary hues or any distracting tinges. There is an amazing simplicity: *either or*; not the thinnest hair could be wedged between *yes* and *no*.

The author's iron logic is oppressive, and the leftist cry of bygone years—Who is not with us is against us—rings in our ears.

But it is too late! We have already had several swallows of the invigorating air of restructuring; and having done so, we have grown bolder, we have been filled with the "liberal spirit." Our thoughts and feelings have begun to protest: Why only black and white, only yes and no? And finally having become bold, we permit ourselves to express an entirely seditious thought: Why can one not become a little pregnant if we are talking about society?

And indeed, why not? Who said so? Was it someone in the last century? A lot of water has passed under the bridge since then. Then there was no socialism; there were only theories and edifying debates in the offices and from the chairs of various academic socialists whom the author mentions in vain.

But today, by the way, we are already *living* under socialism, and we know it not from theory, but from practice. We already know what is good or bad about it, what we do not want in it and what must be gotten rid of: we do not want a socialism that is entangled in the web of administrative coercion; we do not want queues, the abuse of power, unrighteous judges, bureaucracy, the absence of openness [*glasnost'*], the lack of thought. . . . What is the reason for this yes or no, for this either or? Indeed, at a time when so much effort is being exerted today to overcome stagnation in society's economic, social, and spiritual development, statements of the type: either "plan" or "market" are always reminiscent of the position of the "wellwisher" who upon seeing a funeral procession shouts to the coffin bearers: "Well, you'll never run out of customers!"

Where, one asks, would the idea of the market, of which there is so much discussion in the note, come from if in our society and in our objective reality proper there were not a burning need for its broad development? And if this idea has not been properly reflected in society, it is because we have long been dominated by dogmatic thinking. But fortunately, the logic of development is such that when science becomes dogma that begins to impede the development of life, life invariably either rejects it or else corrects it and brings it into line with itself.

But, it seems to me that we have gotten carried away, that we have become didactic, and are beginning to utter banalities. However, we have been forced to do so by the author's simplistic view, which is manifested in its total logic and in the seemingly devastating and irrefutable formula that "one cannot be a little pregnant."

Not every comparison in science can be considered fortunate and, as experience shows, the most unfortunate are comparisons of a living organism to the social organism. It is one thing when such a comparison is used as a metaphor, but it is quite another matter when it expresses a scientific principle. This is precisely what happened in the given instance. For all the unquestionable wittiness and external convincingness of the formula cited above, it does not work when applied to the social organism. Using the same importunate "midwifery" terminology, we note that unlike a living organism, society is in principle *always* "a little pregnant" with something new that is born over a long period of time, slowly, and with difficulty in its depths. And it is possible to be in this "interesting" condition for a very long time. Whether it develops to term, whether it ultimately produces a fetus or ends in nothing depends on a number of concrete historical circumstances that are too numerous to mention. But just as the possibility of unpleasantness and complications does not discourage people from having children, so it is in social organisms that the possibility that a social experiment might fail has never dissuaded people from following the path of daring, reform, and progress, especially when these were dictated by life. Our economy, however, has long been "pregnant" with the idea of radical restructuring based on the integral combination of plan and market—there are few who doubt this today. It would seem that the time has come for it to be delivered of this "child." But as we ourselves see, the matter has proven difficult—so difficult in fact that surgical intervention may be entirely necessary.

Some may take exception, and not without foundation: Is L. Popkova not right in her alternative "either the plan or the market?" No matter what you say, they are different things. They are indeed different, especially as Popkova construes them: she understands "plan" to mean the rigidly centralized plan that dominated our economy for many years, and understands the "market" to mean the spontaneous market forces of capitalism in the times of Dreiser's Cowperwood (at the end of her note, she explicitly states that these spontaneous forces have a serious future). They indeed cannot be combined—here, Popkova is right. But the point is still that neither one nor the other is related to socialism.

Popkova's straightforward but dogmatic approach prevents her from viewing the problem from a different, in our view more correct, important, and, if you will, acute angle. We will do this for her. According to a wise biblical saying: new wine is not put into old wineskins; if it is, the skins burst, the wine is spilled, and the skins are destroyed. This would seem to be the real essence of the "plan-market" problem. The "old skins" are the "plan" in its previous understanding in the spirit of undemocratic centralism, together with the old economic mechanism with its all-encompassing vertical and horizontal monopoly; the "new wine" is full profit-and-loss accounting with self-financing and self-recoupment embodying the idea of the market under socialism. All-embracing bureaucratic centralism, even though it has little relationship to socialism, has become firmly entrenched in practice; profit-and-loss accounting and everything associated with it, on the other hand, as yet exists more in the realm of ideas, even though it is directly related to socialism. Therefore, present attempts to put the new and immature "wine" of profit-and-loss accounting into old but still entirely strong planning and economic "skins" that are unwilling to relinquish their positions are engendering serious contradictions in our economy. Nor are they abstract: they involve living people and passions; they reflect the most vital, frequently opposing interests. After all, it is only in words that everyone is for restructuring. In actuality, however, if we dot the "i's," these "old skins" serve as the broadest social antirestructuring base (does it not nurture views such as those expounded by Popkova?). If the obstructions of bureaucratism and its power that exists to this day, of coercive centralized planning, of administrative and fiat methods of management, of petty guardianship over everything, and finally, of the fear that gnaws at us—What if things go wrong?—are not eliminated in good time, we are firmly convinced that these contradictions will totally discredit the idea of the economic, social, and spiritual restructuring of society and will curb the democratization and openness process. That is how the problem looks to us.

And, finally, where does Popkova get such, let us be frank, presumptuous certainty to paint her socialism as the only possible type, and that it is specifically barracks socialism—neither "market" nor "*pirogi.*" There is not even any discussion of democracy and openness. . . .

"Enough of your verbiage," we hear the voice of the more perspicacious people, "Is the author against all this?" If not, then why the "meaty *pirogi*" that she invitingly includes in the title, that she uses to tease our unsatisfied "socialist" appetite?

Indeed, is Popkova not being cunning? Despite all our disagreements with her, we would be willing to give her consistently uncompromising attitude its due were it not for those ill-fated "meaty *pirogi.*" They have spoiled the whole works, they have destroyed the strictness of her judgments and have reduced principle to questionable ambiguity. Indeed, after constructing her rigid scheme of "either or," and after departing, as it seems to her, from the question she deftly posed at the end concerning her own choice between "plan" and "market," Popkova through various kinds of innuendos engenders in the reader the conviction that she herself is for "meaty *pirogi.*" Whether she wished it or not, Popkova placed herself in a very ambiguous position. Judge for yourselves: under socialism, the "meaty *pirogi*" so desired by her are excluded; the only remaining possibility of obtaining them is under . . . market capitalism. This is why Popkova's position is very far removed from "convinced collectivism," of which she so self-confidently claims to be a true advocate. And Popkova in vain refers to Friedrich Engels to justify herself, and makes him out to be a dry, pedantic schoolteacher devoid of ideals and emotions.

But this is not the most important thing. The entire matter hinges on the actual formulation of the question. It is precisely this formulation that causes genuine astonishment and perplexity. What was the meaning of all these ideas of the author, which are strange to say the least? What was their purpose? Was it to mystify or astonish the reader? Or was it merely a play on words? If this is the case—and we do not see any other rational explanation—it is, as Gogol' said, even foolish to look.

We could conclude on this note. But Popkova's short note, even though we reject all its positions, forced us (and not only us) to take another, more attentive look at the vital problems in our society's economic and social restructuring. And we see once more how complex this matter is, how many obvious and hidden obstacles there are on the road to restructuring that still have to be overcome so as not to limit it, as in the past, to half-measures or, what is still worse, to destroy it entirely. We can be thankful to L. Popkova at least for that.

O. LATSIS

Why Are You Pushing?

To L. Popkova, Author of the Letter "Where Are the *Pirogi* Meatier?"

I found your letter, which was printed in issue five of *Novyi mir*, quite perplexing. And I am not the only one. Many of my acquaintances ask me: "Did you read it? What is it all about?" I was not immediately able to say just what it was in your letter that bothered me. After all, you did not provide material for scholarly discussion by economists. Nor did you cite facts or arguments. The only thing that could be considered an argument was your brief statement about the failure of the social democratic, "third road" in capitalist countries. But is there anything new and surprising in this? Has any Soviet economist predicted that it would be successful? And what relationship does all this have to a socialist economy?

Your assertions cannot fail to evoke bewilderment from your very first words. You write, for example, that neither in practice nor in theory has there ever been a place for "profit-and-loss" socialism in our country. What do you mean by that? What about the USSR in the twenties and the entire group of socialist countries in the sixties through the eighties? And as for theory, what about the works of V. S. Nemchinov, V. V. Novozhilov, L. V. Kantorovich, A. M. Birman, and many others? And what about Soviet economists in the twenties? And what about many of them that are alive and well today? And what about our colleagues in socialist countries?

Russian text © 1987 by "Izvestiia" Publishers. "Zachem zhe pod ruku tolkat'? L. Popkovoi, avtoru pis'ma 'Gde pyshnee pirogi?'" *Novyi mir*, 1987, no. 7, pp. 266–68.

The author holds a doctor's degree in economics.

This may not be important. But the points made in your letter are important. It raises a question that is frequently raised in our country and abroad, a question that many people ask themselves. Even though you did not explicitly formulate the question, it follows from the logic of your letter. I allow myself to state it as follows: Will our plans come to fruition, will we cope with the reform of the economic mechanism, without which we cannot cope with the entire restructuring?

This is a question in which we are all keenly interested. But do you yourself hear the answer you gave? I fear you do not. It has long been known that specialists are like flux. I have noted more than once that many specialists are painfully inept when they discuss their subject with people belonging to other professions. They race through information that is known and comprehensible to them but that is unknown and incomprehensible to others, or do not notice that their audience does not understand them or, still worse, that they misunderstand them. It seems to me that you became so carried away with criticism of dogma that we political economists are all so tired of that you forgot about everything else.

I agree with you that there are those who all their life have opposed commodity-monetary relations ''according to Marx'' but who are now for them—once again ''according to Marx''; this is the sum total of their restructuring. They are unable to speak ''about life.'' But can you really believe that real restructuring is made by the works of such authors? While justly warning us against entertaining excessively high hopes for answers in ready ''quotations,'' did you notice what you said beyond that? After all, you said that the reform that we have commenced is unrealistic and that nothing can be realized. If you, as I believe, said this without wishing to and without noticing, you will argue that you did not say these words. I agree that you did not. But such is the logic. After all, you said that the ''plan'' cannot be combined with the ''market'' (the terminology is imprecise, but we will accept your words for the given conversation; their meaning is understandable). That is, in your view it is possible to build such a mechanism, and the effectiveness of production will grow and the "*pirogi* will be meatier," and you seemingly do not oppose this mechanism (even though you do not seem to be in favor of it), but this will not be socialism. You do not state anything else. The reader must complete the thought himself: we do not want capitalism in any case, so we have to renounce restructuring and "*pirogi*" at the same time. Is this not the case?

Is it not strange that your speech, which is so bold, uninhibited, and unorthodox, turns into the most banal dogmatism? The planned economy is depicted as not connected with the full profit-and-loss accounting of enterprises specifically in the dogmatic view of planning (of planning exclusively in the form in which it existed up to now) and of the "market" (depicted solely as the carrier of indomitable spontaneous forces and nothing more).

Theoretical arguments in favor of the possibility of combining the plan and profit-and-loss accounting are well known. There is a considerable amount of scholarly literature on this subject. We also have some practical experience. But your arguments are more from the realm of social psychology (if not even individual psychology) than from economics. But this is also an important, even very important, plane of analysis. You know from personal experience, but this is natural for all people; so, what we have is a fact that is both personal and at the same time social. But in your account of your personal experience, you unmistakably hint of your disappointment. There was absorption with the little book about the plan and the market. There was enthusiasm in connection with the economic reform. As it turns out, you even took the state exam on it but the reform did not come off.

And so you took a "state exam on the economic reform." Thus, according to my calculations, you received your higher education about ten years after my peers. I took my state exams three months after the Twentieth Party Congress and went to my first place of work filled with the inspiration of the unforgettable year of 1956. I welcomed the first restructuring—the birth of the national economic councils [*sovnarkhozy*]—with the same inspiration. Perhaps I am influenced by my experience at that time, but even now I believe that national economic councils were useful, even though I realized long ago that this question itself— the distribution of the administrative apparatus by branch or by territory—was of tertiary importance in the overall problem of reform.

As an economist, I understand this. As a person, I realize what a shock this was for everyone, the passions that boiled, the fates that were smashed. I was very vividly reminded of all this, incidentally, by A. Bek's most recent novel, as if it were today and as if it were written about the life of today. But here I want to tell not of the merits but of the shortcomings of the national economic councils. You, while preparing for your state examination on the 1965 reform, also had to address the reasons why the national economic councils were abandoned. For you, this was study material, but for my generation it was living material. In the biography of my generation, this was one more disappointment (or if you will, defeat). But after all, a generation that was another ten years older, a generation that lived through 1941 and was ultimately victorious, it would only laugh at our disappointments. And what of those who are even older?

In 1965, the economists of my generation, who saw the beginning of the Virgin Lands, Bratsk, and the rise and fall of the national economic councils, drew what I consider to be the most natural conclusion: since not everything came off the way it should have in 1957, we had to go deeper. And what we learned in our subsequent work (in which many things also did not go the way they should have) makes it possible to look with not less but greater certainty at future work: after all, we have considerable experience behind us.

You correctly link the fate of socialism to the economic reform (and, you add, the entire restructuring). Is your socialism the socialism that Lenin left in his will or not? You say that it is, and you emphasize your point with an exclamation mark. It is the best and consequently cannot be improved upon. I, however, do not believe that it is the best as yet, that we will make it better. I need no arguments other than the fact that this is what I think. This is precisely the point at issue in the given instance. If you, I, he, she, they, if we all think that our socialism must be made better, we will make it better. If we do not think that it can be made better, then we will not make it better.

And this is very important to understand because the times that lie ahead of us will not be easy, and the *pirogi* will not become meatier overnight. You cannot hope to have the *pirogi* if you have not sown the grain. I would compare the present with the beginning of capital repairs on a dilapidated house: we will have to endure many new discomforts before we put things in order. It is a time when we must labor patiently in order to cope with a mountain of work. It is a time for analyzing the details of how best to perform these repairs on our economy.

Knowledgeable people, specialists, and intellectuals today have the great responsibility of conscientiously trying to understand what is happening and of explaining it to others. Lamentably, instead of this, one sees those who add up old literary accounts, others who recall (or invent) injuries inflicted sometime by someone on their nation, while still others simply shout anything at all without regard to the search for the truth but merely to show everyone how bold and original they are. Enough! Does it take courage to shout these days? Courage is needed to think new thoughts, to abandon—if only for oneself—cherished misconceptions.

Twenty years of stagnation pose a difficult task for all of us. We will have to make up for lost time. We will have to pull at the oars with all our might, not where the water runs still but against the current, against the waves. Every pair of hands on the oars is precious. But if someone cannot or does not wish to row, that is up to him. Only why should he push someone else's arm?

T. VALOVAIA

The Difficult Road of Cognition

Reflections on a Timely Book and a Sensational Article

"Not even love has made fools of so many people as the attempt to divine the essence of money."

Karl Marx was fond of quoting this figurative pronouncement by a nineteenth-century English politician. Indeed, only Marxist economic theory could reveal the true essence of the basic categories of the capitalist economy—commodities, value, money, the market, competition—from a truly scientific position. The economic realities of the twentieth century have confronted political economists with new questions relating to the historical process of development of commodity production. One of the most involved questions, which has been the subject of fierce debates among economists, is that of the role of the market under socialism.

Today, at a time when the radical reform of economic management envisages broader use of the economic methods of planned management and commodity-monetary relations, this problem has acquired markedly greater theoretical and practical significance. The June Plenum of the CPSU Central Committee noted that the relationship between centralized planned management of the national economy and the independence of its individual links, between planned development and commodity-monetary relations, requires serious reinterpretation. Very timely in this

Russian text © 1987 by "Pravda" Publishers. "Trudnyi put' poznaniia. Razmyshleniia nad aktual'noi knigoi i nashumevshei stat'ei," *Ekonomicheskaia gazeta*, August 1987, no. 35, p. 9.

The author holds a candidate's degree in economics.

regard is V. Shemiatenkov's book *Between Spontaneity and Planned Development (How Monopolistic Competition "Works")* [in Russian], recently published by "Mysl'" Publishers.

The problems raised in the book regarding the essence of monopolistic competition and monopolistic enterprise and the role of the economic mechanism in the confrontation between the two systems are unquestionably of interest not only to economic specialists, but also to a wide range of readers who of late have been deluged with articles written by their countrymen advocating freedom of the market and maintaining in particular that the "golden age" of free enterprise is still ahead. Is this the case?

The book explores with great depth and thoroughness the capitalist economic mechanism of today, the main principle of which is the interaction between the firm and the market. As the author correctly notes, bourgeois social thought makes a fetish of the market and has blind faith in its miraculous powers. "Of all the stereotypes of bourgeois and reformist propaganda, the myth of the market is the most dangerous." Some of the working people are in the thrall of ideas generated by bourgeois propaganda and link illusory hopes for the rapid and easy improvement of their well-being with the use of spontaneous market forces under socialism. On the basis of in-depth scientific analysis, the monograph shows that this ideological phenomenon is based on certain characteristics of the revolutionary transition from capitalism to socialism and the development of a new formation.

The author notes that the commodity form of the socialist product carries with it the danger of the emergence of partial disparities between personal, group, and social interests. Our class enemy tries to capitalize on this and uses every means to counterpose the plan to the market, to shake the foundations of the socialist economy, and to revive the private ownership mentality among the population of socialist countries.

Some of our economists also try to counterpose the plan to the market. Illustrative in this regard is L. Popkova's publication "Where Are the *Pirogi* Meatier?" in issue five of *Novyi mir*, which has already generated considerable debate. Playing at impartiality, Popkova refrains from openly declaring which side she is on—the plan or the market. But there is hardly any doubt as to where the economist's "ideological sympathies" lie when she states that socialism and the market are incompatible, that the *pirogi* (read standard of living) are meatier where there is more of the market, and finally goes so far as to make the blasphemous statement that the twentieth century was so bloody because "free enterprise was for a long time stifled by the vestiges of feudalism and the activity of all manner of utopians."

The author clearly does not believe in the future of the socialist economy, and gives preference to free enterprise. In her opinion, capitalist *"pirogi"* are better than socialist ones. Well, of course, that is a matter of taste. And it is a good thing that openness in our society permits writing about this openly. It is a good thing that the time of "hanging labels" has passed. But it is not a good thing to distort what one does not believe in to please one's own taste.

> I repeat: where there is socialism, there is no room for the market and the spirit of liberalism. I also extend this certainty of mine to current attempts to orient the national economy toward consumerism. In a planned economy, the law of value cannot operate advantageously; socialism is incompatible with the market. Neither Marx nor Lenin was in error in this regard. Socialism is a planned economic system. The fact that the economic effectiveness of this system and its potential for securing the rapid and stable improvement of [the people's] well-being was evidently slightly exaggerated is another matter.

It seems to me that this short paragraph can compete with the spacious materials of Western newspapers in terms of the number of distortions it contains. We are supposed to be persuaded that the founders of Marxism-Leninism bequeathed us socialism in finished form together with clear indications of how things were to work. But this system is supposedly not effective.

Everything here is turned topsy-turvy. Let us focus attention on the book *Between Spontaneity and Planned Development*. Its author clearly shows that Marx and Engels left the solution to the question of the specific forms and methods of revolutionary restructuring of society's socioeconomic life to subsequent generations of revolutionaries, since the practice of the workers' movement of that time naturally could not shed light on the details of the future revolution. "Preconceived opinions regarding the details of organization of future society? In us, you will not find even a hint of them," Engels wrote.

What an enormous theoretical wealth and what practical experience of real socialism the founders of Marxism-Leninism left us—they are described with innovative boldness in the section "The Economic Program of the Socialist Revolution" of the book *Between Spontaneity and Planned Development*. I heartily recommend this to undiscriminating readers who took at face value L. Popkova's statement that in Lenin's opinion the law of value cannot work to advantage in a planned economy.

Popkova does not believe that the Soviet economy is capable of radical reform. But why refer to the fundamental premises of Vladimir Il'ich Lenin about the need for profit-and-loss accounting and material interest under socialism, which are the basis of restructuring, as a "contrived collection of quotations" from his works? As we know, Lenin spoke of this on more than one occasion and devoted a considerable number of his works to the conceptualization of the experience of the first years of the socialist economic system.

Returning to Popkova's statement about the impracticability of our economic reforms, it should be said that today even bourgeois ideologues are less and less inclined to denigrate the reforms in the Soviet Union. It is indicative that many responses of bourgeois propaganda to the June Plenum of the party's Central Committee emphasize the realism and radical nature of its decisions. Here, for example, is an admission by the *New York Times*, one of the most influential American newspapers. Speaking about the projected reforms in the USSR, it writes: "We must not simply consider whether they are an indication of convergence with

Western ideals and institutions. We should not hasten to proclaim their success or failure or to exaggerate the influence of the West. What is happening will be based on Russian history and *Soviet society*" (*EG* Editors' emphasis).

The author of the article "Where Are the *Pirogi* Meatier?" while defending the conception of the incompatibility of the "plan and the market," attempts to foist the opinion on the reader that we are traveling the path of West European social democracy and to frighten us with the results of the economic policy of social democratic governments—the decline of growth rates, inflation, the declining competitiveness of industry. But an economist who undertakes to elaborate such a sharp and urgent topic should know some common truths: Western Social Democrats are not failing because they try to "redistribute the wealth and bring social justice," but because they are pursuing their economic policy from petty bourgeois, reformist positions. What is more, impartial statistics show that when Social Democrats are in power, a country's economy does not invariably suffer ruinous consequences. Thus, in the seventies, when the coalition of the Social Democratic Party of Germany and the Free Democratic Party was in power, West Germany, despite the deterioration of the general conditions of development in the world capitalist economy, retained and even strengthened its economic positions and surpassed its competitors with respect to a number of indicators.

To all appearances, readers should be frightened still more by Popkova's thesis that "all manner of utopians" who stifled free enterprise were to blame for the fact that the twentieth century was bloody. Isn't it obvious that Popkova is once again thinking of Western social democrats? And what is meant by "vestiges of feudalism?" In any case, the author's article was extremely rough on the social democrats, who in the given instance appeared to be extreme right-wingers. After all, neither the American Republicans nor the British Conservatives have ever tried to dump the blame for the difficult, sometimes even terrible fate of the last century of the present millennium on the social democrats.

I do not deny that I wanted to learn in greater detail about the author's stand on this question, about her "experience in studying the path" of West European social democracy. Guessing that her candidate dissertation was devoted to this topic, I visited the V. I. Lenin State Library. But I met with failure: such a work was not to be found. Does this mean that she used a pseudonym? But why then did she add "candidate degree in economics?" I do not doubt that the author has an academic degree. But nevertheless, it seems to me that to use a pseudonym—while this is the sacred right of every publicist—and to add an academic degree for the sake of greater convincingness is nothing more nor less than "sitting on two chairs," to use Popkova's own expression.

Using the plan to frighten and the market as a lure, the author employs one distortion after another. "Look at the socialist countries," the author of the journal publication writes, "where there is more market, the *pirogi* are meatier." Is that true? Of course, it is not surprising to hear something of this sort from the average tourist returning home from a short visit abroad. But a candidate of economics who is teaching us how carefully we must treat the classics and who laments that the highest grade received by political economists is a "C" should probably know that the state of a nation's economy cannot be judged entirely on the basis of the glitter of the shop windows and the assortment of the stores. I would very much like to advise Popkova to read the section of the book *Between Spontaneity and Planned Development* entitled "Are Appearances Real?" which reveals the deep Marxist idea that the conceptions of people who are directly involved in capitalist production relations are phenomena that distort the essence of real economic relations. And some "scholars" try to present these distortions as reality.

In conclusion, the author of these lines does not conceal the fact that she sees no antagonism between the plan and the market. I believe that the socialist economy will sooner or later find their optimal combination. And let there be a little more plan in one socialist country and a little more market in another. And let this correlation be flexible. This will only enrich socialism. Ultimately, may L. Popkova forgive me for the "quotation," Marxism-Leninism is not a dogma.

Incidentally, a word about quotations. Even if one does not like quotations, it is not good to distort their content. Thus, Popkova writes in her conclusion: " The second comment concerns the possible question as to where the ideological sympathies of the author predominantly lie: on the side of the plan or the side of the market. For the benefit of those interested in this question, I would like to recall Engels's famous words to the effect that a person of science should not have ideals, because having ideals means being prejudiced and makes it difficult to see reality as it actually is."

In this instance, Popkova resorts to a "marshaling of the facts"—a principle which she condemned. Let us recall to whom Engels's words apply. As is known, Marx resolutely opposed attempts to glorify his person. After his death, Engels saw to this. Presenting Paul Lafarge with his remarks on his review of a book by a French bourgeois economist, Engels wrote: "Marx would have protested against 'the political and social ideal' that you ascribe to him. Just as soon as it is a question of a 'man of science,' of economic science, he must not have an ideal. He elaborates scientific results, and when he is, moreover, also a partisan man, he struggles to see to it that these results be applied in practice. A person who has an ideal cannot be a man of science because he proceeds from a preconceived opinion" (vol. 36, p. 170). In other words, Engels warns Marxists against blindly submitting to Marx's authority, demands that he not be transformed into a "political and social ideal," but that they act in accordance with the circumstances, and that they be guided not by an ideal individual, but by partisanship based on knowledge, not feelings. This is the essence of the remarks of one of the founders of Marxism. But our learned "person of science," intoxicated with the "spontaneous forces of the market," did not understand the true sense of Engels's words or, what is still worse, deliberately manipulated them in her own interests. And this prevents her from seeing "reality as it is."

I heartily urge everyone who has read this sensational journal article to become familiar with the profound, intelligent book *Between Spontaneity and Planned Development*, which shows in particular how difficult and thorny is the path to divining the socioeconomic realities of society and how difficult it is to understand the nature of the plan and the market. Knowledge of the strengths and weaknesses of the opposing economic system, V. Shemiatenkov emphasizes, is one of the prerequisites to the successful improvement of socialist economic management and further progress in the economic competition with capitalism. To this, it can be added that only by knowing the true and not the apparent essence of spontaneous market forces can one judge the "meatiness of the *pirogi.*" Of course, not forgetting in the process who eats them.

Price
Reform

G. A. KULAGIN

Product Mix, Price, Profit

The preliminary results of the large-scale experiment are currently the subject of discussion in the pages of the central newspapers
and economic journals. At the same time, the range of enterprises
converted to the new conditions has been significantly expanded
since 1985.

Most industrial workers participating in the first phase of
the experiment clearly expressed the desire to reduce decisively the number of plan and performance-evaluation indicators
(which, incidentally, are far more numerous than intended in
the 1965 economic reform), to dramatically improve supply, and
to consolidate supply contracts which, in our view, is the reverse side of the same problem of increasing the reliability of
supply.

Economic scholars, while agreeing with these wishes, are engaged in a lively debate on another topic: precisely which indicators—physical or value—should be given priority and what
should be the specific set of these indicators? Very interesting in
this regard are articles by economic scholars A. M. Birman
("Tons, Units, Rubles") and D. V. Valovoi ("Specialization and

Russian text © 1985 by "Ekonomika i organizatsiia promyshlennogo
proizvodstva." "Nomenklatura, tsena, pribyl'," *Ekonomika i organizatsiia
promyshlennogo proizvodstva*, 1985, no. 11, pp. 89–106.

The author lives and works in Leningrad.

This article is published for purposes of discussion.

Realization'') published in the pages of *EKO** for discussion purposes.[1]

The thrust of the first article is directed against the emphasis on physical indicators [*naturofil'stvo*]. Its author shows the utopian nature of the idea of direct calculation of the physical needs of our gigantic national economy even with the aid of the most sophisticated computers, protests attempts to create artificial general indicators based on the arbitrary ''ranking'' of dissimilar components, and advances value categories to first place.

Conversely, D. V. Valovoi, the author of the second article, cites very colorful examples of the fictitious growth of gross output and sales by means of manipulations with totally unneeded cooperation, and, while not denying that value categories have a certain amount of significance, he believes that physical and labor indicators must occupy the main place in the system of plan indicators and that NNO [normative net output] must take the place of gross output as an indicator.

Paradoxical as it may be, even though at first glance both concepts are direct opposites, both authors are correct in criticizing the existing system of indicators. While their proposals to improve the planning and evaluation of enterprises' work were substantially different from one another, they were also quite convincing, even though they were formulated less clearly.

It seems to me, a practical person who has worked more than 40 years in industrial enterprises, that there is the possibility, and above all the necessity, to reconcile these two different approaches and to find the synthesis that will facilitate the more complete utilization of the vast reserves of our production collectives.

For the beginning, I would like to support the opinion that the role of economic methods in economic management must not be underestimated. Figuratively speaking, the economy of devel-

---

*Translator's note: *EKO* is the acronym commonly used by Soviet specialists to denote the journal *Ekonomika i organizatsiia promyshlennogo proizvodstva*.

oped socialism rests on three whales: state-public ownership of the means of production, centralized planning, and commodity-monetary relations. The advantages of the socialist mode of production consist specifically in the combination and full utilization of all three principles. We cannot ignore the laws of the commodity-monetary relations that actually exist. What is more, if they are not correctly used, it is impossible to measure the labor contribution of each worker, i.e., to realize the main socialist principle "to each according to his labor," and to determine the effectiveness of the work of production collectives. This is a generally recognized axiom.

But D. V. Valovoi is also right when he blames the existing value indicators, particularly the sales indicator, which is nothing more than the "second I" in notorious gross output, for many sins: for impoverishing the consumer goods mix, for the disappearance of many necessary but inexpensive items in the quest of "others' labor," for the increase in material-intensiveness and the decline of the output-capital ratio, and for the reduction of the actual effectiveness of social production.

As already stated, both authors recognize the need for the "coexistence of physical and value indicators." Neither of them deny the necessity of planning the product mix and the usefulness of raising the responsibility of enterprises for the fulfillment of delivery contracts, because this is essential to the normal operation of individual enterprises and the national economy as a whole. The only question is the degree of detail of "physical planning" at the various levels of economic management.

The principal disagreement lies in the answer to two questions. The first: how to evaluate the dynamics of change in the volume of output, because physical indicators are not always suitable for doing so or, more precisely, are clearly unsuitable for the majority of our multispecialty enterprises? The second: how to evaluate the ultimate effectiveness of production?

A. M. Birman believes that this is best achieved by the sales and profit indicators that are actually reflected in accounting balances and bank accounts, and objects to the construction of artificial indicators such as NNO.

His opponent, on the contrary, considers NNO the most suitable yardstick of the dynamics of output because when correctly "designed," this indicator most precisely reflects the collective's own contribution to the social product and excludes the quest for "hired," for "others' " labor and for the fictitious growth of the volume of production. For the evaluation of the effectiveness of production, on the other hand, a system of different kinds of indicators, among which profits are not mentioned, is proposed.

Also, both authors skirt or say very little about what we consider to be the main issues: prices and pricing. And yet, under the conditions of a planned economy in which market relationships are not price regulators, it seems to us that correct pricing is the basic issue in the further improvement of the economic mechanism. Saying nothing of the fact that all distribution relations rest on prices, all presently active plan and performance-evaluation indicators are derived from price: sales are the sum of prices of sold goods; NNO is the same sum minus "past labor"; profit is price minus production costs; productivity is the sum of the prices of products divided by the industrial work force, etc.

Before discussing the role of prices and pricing in detail, in our view it is useful to consult the experience of the 1965 economic reform, which advanced the profit indicator to one of the leading places. Today, one can frequently read articles criticizing that indicator. The fact that the 1965 reform did not produce the anticipated effect is cited as a substantiation of this criticism. At the same time, it was precisely in the course of the reform that there was a considerable increase in the growth rate of labor productivity; fixed and working capital indicators improved; production costs declined at a faster rate; and there was much more growth in profits. At the same time, as one who took an active part in the discussion of that reform's principles in the stage of its preparation and who also managed a production association under pre- and post-reform conditions, I can testify that it did not actually justify all the hopes that were placed in it.

But let us ask ourselves: why? Because the reform incorporated false principles, or were there other reasons?

I wish to decisively support A. M. Birman's opinion: the reform principles were absolutely correct and its partial failures were due exclusively to the inconsistent, indecisive implementation of these principles. There were two critical errors. First, tight state control over pricing was not established from the very beginning (even though the pricing system was improved in the course of the 1967 wholesale price reform). As a result, many enterprises began increasing their profits not as a result of actual increases in the volume of production and the lowering of production costs, but by jacking up prices. In many instances, the money incomes of the working people began growing at a faster rate than the productivity of their labor.

Second, since heavy industry enterprises were better organized, they were the first to be converted to the new conditions. Only then were enterprises in light industry, the food industry, and the service sphere, i.e., branches that create the material goods on which the population spends its available cash, converted. Moreover, prices on the goods that determine the people's living standard were more closely monitored.

The result was that the wage level and the quantity of money in the population's possession began to rise faster than the volume of consumer goods. The central planning and finance organs, rightfully concerned over this gap, began issuing one set of additional instructions after another restricting the growth of incentive funds and average wages and introducing additional indicators that gradually reduced the entire idea of the reform to naught instead of instituting stricter price controls. In addition to payments for capital, enterprises also had to surrender their free profit remainder. The terms governing payments to incentive funds gradually became more complicated, and eventually there was no connection whatsoever between the size of these funds and the performance of the enterprise collective. Then, ceilings were placed on bonuses, and they, too, were lowered from year to year.

The September (1965) Plenum of the CPSU Central Committee indicated that in time the enterprise development funds would become the principal source for renovating the means of production, and that enterprises would thus cease to be the dependents of the state budget and would themselves be responsible for the entire reproduction cycle. In practice, however, development funds were set at such a low level that not only reconstruction but also the current renovation of equipment continued to depend on centralized allocations. However, even these meager funds were soon "centralized," and enterprises were deprived of the possibility of disposing over them as they saw fit. The same fate also befell currency proceeds from exports.

But in itself, the idea of the self-renovation of enterprises was absolutely correct not only from the standpoint of increasing the responsibility of managers for keeping the enterprises entrusted to them up to date, but, what is even more important, it was very useful as a factor restraining the rise of equipment prices. If a manager acquires a new machine using budget allocations that are "lost" after January 1, and if, moreover, he will "catch it" if he does not utilize all his resources, the cost of the machine is a matter of indifference to him. But if he uses his own, earned funds to buy the machine, he will think thrice whether the machine is worth the asking price. The result is a powerful feedback that enables organs of the State Committee for Prices to keep those who have a penchant for jacking up prices in check.

Unfortunately, this did not happen, and prices on equipment crept upward. Strange as it may seem, there was no agency truly interested in counteracting this trend. Neither the manufacturer, nor the customer, nor even the Ministry of Finance proved to be interested in stabilizing and lowering prices. I cite an example from the practice of the association in which I worked. A machine that we successfully developed in a short time began yielding indecently high profits after a while. Since the free profit remainder went to the budget and the increase in profits did not in any way increase the size of our incentive funds, we ourselves suggested that the price of the machine be lowered. The ministry reluctantly agreed. The State Committee for Prices also agreed. Strange as it seems, the Ministry of Finance objected strongly. At first we could not understand this paradox: it seemed to us that the financial department should be keenly interested in lowering prices. But then everything became clear: when the Ministry of Finance collected surplus profits in the form of the free remainder, it simply and easily accumulated it in the form of budget revenues. But when prices are reduced, budget revenues decrease and the Ministry of Finance is unable to determine whose budget allocations for these machines should be reduced accordingly, because the allocations are made to tens and even hundreds of addresses.

Let us sum up. In our view, the aforementioned failures of the 1965 reform are by no means associated with the reappraisal of the role of profits and value indicators, but are exclusively linked to its indecisive and inconsistent implementation. Instead of concentrating all efforts on the central issue—price control, we imposed petty restrictions on the rights of enterprises and increased the number of indicators, as a result of which the initial sense of the reform was distorted, and to a considerable degree it lost its effectiveness. It is necessary and useful to recall this now, at a time when the large-scale experiment is expanding, so as not to repeat past mistakes.

Thus, experience and common sense indicate that without strict price controls, it is impossible to create a system of indicators that will motivate the enterprise to struggle to make production effective. How can this be done?

Prices must above all reflect socially necessary labor inputs per unit of use value. However, it is also possible to deliberately make price deviate from this level for the sake of economizing scarce raw materials or encouraging the production of particularly essential products and new machinery. Above all, the determination of the price level must be in the hands of the socialist state, and it must be free of departmental and local influence.

It is also clear that price must be based on labor norms that in turn are based on technically substantiated norms and approved rates and scales. There is no disagreement on these issues among economists or among production workers. Disagreements arise concerning the practical implementation of these principles. The principal disagreements are over three main questions:

—in our fast-moving age, is it necessary and possible to create uniform national, or at least branchwide labor norms as a firm basis for pricing? (We note, incidentally, that this question equally concerns NNO as well.)

—Is a single state organ in the person of the State Committee for Prices, even if its rights and apparatus are expanded to the maximum, capable of determining, or at least monitoring the many millions of prices in effect in the national economy?

—What is the correct way of designing a price so that it encourages production of the particularly essential products and also correctly reflect the real contribution of the production collective to the summary social product?

It is most difficult to answer the first question. In some branches that have a relatively uniform and stable technology, let us say the textile industry or petrochemistry, uniform branch norms are established and are being successfully applied. However, in many other branches, especially in machine building and instrument making, the high degree of changeability and the varying character of production, the different organizational structure, and the different levels of technical inputs per enterprise worker make it hardly possible to establish stable branchwide norms. But there is no need to do so. In such a case, it is possible to draw upon the normative base of each individual enterprise, but at the same time it is necessary to see to it that the level actually attained is not "diluted" and that the labor costs of new products do not become more expensive per unit of useful effect. This can be achieved even by the existing pricing methods if they are applied honestly and uncompromisingly.

Regarding the ability of the State Committee for Prices to keep a firm hold on pricing, this also seems entirely solvable, despite the complexity of the problem. But above all, no matter how difficult this problem is, it must be solved. Here, one must agree with D. V. Valovoi that it is not by any means absolutely necessary to focus our attention on all 12 million prices. We will not say whether it is sufficient to focus our attention on 500 prices, as D. V. Valovoi proposes, or 1,000 prices, but we unquestionably can and must single out a group of the most important products such as metal, fuel, energy, machine tools and equipment, and agricultural staples, the prices on which must be scrupulously examined and approved by the State Committee for Prices. For the remaining types of products, it is enough that the State Committee for Prices approve the appropriate guidelines and that it indicate the agencies that are entrusted with approving prices. It is above all essential to establish an inspection apparatus possessing the right to conduct periodic checks on all organizations and the right to strictly punish all violators of these guidelines.

How can the third problem—to establish prices that are equally profitable to the producers on all their products so as to remove the temptation to manipulate the product mix for the sake of improving their indicators—be resolved?

A. M. Birman proposes establishing a close to equal level of profitability in the sales price. But then, the more hired labor, expensive materials, and components included in it, the more profitable it will be to the manufacturer. Our restaurant menus, then, will never feature cabbage cutlets but will always list only chicken-*tabaka*! This proposal is the most vulnerable aspect of A. M. Birman's whole, harmonious concept.

On this question, we also agree with D. V. Valovoi who, in substantiating the advantages of the NNO, proposes calculating profit in equal percent of expenditures of only [the production unit's] own live labor. An incidental note: the practice of making the transition to NNO shows that where this principle has been violated and NNO has been "made" by simply subtracting the costs of hired labor from the old existing prices, there was a sharp increase in the gap in the evaluation of the growth of ouput based on sales and that based on NNO, and, most important, the difference between products that were profitable and unprofitable for the enterprise was not eliminated. It was specifically this circumstance and not merely the fact that the NNO, as A. M. Birman correctly notes, was not reflected in accounting, that resulted in a situation in which the NNO indicator did not work well everywhere and the initial enthusiasm that greeted its introduction dulled significantly.

It seems to us that these contradictions not only can but should be attenuated through a "lawful marriage" between the NNO indicator and the sales indicator. **This requires revising all prices based on the principle inherent in NNO; i.e., in the process of calculating price, profit must be calculated in equal percent only for one's labor costs.** This does not by any means exclude conscious deviation from the given principle in necessary cases for the sake of encouraging the production of a given product by introducing price markups for exports or for use in the index "N," by establishing temporary higher prices during the running-in period for new, sophisticated machines and instruments, etc. Nevertheless, we emphasize once more, the principle of equal profitability must be fundamental in pricing policy. Only the sales indicator is free of a considerable part of the shortcomings that D. V. Valovoi correctly identifies, and draws closer to NNO, while profit becomes the principal yardstick to the effectiveness of production, as proposed by A. M. Birman. Main, but not only. And here, we agree that full evaluation **requires a system of indicators, with the mandatory condition that these indicators will be mutually noncontradictory and that their number will be minimal.**

However, many existing indicators are not only superfluous, but clearly contradict one another, tie the hands of enterprise managers, and transform them from fighters for real effectiveness into skillful jugglers of various figures.

Let us attempt to show this on the basis of examples. Designers at the Leningrad Metal Plant proved that it was more profitable to weld large hydroturbine assemblies than to make them from steel castings which the plant received from the outside. And that is what they did. Production costs declined, profits increased, and total production cycles accelerated. But the labor productivity indicator declined: in the past, it was only necessary to remove the turnings from the casting received from "uncle," and the part was ready. Now it was necessary to mark and cut the sheet and weld the blank. Only then did the piece reach the machine. The plant's own labor costs rose sharply. After doing what was profitable for the state, the plant suffered for a long time until its base was adjusted for labor productivity.

A second example. For a long time, the Leningrad Ia. M. Sverdlov Machine-Tool Construction Association fabricated rotating tables for boring machines produced by the association. Then we started receiving them from a specialized plant, and the productivity indicator rose without any effort on our part.

An infinite number of such examples could be cited. Today, for example, the enterprise is assigned separate quotas for saving materials and for lowering labor intensiveness. But sometimes it is more profitable to increase the expenditure of materials in order to economize more [the enterprise's] own live labor. Other times, conversely, it is better to invest more of one's own labor in order to save more expensive material. After all, material is ultimately the same embodied labor of workers of the supplying plant. While as a rule it is necessary to reduce production costs, sometimes it is advantageous to raise them for the sake of improving quality, because the customer will not accept a cheap but inferior product. Our light industry is encountering this situation more and more frequently. It is often necessary to increase sharply the production of scarce products even at the cost of acquiring expensive equipment and hiring additional manpower. It may be that the production costs will not decline, but the national economy will receive the products it urgently needs. Nor will the enterprise be the worse for it, because the volume of sales and the profit mass will grow.

The system of indicators must first of all secure the interests of the state and society as a whole; at the same time, it must not prevent the enterprise from freely maneuvering the resources entrusted to it but motivate it to do its utmost to increase the effectiveness of its production.

This general demand of a socialist economy can be expressed by the following rule: the state and higher-echelon organizations must dictate to the enterprise "what to do," and they must define the terms that stimulate the effectiveness of its work while at the same time giving it the freedom to choose "how to do" what was assigned.

To this end, in our view it is necessary and sufficient to leave higher-echelon agencies the following functions in the area of planning and monitoring the production activity of a cost-accounting enterprise:

—determination of the profile (specialization) of production;

—approval of the product-mix plan and monitoring the fulfillment of deliveries of these products (observance of contracts);

—approval of prices for entire planned product mix;

—approval of long-term rules having the force of law for distributing profit obtained by the enterprise.

The fulfillment of the plan in physical form (product mix) and profit become the principal performance-evaluation indicators.

The question might arise: and what of production costs, labor productivity, wage funds, work-force size, and many other indicators that are presently mandatory? It is our deep conviction that with strict control over prices and the product mix and with the motivation of the enterprise to realize maximum profit, all these and many other indicators are not needed. The enterprise itself will not expend extra materials, maintain extra people, and pay them money needlessly.

Considering the inertia of the habits of many years and the existing demographic situation, it might be well initially to assign manpower ceilings from above. But the enterprise must unquestionably be given the right to decide within the limits of the ceiling the number of workers, ENP [engineering-technical personnel],and employees, including managerial personnel. It would seem expedient to have these ceilings established not by ministries, but by local organs of Soviet power in agreement with Gosplan. We repeat: **if consistent and firm controls are exercised over prices, and if profit is made the basic criterion of economic effectiveness, in time almost all the indicators**

**named will become unnecessary or, more precisely, will retain
only an analytical rather than a directive function.**

From the foregoing, it is obvious that the author, following
A. M. Birman, attaches decisive importance to the profit indicator. As is known, some economists disapprove of this concept,
finding that it has a "bad aftertaste," evidently remembering that
the profit motive is the basic goal of capitalist production. But
nothing could be more erroneous than to fail to distinguish between the nature of capitalist and socialist profits. The difference
is how it is obtained and who appropriates it. The capitalist
creates profit through the unlimited exploitation of his workers
and sometimes his customers as well. And most important is the
partial appropriation of the profits created by the working people
by the owner of capital and the use of it for his interests. Under
socialism, profit is placed at the disposal of all society and is used
in the interests of all the working people. In his *Critique of the
Gotha Program*, Karl Marx stated that even in a future socialist
society based on collectivist principles, it will be impossible to
distribute all "earned income" among its creators, and that it
will be necessary to subtract a certain part from it to compensate
and to expand consumed means of production, to create a contin-
gency fund to cover accidents and natural disasters, to defray
general management costs, to finance the maintenance of schools
and public health institutions, to create funds for the disabled,
etc.

At the same time, with proper price control, the growth of
profits adequately reflects all positive changes in the activity of
the enterprise. Thus, when the workers' productivity increases,
profits rise; conservation of supplies, energy, and fuel results in
higher profits; improved utilization of productive capital as well
means profit growth. . . . And, finally, profits also rise when the
volume of production increases even when production costs remain the same.

But so that profit "works" correctly, it is essential to observe
one more condition in addition to price controls. "Iron" rules
must be established for the distribution of the share of the profits

that is taken from the enterprise and of the share that is left at the disposal of the enterprise. These norms need not be standard or uniform—they can be tailored to meet the particular conditions of each enterprise. But it is essential that they be of a long-term nature and that they have the force of law not only where the enterprise is concerned, but also for all higher organizations. In other words, they should be changed, legislatively, as seldom as possible, at the most once every five or ten years.

Only with the observance of such conditions will economic, party, and trade union leaders be truly able to mobilize collectives for the full discovery and utilization of all reserves.

In our opinion, the profits that are left to the enterprise should be used first of all to pay fines for failures to adhere to the delivery schedule or for inferior output. This will be a powerful impetus to observe contract discipline more strictly. Then, once again according to firm rules, the remaining sums are divided into two parts: the development fund and the collective's material incentive fund. Naturally, depreciation allowances—in addition to part of the profits—must also be paid into the development fund and, what is more, in substantially larger amounts than is presently the case.

The scientific-technological revolution makes the retooling and reconstruction of enterprises a continuous rather than a one-time necessity. As long as enterprises are dependent on the decisions of higher organizations, the manager's responsibility for the enterprise entrusted to him is very conditional: if he receives the money, he renovates; if he does not, he throws up his hands as if to say "what do you expect me to do?"

As a result, we build new plants that take many years to reach their rated capacity and that have difficulty putting together collectives able to do the work, and at the same time we doom enterprises that have amassed invaluable production know-how to grow old before their time. It would seem that budget and other centralized sources of financing should primarily be used to develop the infrastructure and to build new enterprises in the eastern regions of the country. And only in certain situations, when an existing enterprise must tool up for fundamentally different output, should the use of state budget funds be permitted.

As the intention was from the very beginning, **material incentive funds** will become, in addition to the growth of individual output, the **main source for increasing the incomes of the working people.** I would also like to call attention to this aspect of the problem: if the growth of wages and other benefits depend on the size of the funds, this will dramatically enhance the role of such forms of incentives as the thirteenth payday, bonuses for winners in the socialist competition, the construction of housing, children's institutions, holiday homes, etc. All this will help to consolidate the collective, strengthen discipline, reduce turnover, and foster communist consciousness.

In addition to reducing the number of planned indicators, **we should,** in our opinion, **no longer evaluate an enterprise's performance solely on the basis of the percent of plan fulfillment. Instead, the evaluation should depend primarily on the collective's progress compared with the preceding period.** As long as 100-percent fulfillment is the fatal dividing line, one side of which is paradise and the other is hell, we will never eliminate the enterprise's striving for less intensive plans and its attempt to conceal its reserves.

If there are no constraints on raw materials and sales, progress can be measured on the basis of increased output in physical terms, and also on the basis of higher profits, which reflect all aspects of an enterprise's performance.

The measurement of the performance of production collectives on the basis of their increased output in physical terms is most reliable and graphic, but unfortunately it can be applied only if the enterprise's product mix is small and stable and if the quality of the primary raw materials is constant. Such conditions exist in petrochemistry, at dairy plants, in the production of standard fasteners, bearings, phonograph records, etc. But this approach is less suitable for multiple-specialty machine-building enterprises with a constantly changing product mix and for many mining and timber industry enterprises with sharply changing geological and natural-geographical conditions in their work.

What is more, with the transition to intensive methods of economic management, there will be more enterprises whose task of increasing output will give way to the task of improving product quality and increasing the effectiveness of production.

This is why we believe that the profit-growth indicator must become increasingly important on a par with the observance of contracts in the evaluation of enterprise performance. But we emphasize once more that the accuracy of this indicator, like the accuracy of all other economic indicators, will depend entirely on improvements in pricing.

The author is fully aware that the ideas presented in this article do not exhaust all the important measures relating to the further improvement of the management of industrial production. The policy of strengthening delivery discipline poses the urgent question of making the enterprise-supply system more reliable. It would appear that this problem should be resolved primarily through the all-around development of the warehouse form of supply and wholesale trade in the system of territorial administrations of Gossnab [the State Committee for Material and Technical Supply]. This will increase the size of orders placed with the suppliers of materials, thereby making it easier for them to fulfill their contractual obligations, will also reduce the load borne by transport, and will permit the more efficient maneuvering of materials in the regions where they are used. Obviously, no matter how hard it tries, a multiple-specialty enterprise that has hundreds and even thousands of customers and that is compelled to make many small shipments that do not fill a standard freight car can never fulfill its contractual obligations one hundred percent.

It is extremely important that, as envisaged in the school reform, the enrollment of youth in secondary vocational-technical training schools (SPTUs) double with the aim of reinforcing the working class. Evidently, the time is also ripe for the reform of higher and secondary specialized education. In the area of engineer training, in particular, intensive methods should have taken the place of extensive methods long ago. We recall that we already have more than five million engineers with diplomas. We believe that we should have long ago reduced enrollment in advanced technical institutions and improved the quality of specialist training by means of more rigorous screening and by flunking out mediocre students. Nor would it be a bad idea to convert a number of technicums to the training of highly skilled specialists who know how to work with their hands as well as their heads.

Modern production is extremely interested in specialists capable of working as adjusters of NC machine tools, robots, and flexible manufacturing systems, as operators of gigantic converters and rolling mills, and as wide-ranging specialists in the laboratory or at the testing facility. But we continue to train technicians as a "cheaper edition" of an engineer, who is unable to operate a modern machine in a shop and who is not very useful in a design office because of the obvious oversupply of engineers.

The time has also come for the more energetic fulfillment of the decisions of party congresses on bringing research and development closer to production by incorporating independent design offices and many applied scientific-research institutes in production and science-production associations. This must be done not formally but in fact, with the personnel of design offices and scientific-research institutes being transferred to an industrial group, because the design engineer and the practical researcher perform operation number one in modern production and in that capacity must unquestionably be a part of the aggregate work force.

There are also other important problems that await solution.

But first of all, as the experience of enterprises participating in the large-scale experiment shows, we must clearly articulate the actual principles underlying the further improvement of the economic mechanism, firmly outline the rights and obligations of the socialist enterprise, give it sufficient room to maneuver all its resources, and assign it full responsibility for its performance.

Note

1. *EKO*, 1983, no. 9 and 1984, no. 8.

D. M. KAZAKEVICH

Improving Consumer Prices

The formulation and implementation of scientifically substantiated pricing principles are among the most important elements today in improving the economic mechanism. "Pricing must be dramatically improved so that it will promote the successful implementation of economic policy."[1] This applies to both producer and consumer prices.

Producer prices include: prices for which industrial enterprises sell their products to state and cooperative production enterprises (means of production) or to state and cooperative trade enterprises (consumer goods); procurement prices on agricultural products sold to collective and state farms; estimated prices on the output of the construction industry; prices and rates on freight shipments and productive services. Consumer prices are the final prices on goods and services sold to the population.

The particulars of state planned regulation of consumer prices stem from its interrelationship with such areas of economic policy as the implementation of programs for securing the more complete satisfaction of the population's needs and for raising the population's living standards; maintaining a constant balance of the dimensions of production, market stocks of consumer goods and services, and the population's money incomes; shaping the

Russian text © 1986 by Ekonomika i organizatsiia promyshlennogo proizvodstva. "K sovershenstvovaniiu potrebitels'skikh tsen," *Ekonomika i organizatsiia promyshlennogo proizvodstva*, 1986, no. 1, pp. 33–43.

Professor Kazakevich holds a doctorate in economics, is affiliated with the Institute of Economics and Organization of Industrial Production, Siberian Department, USSR Academy of Sciences, and lives in Novosibirsk.

structure of consumption; and the inculcation of rational consumer behavior. The improvement of consumer prices is of exceptionally great importance not only from the standpoint of raising the people's living standards, but also as a factor in the material stimulation of more productive labor, in strengthening cost accounting, and ultimately in increasing the effectiveness of social production.

Nevertheless, scholarly treatises on pricing as well as the economic press fail to devote sufficient attention to the problem of improving consumer prices. The feasibility of preserving existing prices on such foodstuffs as bread, groat and flour products, and meat and dairy products that do not compensate socially necessary production costs, is a question that merits particular discussion. There is a considerable gap between procurement prices reflecting agricultural production costs on the one hand, and final, consumer prices on these foods on the other. Our stores, for example, sell meat at a price that is two to three times lower than cost. [2]

Regulation is effected with the aid of a special USSR Gosbank [State Bank] account. This account defrays all agricultural procurement costs, including: the payment of zonal prices (plus markups for the overfulfillment of the procurement plan) to collective and state farms for their products; the costs of procurement organizations, including transport costs; and the profit of procurement organizations. All income from the sale of agricultural products by procurement organizations to enterprises in the processing industry for wholesale prices (unified or differentiated) is paid into this account. The negative difference between wholesale prices and procurement prices in sum with the procurement cost, derived by comparing total receipts in the special bank account and total expenditures, is made up by a subsidy from the state budget. The amount of this subsidy is deposited into the special bank account.

While processing-industry enterprises themselves may also perform procurement functions, this does not alter the general procedure for regulating prices through the special bank account.

For example, livestock delivered to meat combines are paid for on the basis of zonal purchase prices. The prices of meat products leaving the meat combine for further processing or for delivery to the consumer are based on retail prices minus trade discount. The difference between them and the purchase prices on livestock is compensated by a subsidy from the state budget with the aid of the same special USSR Gosbank account.

According to data cited by N. T. Glushkov at the beginning of 1980, the annual state subsidy to compensate the difference between production costs and proceeds from sales of meat, dairy, and certain other consumer goods for retail prices was 25 billion rubles.[3] Since then it has increased substantially, because the purchase prices on livestock, milk, grain, sugar beets, and certain other agricultural products were raised on January 1, 1983, in accordance with the resolution of the May (1982) Plenum of the CPSU Central Committee, while the retail prices on food remained the same and the state allocated an additional 16 billion rubles a year for this purpose.[4] The current subsidy for meat alone is almost 20 billion rubles a year.[5]

Retail prices on bread, on groat and flour products, and on sugar have been stable in the USSR for 30 years, while prices on meat and dairy products have been stable for 23 years, despite the higher cost of producing these staple foods.[6] The average price of bread in the Soviet Union is considerably lower than in other socialist countries, and it is still lower (by 4–5 times) compared with capitalist countries with the highest level of agricultural development. Prices on meat and dairy products are also substantially lower.

There are advantages to stable food prices in that at these prices, all groups of the population can purchase the vital necessities. Consequently, the preservation of stable prices coupled with the steady growth of the population's money incomes (the average monthly wage in 1984 was 185 rubles, compared with 71.8 rubles in 1955 and 86.7 rubles in 1962,[7] the last time food prices were revised) is a factor in raising the living standards of all working people. This is also the basis of the orientation of recent

Party congresses—that the necessary saturation of the market with consumer goods take place while maintaining a stable level of state retail prices.[8]

Unquestionably, the best way to bring consumer prices on food into line with food production costs and to balance supply and demand is to reduce costs and to increase food production to the extent that the effective demand for food with the existing level of the population's money income is saturated. But this will take a long time and will require economic conditions that in our view will require some changes in current food prices.

At a meeting of party and economic activists in Tselinograd, M. S. Gorbachev referred to numerous letters written to the CPSU Central Committee by working people citing barbaric attitudes toward bread and noted that "this is something for work collectives and for the central organs to think about."[9]

Naturally, economic science must become involved and must come up with recommendations for solving this problem.

In our view, the current prices that are presently preserved as stable prices on food staples have both advantages and disadvantages. Bread comprises 2–4% of the price of a meal in a workers' canteen and 0.5–1% of the price of a restaurant meal. Since these prices are so low as to be negligible, it is inevitable that an enormous quantity of bread that is paid for in public dining establishments ends up as garbage. Obviously, losses of bread are no less if indeed not more throughout the country and in the home, since the price of bread is negligible in the budget of most families, especially in comparison with prices on clothing, footwear, and household items. The Institute of Psychology of the USSR Academy Sciences polled the population in various cities and villages and found that 92% of the respondents judged the social value of any commodity, including bread, on the basis of its retail price.[10] This connection has been firmly established in the public mind. Symbolic prices are largely detrimental to efforts to reduce the losses of bread and to educating people to be thrifty in their use of this most important food.

In view of the low prices, a considerable quantity of baked

bread and groat and flour products are fed to livestock and poultry maintained on private plots by the population and by collective farms, despite existing legal sanctions against this practice. This is economically profitable, even highly profitable if one compares the state retail prices on these products and the price of meat in the unorganized market.

This also makes it possible for speculative elements to acquire unearned income as a result of the price scissors; i.e., this opens a valve for the uncontrolled flow of a certain part of the national income, which then circulates uncontrollably in the so-called shadow economy.

The low state retail prices on meat and dairy products make it difficult to balance supply and demand, and they artifically maintain and increase the partial scarcity of these products, which is self-perpetuating to a considerable degree. The result of low prices on food staples over a long period of time concomitant with the considerable growth of the population's money incomes is that the effective demand increasingly shifts to other products—high-quality, fashionable clothing and footwear, high-quality furniture, cars, etc., thereby generating scarcity of, and hence higher prices on, these products (the income from these increases partly offset the enormous state subsidies that were discussed above). The result is a still greater degree of skewness in pricing, while some high-quality products gradually become unattainable to working people in the relatively low income brackets for whom the low food prices are preserved.

The general availability in stores of all food products (and other consumer goods) for prices that compensate the cost of their production and the balance of the market are among the most powerful factors in maintaining the economic and moral health of society at a high level, in strengthening labor discipline and material incentives for increasing labor productivity, in strengthening the authority of the ruble and the nation's monetary system, in eliminating the need for the socially unjustified administrative distribution of some of the consumer goods among the population, in strengthening cost accounting in production and in promoting conservation throughout the entire economy, and in entirely eradicating elements of the black market, speculation, and similar phenomena alien to the nature of socialist society. The continued scarcity of some consumer goods, on the other hand, has the opposite effect.

The question we are addressing here has already been raised by a number of authors. Thus, V. A. Volkonskii writes: "The budget mechanism for regulating the difference in prices (the conclusion follows the mention of the difference in prices on meat and dairy products.—D. K.) and the actual deviations of prices from the level of socially necessary costs cannot be considered a necessary and permanent element of the socialist economic system, since they do not correspond to the principles of the maximum effectiveness of management."[11]

This does not mean that we should abandon the policy of maintaining stable prices on basic consumer goods and switch to constantly changing prices. But it would be a good idea to make a one-time adjustment of consumer goods prices and their structure in order to have better stable base prices that would be free of the shortcomings of existing prices. Consumer goods prices should be raised when they do not cover the socially necessary expenditures incurred in their production and delivery to the consumer. State subsidies of retail prices should be eliminated, and all the funds released thereby should be used to raise the wages and salaries of the working people, as well as pensions, scholarships, and other of the population's incomes. In budget institutions, these state budget funds can be used directly for raising salaries. Cost-accounting units in which higher wages are reflected in production costs will begin paying correspondingly less profit to the budget, which will mean that the former budget subsidies are being indirectly used to raise wages.

Raising the working people's wages and salaries, as well as pensions and scholarsips, and raising prices by the sum of the reduction of state budget subsidies, i.e., compensating the population for additional costs associated with increased prices, will ensure that the working people's standard of living will not be affected. Subsequently, this measure may even help to raise the standard of living due to its positive impact on the economy.

If necessary, the raising of wages and salaries can be carried out as a differentiated measure or as a measure associated with the rectification of consumer prices, and it may also be used at the same time in the interest of improving the remuneration of labor.

A one-time measure to rectify consumer prices and to raise the working people's incomes does not contradict the basic policy of the Party and the Soviet state regarding price formation and raising the people's standard of living, and it would have a positive impact on the economy in many respects: it would improve the structure of consumer goods prices; would eliminate the contradiction between prices on interrelated products (for example, prices on bread, groat, flour, and meat and dairy products); would reduce differences between food prices in state and cooperative trade and in the unorganized market; as a result of a better balance between supply and demand, the scarcity of a number of consumer goods would be lessened and eliminated; and all the positive features of the satisfaction of the population's effective demand that were discussed above would begin to show through.

The stability of consumer prices should not be construed to mean that they are inflexible. After the transition to a new, stable level of consumer goods prices, it is inevitable that the dynamics of production costs, the need to balance the supply and demand for different products, and other factors will necessitate the modification of some of them. The documents of the April (1985) Plenum of the CPSU Central Committee discuss the need for ''greater flexibility in the system of prices'' on goods and services for the population.[12]

We believe that the rectification of consumer prices must also touch another important aspect of the people's well-being—apartment rents. Rents have remained the same in the USSR for several decades. It is appropriate to note that the July 23, 1926 resolution of the Joint Plenum of the Central Committee and Central Control Commission of the All-Union Communist Party (of Bolsheviks), which layed down the principles for fixing apartment rents in the

USSR, formulated in particular the principle of the self-recoupment of housing as the point of departure in determining the level of apartment rents. In accordance with the resolution of the Central Executive Committee and Council of People's Commissars of the USSR, "On Housing Policy"(1928), apartment rent was to average no more than 10% of wages. The rent level of 13.2 kopecks per square meter of housing, which was raised to 16.5 kopecks for rent in new buildings, corresponded to these principles. To maintain rents at the same level today corresponds to neither the first nor the second principle. It does not even compensate one-third of the cost of housing maintenance and requires an annual subsidy from the state budget in the amount of approximately six billion rubles, to say nothing of compensating capital investments in housing construction, which are many fold higher than operating costs. Apartment rent today amounts to not 10%, but only 2–3% of wages. In view of the increase in income in recent years, apartment rent in state dwellings has by and large become merely symbolic.

While such a level of rents has advantages, it also has serious drawbacks. With low rents and large subsidies from social consumption funds for housing maintenance, these benefits are enjoyed more by that part of the population that is better supplied with housing, i.e., persons having more apartment space and a higher level of amenities (since apartment rent is not differentiated according to the quality of housing). It is hard to maintain that it is mainly lower-income families who occupy the more spacious, better appointed apartments, which is the rationale for preserving low apartment rents and housing subsidies from social consumption funds.

The preservation of low rents that are not differentiated according to the quality of housing will not help to eliminate the housing shortage in the shortest possible time or to eliminate many of the unhealthy phenomena associated with them. It is no secret, for example, that some of the population is prepared to hold onto surplus housing space until such time as it becomes scarce. (The point is not only the psychological effect of scarcity as a phenomenon, but, most importantly, the difficulty of expanding housing area in the future when this need may arise as a result of increase in family size or due to other factors.) This is at a time when the rate of payment for living accomodations, for heating, for water supply, etc., have little impact on the family budget.

The scarcity of housing and the desire to hold onto it reduces the population's mobility considerably and does not encourage the migration of manpower to newly developing regions, as the country requires. The reservation of inhabitable state apartments in such cases is not the best solution to the problem: the housing shortage is thus artificially maintained, because a family consequently receives two apartments instead of one, and instead of settling in a new region permanently, they return to their old apartment in a region that has a manpower surplus.

The problem posed by the low rents that are charged for state apartments was aggravated with the advent and rapid development of cooperative housing construction. Families' expenditures on cooperative housing fully compensate the cost of cooperative housing construction and maintenance and are several times higher than apartment rent in state buildings. But after all, the apartments in cooperative buildings go to the same working people, and there is no rule that apartments in state buildings be assigned to families with relatively lower per capita income and that apartments in cooperative buildings be assigned to families with relatively higher per capita income. The existing situation does not entirely correspond to the policy of social justice operative in all areas of socialist society.

The preservation of low apartment rents in state buildings, which is, moreover, not differentiated according to the quality of the apartments, and the existence of state housing subsidies that exceed many fold the income from the housing rents, prevent the transition to true cost accounting in housing and municipal services. Also attributable to the low rents are shortcomings in securing the proper level of housing maintenance for the sums expended on this purpose.

The self-evident solution to the problem does not require the revision of the Soviet state's policy of providing the working people with housing in accordance with their constitutional right to it. On the contrary, it lies within the framework of this socially just policy of the socialist state. State housing subsidies should be used not to keep apartment rents low, but rather to increase the working people's incomes and to set the rates of apartment rent and municipal services at a level that will cover the cost-accounting costs [*khozraschetnye izderzhki*] of housing and municipal services.

But it seems to us that the analogy of reassigning subsidies to retail prices on food must not be fully applied here. It would not be entirely correct to use former housing subsidies to raise wages.

For example, it would be expedient to use social consumption funds previously utilized for housing subsidies to increase monetary payments to large families in an amount that would cover the increase in their apartment rent and create for them the possibility of maintaining an apartment for a large family.

In a word, the funds that are released upon the elimination of rent subsidies should be used in accordance with programs for the social development of society through local soviets of people's deputies. They should be used according to established material assistance rules to help some families to pay for their apartments.

Here we proceed from a situation in which all housing is transferred to the local soviets and maintained on a cost-accounting basis by housing and municipal service organizations subordinate to them. The transition to true cost-accounting methods for managing the functioning and development of the social and service infrastructure, like the production infrastructure, is an important element in improving the economic mechanism, and it is taking on increasing importance.[13]

It would seem appropriate to increase local budget revenues substantially on the basis of profits from all production units regardless of departmental affiliation. Local soviets of people's deputies enjoy the right to create subordinate enterprises in the production and social-service infrastructure; they could use part of this income for the further development of the district infrastructure, including housing construction. If the all-union budget allocates a subsidy for this purpose, it must be awarded to the local soviets. They in turn must also have economic interrelations with contractor organizations that are constructing the infrastructure in the districts.

Rent reform is one of the main prerequisites to the total abandonment of the departmental principle in housing construction and maintainance and to placing its operation on a cost-accounting basis.

The draft of the "Guidelines for the Economic and Social Development of the USSR for 1986–1990 and the Period Ending in 2000" states that we must "improve the system of state retail prices and rates and see to it that they more completely reflect the socially necessary costs, quality, and consumer properties of goods and services.[14]. This statement is very timely. Housing and municipal services are among the most important sectors of our economy. Rents, like consumer goods prices, should be reformed in accordance with the enumerated principles.

Notes

1. M. S. Gorbachev, *Korennoi vopros ekonomicheskoi politiki partii. Doklad na soveshchanii v TsK KPSS po voprosam uskoreniia nauchno-tekhnicheskeskogo progressa 11 iiunia 1985 goda*, Moscow, Politizdat, 1985, p. 27.

2. See M. S. Gorbachev's speech at a meeting of Party and economic activists in Tselinograd on September 7, 1985 (*Pravda*, September 11, 1985).

3. N. T. Glushkov, "O razrabotke novykh optovykh tsen," *Ekonomicheskaia gazeta*, 1980, no. 17.

4. N. Glushkov, "Planovoe tsenoobrazovanie i upravlenie ekonomikoi," *Voprosy ekonomiki*, 1982, no. 8, p. 12.

5. See M. S. Gorbachev's speech in Tselinograd, *Pravda,* September 11, 1985.

6. Ibid.

7. *Narodnoe khoziaistvo SSSR v 1970 g. Statisticheskii ezhegodnik*, Moscow, "Statistika" Publishers, 1971, p. 519; "Ob itogakh vypolneniia Gosudarstvennogo plana ekonomicheskogo i sotsial'nogo razvitiia SSSR v 1984 godu. Soobshchenie TsSU SSSR," *Pravda*, January 26, 1985.

8. See *Materialy XXVI s"ezda KPSS*, Moscow, Politizdat, 1981, p. 179.

9. *Pravda*, September 11, 1985.

10. See: P. El'chaninov, "Tsena khlebu nekopeika," *Pravda*, April 24, 1978.

11. V. A. Volkonskii, *Problemy sovershenstvovaniia khoziaistvennogo mekhanizma*, Moscow, "Nauka" Publishers, 1981, p. 90. See also: E. G. Iasin, "Raspredelitel'nye otnosheniia v strukture khoziaistvennogo mekhaniz- ma," *Ekonomika i matematicheskie metody*, 1983, vol. 19, no. 3.

12. *Materialy Plenuma Tsentral'nogo Komiteta KPSS 23 aprelia 1985 goda*, Moscow, Politizdat, 1985, p. 14.

13. "Life more and more urgently requires that we resolve the problem of dividing the resources allocated for productive purposes and for the creation of the infrastructure (especially the social infrastructure) between branch and territorial organs of management. Allocations for the urban and rural infra- structure must go to the direct satisfaction of the needs of the working people and should, as a rule, be given to territorial organs of management" (V. P. Mozhin, "Ratsional'noe sochetanie otraslevogo i territorial'nogo planirovaniia i upravleniia narodnym khoziaistvom," *Planovoe khoziaistvo*, 1980, no. 3, pp. 108–09.

14. *Pravda*, November 9, 1985.

Labor
Incentives

VLADIMIR G. KOSTAKOV

Employment:
Scarcity or Surplus?

The problem of labor resources and employment has become a topic of discussion in the wake of Tat′iana I. Zaslavskaia's article in *Kommunist* (1986, no. 13).† This problem would seem to require more detailed examination when we discuss the human factor in economic development and the active participation of man himself in the restructuring process.

It is widely believed (in our view, wrongfully) that the country's labor resource problem is the result of a "shortage" of manpower. It is worthwhile to address the very nature of this shortage, as well as the broader problems of employment under socialism. The view of the labor resources problem has obviously been affected in no small measure by the lack of theoretical and practical elaboration of such issues as the interaction of demographic processes and employment, the maintenance of full employment in the intensification of social production and the dramatic acceleration of the growth of labor productivity, and regional aspects of the utilization of labor resources under conditions of intensification.

Let us discuss these questions.

Imaginary and real causes

When our economy encountered the so-called manpower shortage, specialists' studies and official documents initially gave the problem a

Russian text © 1987 by "Pravda" Publishers. "Zaniatost′: defitsit ili izbytok?" *Kommunist*, 1987, no. 2, pp. 78-89.

Prof. Vladimir Georgievich Kostakov holds a doctor's degree in economics and is assistant director of the Scientific Research Economics Institute attached to USSR Gosplan.

†For the English translation of this article, see Tat′iana Zaslavskaia, "Social Justice and the Human Factor in Economic Development," *Problems of Economics*, vol. 30, no. 1 (May 1987).

demographic interpretation (A. Vishnevskii called attention to this fact in the article "The Human Factor in Demographic Measurement," *Kommunist*, 1986, no. 17).* There was a simple, superficial explanation: the increase in population had slackened; more concretely, the birthrate declined and a labor resources problem was the result. However, this relationship is not so obvious. The potential number of workers depends above all on the number of people of working age. Its dynamics may be at considerable variance with the dynamics of the total population.

Statistical data show that in the first half of the 1970s, when the manpower shortage was particularly pronounced, the average annual increase in population of working age was 2.4 times higher than in the 1960s. It is noteworthy that in the '60s, or more precisely, in the first half of the '60s, when the number of people entering the workforce was even lower (the result of the demographic echo of the war), there arose quite unexpectedly the urgent problem of finding employment for the population, which required sweeping, energetic measures. New enterprises were established and existing enterprises were expanded in small and medium-size towns. This fact is graphic evidence of the way in which labor and demographic processes sometimes operate in diametrically opposite directions.

In the '70s there was an extraordinary increase in the national economy's manpower requirement. Given the high level of employment at the beginning of that period—nine-tenths of the nation's labor resources were either employed in the national economy or involved in studies—even a considerable natural increase in the able-bodied population was simply no longer enough.

The productivity of social labor sharply declined. On an annual average, this indicator (national income per worker in material production) rose by 6.4 percent in 1961-70; by 4.5 percent in 1971-75; by 3.3 percent in 1976-80; and by 3.1 percent in 1981-85. If we also consider product quality, which dropped markedly during that time, and the production of many unsaleable consumer goods, the real state of affairs was even worse.

Thus, the thesis of the demographic nature of the labor resources problem is without foundation. Economic science, which initially was not up to the mark in explaining the new conditions of demographic development and manpower utilization, is primarily to blame for its very emergence. However, the main reason for the "longevity" of the demographic interpretation of labor problems has probably been the

---

*See *Problems of Economics*, vol. 30, no. 2 (June 1987).

fact that this interpretation suited many. After all, the demographic factor—something objective and insurmountable—has frequently been used to explain the manpower shortage (by virtue of the adverse demographic situation), personal miscalculations, inability, and the simple reluctance to manage effectively.

But does there exist a so-called adverse demographic situation, about which there is still so much discussion? And if so, wherein does it consist, what relationship does it have to labor problems?

The sharp drop in the growth of the working-age population is considered to be an extremely adverse factor. In actuality, it began in the late '70s and should continue until the mid-'90s. We will not examine this process in detail. We shall merely note that over fifteen years (1981–95), the increase in working-age population will amount to less than during the five-year period 1976–80, which in turn registered less than in 1971–75. This is the first time in all its years of peacetime construction that the nation has encountered such an extraordinary situation of a long decline. It is this situation that is characterized as extremely adverse. But the question arises: What is meant by adverse, from what positions?

Was this [situation] unexpected? No. The future dynamics of the working-age population were well known fifteen years ago from demographic forecasts made by the USSR Central Statistical Administration and USSR Gosplan in the late '50s and early '60s. There was more than enough time to evaluate everything and to draw the necessary conclusions of how to manage affairs: the whole idea of a planned economy is to prevent all manner of shortages. The present dynamics of labor resources and those anticipated up to the year 1995 may prove to be adverse only if the national economy's workforce grows at the same rate and with the same intensiveness as in 1976–85, for example. In such a case, there will indeed be a shortage of labor resources.

However, according to data in the Guidelines for Economic and Social Development, in the next fifteen years (1986–2000) the productivity of social labor will grow at a faster rate than national income (2.3–2.5-fold and 2-fold, respectively). This is a new situation which means that the number of workers in material production will not only not increase but will decrease by approximately 13–20 percent, which in absolute terms will mean a reduction in the workforce in this sphere of the national economy by 13–19 million persons, or by approximately 16 million on the average. This is an unprecedented phenomenon in our economy. From this standpoint, the slackening growth rate of labor resources is extremely favorable because it alleviates to a considerable degree the difficult problem of finding jobs for laid-off workers.

As demographic analyses show, the reduced increase in the working-age population will to a considerable degree take the form of an increase in the number of people reaching pension age. Among the favorable developments for the economy is the equalization of the sexes in the able-bodied population, which occurred at the beginning of the current five-year plan (for a long time women outnumbered men; today men account for slightly more than half of the population). It is difficult to exaggerate the importance of such positive changes, since the disruption of the normal ratio of the sexes forced women to take the place of men in many occupations, which was by no means always in their best interest or that of the national economy.

Thus, in our view the parameters of natural movement of the working-age population should be considered favorable for the effective utilization of labor resources.

Nevertheless, negative factors in the demographic situation, very serious negative factors, exist and have existed for a long time. Unfortunately, this situation has for the most part been viewed through the prism of manpower for the national economy, and attention has been concentrated on the quantitative aspect—the size of the working-age population. The social aspect has remained in the shadow. Publicity about the ''shortage'' of people required to carry out our plans has been effective. But the negative processes associated primarily with the life span, which have deep social roots attesting to serious problems in people's living conditions, mode of life, and working conditions have remained outside public scrutiny. And only now is it possible for a wide circle of specialists to see what is happening here. The corresponding data are once again being published in statistical publications (see *Statistics Herald* [*Vestnik statistiki*], 1986, no. 12).

It is noteworthy that the negative aspects of demographic processes and adverse trends in labor productivity have, as the saying goes, gone hand in hand, have occurred simultaneously. This is a reflection of one of the numerous interrelationships between the utilization of labor resources and demographic processes. It can be said with certainty that the human factor in its ''demographic measurement'' has worked against the effectiveness of labor in the last fifteen years. The deceleration of the growth of labor productivity in turn has had an adverse impact on demographic processes because there has been less opportunity to solve social problems.

How is labor utilized?

If we assess the present manpower situation, we ought to say that what we have is not a manpower shortage, but rather that the national economy has an overabundance of manpower due to the extremely ineffective utilization of labor in all branches.

The level of labor intensiveness in most enterprises, institutions, and organizations, which would hardly have satisfied us in the past, has in our view appreciably declined in roughly the last fifteen years. As a result of the routine we have established (or more precisely the ideas that have become entrenched regarding the normal work routine) we often assign two and even three people to do a job that could be handled by one worker performing several occupational functions and using every minute of the working day. Experience shows that we staff enterprises that we purchase from abroad with a considerably larger workforce [than is needed], one that is significantly—even several times—larger. The absence of an intensive work routine leads to the artificial creation of extraneous jobs. This is the primary reason why it is impossible to implement the principle of material remuneration of people in accordance with their labor contribution.

The situation can be corrected by making high demands on every worker, by instituting strict labor discipline, and by eliminating overstaffing. Sometimes all that is needed is elementary order. Efforts in this direction of late have promoted a certain degree of acceleration in the growth of labor productivity in 1985 and 1986. People will also have to restructure their thinking away from the customary work intensiveness norm to labor with maximum return.

So-called patronly aid [*shefskaia pomoshch'*] to collective farms, state farms, vegetable farms, etc., is one more powerful channel contributing to the formation of manpower surpluses. The mass diversion of people from their basic jobs has grown at an extraordinary rate in the last fifteen years. In addition to economic losses, "patronly aid" causes enormous social harm in that it impairs people's performance of their basic job. Agriculture, vegetable farms, and other entities can and must be supplied with working hands during their "peak" loads by other, economically and socially justified avenues. All this work should be converted to a cost-accounting basis. Those having a need for additional manpower should conclude contracts with citizens, but not with enterprises (as is sometimes proposed) because this will once again encourage enterprises to maintain extra personnel. It is prudent to proceed from the premise that people desiring to work—high school upper-classmen, college students, housewives, pensioners, as well as employed people wishing to earn extra money in their spare time—will be found if the pay is good. This will be economically justified. Then the requirement for people will be as much as are really needed, rather than the more the better.

Many surplus workers are maintained in the national economy due to the lack of uniformity in the activity of enterprises. The absence of balanced, rhythmic activity compels many industrial and construction facilities to maintain a reserve of people for the "crash" effort to meet the plan, which is by no means required when production and the system of material-technical supply are well-organized. There are also "surplus" workers in agriculture due to the seasonal nature of agricultural production. It might seem that since this is a fact of nature there is nothing that can be done about it. But here too there is a known, but very seldom practiced potential for fully satisfying the manpower needs of agricultural production while at the same time uniformly utilizing the labor of rural dwellers. This requires a sufficiency of other spheres of employment aside from agriculture, both in the rural area and in nearby small and medium-size towns (within the radius of public transportation). Conditions will then be created for the rational combination of agrarian and other types of labor. We are clearly lagging in this respect.

The maintenance of "surplus" workers in the national economy is in no small measure associated with unsatisfactory product quality. An entire "labor army" does nothing else than bring fleets of machinery and equipment up to the required level and to keep them in working condition. An experiment involving state acceptance of products that was carried out at the end of last year at a number of enterprises showed that as much as half or even more of the finished product (finished from the enterprise's point of view) was rejected. Nor can it be forgotten that roughly one million persons are engaged in quality control work in industry. Large losses of products due to poor storage, warehousing, transportation, and certain other circumstances are yet another channel through which the "surplus" workforce forms. For example, in agriculture alone, where one-fifth of the output is lost annually, approximately five million persons "work" on the losses.

The abovementioned channels through which manpower surpluses form are connected to age-old shortcomings in the system of management. Yet another channel, which has acquired ever greater significance, clearly emerged somewhere in the mid-'70s: the production of unsaleable consumer goods, or what came to be called "working for the warehouse."

The oversaturation of the national economy with manpower is not of a general, absolute nature. We are speaking only of the quantitative aspect of the matter and of the fact that labor resources are entirely sufficient for the present volume of production and the service sphere. This does not preclude an actual manpower shortage of a structural nature (in individual occupations, in individual regions of new development).

It will be entirely possible to eliminate a considerable percentage of the surplus manpower from the national economy in the immediate future. This merely requires elementary order in the appropriate areas. Even the author's cautious estimate shows that the manpower surplus is at the very least ten million persons (out of the 130-plus million persons employed in the national economy).

The attempt to ascribe the shortage to demographic factors, or in other words, to the possibility of an absolute manpower shortage in the planning system, has inflicted considerable harm on the utilization of labor resources. It is oriented toward the search for additional, not yet activated sources for supplying the national economy with additional working hands. For this reason, there was a substantial increase in the number of working pensioners in the '70s. Progress in solving the problem of reducing women's aggregate workload has been slow. In sum, efforts to increase the size of the workforce have been among the strong factors that have impeded mechanization, and as a result, the growth of labor productivity.

The theory of the manpower "shortage" maintains some popularity and still causes harm. Even now, some specialists, managers, and planners believe that the growth of labor productivity is important because of the manpower "shortage." This does not encourage correct, energetic action. Instead, it generates the illusion that since there are not enough people, manpower surpluses will automatically be "absorbed" at the enterprises and the rate of labor productivity will grow. However, nothing occurs automatically here; experience has demonstrated this fact. The labor utilization system in the national economy is improving very slowly, and enterprises are still highly inclined to maintain reserve manpower (being encouraged to do so by the manpower "shortage").

The attitude toward labor— psychological and economic aspects

The erroneous interpretation of the nature of the so-called manpower shortage shows how important it is to step up the scientific analysis of the interrelationship between demographic processes and the utilization of labor resources. Also in need of thorough interpretation are the circumstances that have sharply decelerated the growth of productivity of social labor over the last fifteen years. Attention is sometimes focused exclusively on the insufficiently energetic effort to improve technology, on the lag in the modernization of existing production, on heavy losses of working time, and on the laxity of labor discipline. In other words, the emphasis is predominantly on production factors and also on imperfections in the economic mechanism, which are connected to the extremely low incentive of all links of the national economy to manage effectively.

In our view—and this is confirmed by the entire course of the discussion occasioned by Zaslavskaia's article—little has been done to study the factors that depend directly on the worker, that determine his attitude toward his work and toward the fulfillment of the functions for which he is responsible. The replacement of one generation by another, the rise of the educational level, and the higher level of development of the individual associated therewith have lent and continue to lend extraordinary significance to the psychological factor, which we as yet do not take into account in our evaluation of the state of labor resources, and consequently, in the determination of the directions of our actions.[1] And yet never before has the final result of labor depended so much on such purely human considerations as the attitude toward one's job, the desire to give one's all, and on the satisfaction with the moral climate in which man works.

We can note several of the most important factors that explain why the psychological factor has still not come into play.

We have lost much and continue to lose by virtue of the fact that the person, who is justly considered the goal of our social and economic development and the ultimate goal of all our plans, is primarily regarded as a worker when we address practical problems. The concern for the person is in fact replaced by the concern for personnel. And even though they are close in meaning, they are by no means one and the same thing. The result is that the worker receives less respect as an individual. For this reason, there is a great lag in the development of the social infrastructure, which is intended to make people's lives easier and better. The existence of all manner of shortages that man encounters in the process of satisfying his material and nonmaterial needs is also associated with this to a considerable degree. Conditions in many workplaces are far from perfect. It is a common practice to offer additional benefits and compensation to attract and keep workers in jobs that should simply be eliminated. Ideological efforts are also frequently employed to this end. A graphic example of this is the customary appeal to keep youth in agriculture even though it is this very branch that employs the most manual laborers (approximately 15 million out of agriculture's total workforce of 20-plus million are engaged in manual labor). It is here that our lag in the level of labor productivity is especially great, vis-à-vis the United States, for example; in this branch it is especially important to transform production, to improve the content of the work dramatically, and in many cases to mechanize those jobs that today's generations simply do not wish to perform.

A unique feature of today is the total "adaptation" of production to man, and if we are deciding whether or not to give the go-ahead to one or another type of new machinery, one of the most important criteria should be human engineering. The view of man as a worker is also manifested in the fact that the worker in our economic affairs is regarded as a kind of average "labor" resource. We can hope for a high effect in production if we also see workers as men and women of different ages and abilities. The average approach is obviously to the liking of the creators of machinery that is designed primarily for strong, healthy men between the ages of twenty-five and forty.

We must also note the sharp decline in the prestige of many occupations—engineer, physician, teacher, other specialists with higher and secondary specialized education and, on a broader plane, brainworkers and the intelligentsia—on which successful socioeconomic development depends to a decisive and ever increasing degree. The decline of prestige has been the result of the loss of the previous advantage in the pay of these categories compared with other, less qualified workers, and is connected with the fact that specialists are compelled to perform work outside their area of specialization. Naturally, the attraction of the corresponding educational institutions has lessened for youth who are completing school. As a result, for a long time now the ranks of specialists have been filled with people with a diploma incidental to the job, who lack the necessary ability and calling. The untoward situation in this area has already had an appreciable negative impact on technological progress and on the health and education of the people. It is extremely urgent that this situation be altered in the shortest possible time. The wages of specialists can be improved with the mandatory presence of two conditions: (1) certification (not all specialists can perform the appropriate functions properly); and (2) the regularization of the very content of their work.

When we speak of the psychological aspects of labor productivity, we must not fail to note that they have acquired exceptional urgency as a result of the significant change in the age of the workforce in these same fifteen years. This has been the result of the natural course of events. In 1985, approximately 60 percent of the entire workforce in the national economy consisted of men and women born in the '50s or later who had not known the hardships of the war years and postwar reconstruction. It is their attitude to life, their demands on production, and their views of good and bad, of what is desirable and what is inadmissible, that presently "determine the weather" in work collectives, that determine the "standards" that gradually become obligatory for everyone. In 1970, representatives of this generation comprised less than one-sixth of the workforce. The majority of the workforce at that time had incomparably more modest demands both on production itself and on things outside production. The present generation, especially the youngest, are particularly sensitive to shortcomings in the organization of work, to being diverted from their basic activity, to all types of shortages, and to the inattention that is sometimes shown to the individual's demands. Young people are sometimes not prepared for the difficulties of life and are not oriented toward tenacious, conscientious labor. However, together with the attainments of the scientific-technological revolution, there is a clear understanding that the orientations of youth are natural and, above all, highly progressive. The notions concerning the logic upon which one's working life or professional career should be organized are changing. In all times, the value of a worker has been determined by experience. Consequently, authority, the right to interesting, independent work, and higher material remuneration came to a person only with the passage of years. Under present conditions, this tie has been broken. In many types of activity, the newcomer may be a no less valuable worker than his experienced colleague because of the vigor of his young mind and his greater capacity to adapt to novel situations.

There has arisen the difficult but urgent problem of bringing the rules governing the remuneration of labor, professional advancement, etc., into line with this new reality. However, to a considerable degree, the attitude toward the young and the mode of dealing with them are based on traditional views that are rooted in the early years of industrialization. This would seem to be one of the principal reasons for the lessening of people's interest in the results of their labor, for the relaxation of discipline, and for other negative phenomena.

Full employment and the intensification of social production

Until very recently, full employment of our country's population seemed to be a natural concomitant of economic and social development. Production increased not only as a result of higher labor productivity but also (as already noted) as a result of the increase in the size of the workforce. The nonproductive sphere also had a constant demand for people, but it absorbed less than half of all additional workers. There was also an increase in the total size of the workforce as a result of the introduction of the shorter work week, the increase in the length of paid vacation time, etc.

The implementation of the intensification policy means that the conditions of securing full employment are radically changing. In the next fifteen years (1986–2000), the productivity of social labor will, for the first time, grow at a much faster rate than national income. This will lead to a situation that is unusual for our economy, a situation in which material production will have to "toss out" working hands. The scale of the process has already been described with the figures previously cited. Naturally, new methods will be required for the systematic utilization of labor resources. The sense of these methods will be that workers must be released without delay. Their sense is also that another problem—that of full employment—must be successfully resolved at the same time. Under socialism, both one and the other are a mighty factor in increasing labor productivity: release—by removing the obstacles to such growth; and full employment—by creating a favorable social atmosphere and by giving people confidence in the future.

However, it appears that we are not as yet economically, socially, or psychologically prepared to make decisive changes in the utilization of labor resources, and consequently, we are also not prepared to achieve the dramatic acceleration of the growth of labor productivity slated by the year 2000.

In our view, difficulties with the release of manpower have, for a long time, worked in the direction of increasing manpower surpluses in the national economy and have substantially hindered the growth of labor productivity. In the capitalist world, the word "release" is practically synonymous with unemployment. It is evidentially for this reason that we refrain from using this term. And if we use it, we do so only in the sense that so and so many people have been released from such and such a sector of production and have been sent to other sectors at the same enterprise. But "release" will take place only when the worker goes outside the enterprise's walls. The acuity of this problem will grow enormously as soon as enterprises have been converted to full cost accounting and self-financing. The logical consequence of this should be the elimination of those [enterprises] that are unable to break even. Naturally, this will require a much more reliable measurement of profitability than at the present, when prices, payments to the budget, etc., are frequently very remote from the socially recognized norms. It is also clear that the decision to shut down a chronically unprofitable enterprise will not be made automatically or hastily—it must be made after a careful, comprehensive examination of the question. Nevertheless, it is obvious that such decisions will be encountered in practice. In these cases, the question arises: What should be the fate of the work collective of the given enterprise, bearing in mind the need to observe the principles of socialist society?

There are numerous problems here. The occupational structure of those who are "released" and those who are in demand usually does not coincide. There may also be discrepancies in territory and in time— manpower is released somewhere but the need for personnel arises elsewhere some time later. Finally, problems also arise because of the fact that they involve specific people who have their own views of where they want to work and the kind of work they would best like to do.

While these are all complex problems, planned economic management makes it entirely possible, albeit not without certain social difficulties, to secure both economic interests—the growth of labor productivity—and social interests— full employment of the population. This requires the implementation of numerous measures. Let us list the most important of them that will fundamentally alter the utilization of labor resources.

It is important to supply manpower to the service sphere, whose development is very promising and whose workforce will grow systematically. It is essential to raise substantially the prestige of the workforce in the service sphere. This will depend in large measure on the nature of the material-technological base of this sphere. Here, much remains to be done, as provided in the Comprehensive Program for the Development of Consumer Goods Production and the Service Sphere in 1986–2000. It is also important to eliminate unjustified distinctions in the pay of workers in this sphere compared with those in material production (in the last fifteen years, this gap has more than doubled).

The planned mechanism for releasing and redistributing manpower should be improved. It is essential to relieve enterprise managers of the responsibility of finding jobs for people; this is the business of specialized labor agencies at the local level (enterprises are responsible for the effectiveness of employment; full employment is the concern of the state). The advanced training and retraining system must be substantially expanded and improved. Within the framework of the wage fund, a centralized fund (outside the enterprise) should be created throughout the national economy to finance retraining and job placement.

Finally, there is a need for improvement in the area of vocational guidance. It is important to provide assistance in occupational selection not only to young people, who are embarking on their working career, but also to other workers of all ages, including pensioners desiring to work for the common good.

The need to eliminate social obstacles to the growth of labor productivity also dictates a new approach to full employment. The concept of full employment is frequently based on a misconception of the universality of labor under socialism, which means that labor alone can be the means of every person's livelihood in socialist society. However, participation of everyone down to the last man in labor for the good of society would mean "100-percent employment" rather than "full employment." There will always be some people who for objective reasons cannot work at least part of the time (for example, young people attending school, women shortly after giving birth, mothers of large families, and certain others). We believe that it would be proper to consider as full employment a situation that fulfills the population's job needs. In the past, we knew only one way of ensuring full employment—increasing the number of workplaces. Today, another avenue—the stabilization, and even the reduction of the labor application sphere in individual areas of the national economy and in entire branches, and reducing the population's requirement for workplaces—is acquiring paramount importance in the interests of effective production, at least in the greater part of the nation. The effect here can be great since there is overemployment of some categories of the population—youth, women (especially women with small children), and pensioners. This requirement can be reduced with the aid of a distribution policy. Presently, more than one-third of those attending higher and secondary specialized, vocational-technical institutions (more than 4.5 million persons) acquire an occupation on a part-time basis. Obviously, an increase in the size of scholarships (if we think of reducing the "scissors" between it and the average wage, and they have almost doubled in twenty-five years) will alter the proportions of vocational training for youth in favor of full-time education. There will be a decline in female employment if maternity grants and leave time are increased. Employment of pensioners will decline if the size of pensions is increased.

It would seem that such a channel for securing full employment as satisfying the requirement of a considerable segment of the population to work an abbreviated work week or day should be utilized to a considerably greater degree. But this requires the creation of conditions in which managers are not as yet interested.

The successful resolution of employment problems will require the serious restructuring of everyone's thinking. It is presently considered natural that if a workplace become unnecessary, the worker should then and there be assigned to another job, preferably at the same enterprise. The constitutional guarantee that everyone shall have the right to choose employment on the basis of his personal aptitudes remains unshakable. But in the process of making the choice, everyone should reckon to a greater degree both with his actual ability and with society's needs. In this process, there are many who will have to seriously reexamine and reappraise their views and their attitudes toward various types of employment.

The improvement of this entire mechanism and the normalization of the population's needs for jobs will increase everyone's responsibility and will create conditions under which people will prize their jobs.

Regional aspects of labor resource utilization

The intensification of social production requires as one of its main conditions acceleration of the growth of labor productivity everywhere, regardless of the degree to which or whether labor resources are increased in one or another region. Attention should be focused on this point because the demographic approach to the labor resource problem also manifests itself in this question: labor productivity should be increased more rapidly where labor resources are few, while where labor resources are numerous there is no hurry to increase productivity, since it is more important to find work for the population. It is hardly necessary to prove that such an interpretation of the growth of labor productivity, and all the more so its contraposition to full employment, are not legitimate. One of the most important principles of economic theory is that labor productivity is the source of accumulation, and that the higher its level, the more resources society has at its disposal in order to maintain the balance between the existence of labor resources and the national economy's need for them, and between the demand for jobs by the population and the availability of jobs in the national economy.

It is specifically the deceleration of the growth of social labor productivity that led to the manpower "shortage" in the European USSR, which also determined the general manpower situation in the nation as a whole. In a number of other regions, especially the Central Asian republics, the sharp decline in the growth rate of productivity (and in agriculture its level has been declining for a long time) was accompanied by the worsening of the job placement problem, particularly in Turkmenia, where the productivity of social labor has not risen at all in fifteen years. This is a perfect example of when the adverse labor productivity situation ultimately complicates the effort to provide full employment for the population.

Labor productivity only plays the role assigned to it in intensification when, in addition to the general processes and trends that are characteristic of the entire economy, full consideration is also given to the specific features of utilization of the labor resources of every territory. These features are primarily associated with the place that every territory should occupy in the all-union division of labor. And it in turn depends on the level of industrial development and on the quality of the workforce (the adaptability of the workforce to different types of production). Demographic processes and national traditions also have considerable impact.

As it follows from the five-year plan (1986–90), the acceleration of the growth of labor productivity in the European part of the country, where the scientific-technological and industrial potential is highest and where the greatest amount of experience of skilled labor has been accumulated, will be based on the technical retooling of existing enterprises. This will lead to the release of workers from material production, which is in line with the all-union dynamics in this sphere of employment. The same approach in these regions will retain its force in subsequent years; in order to fully utilize the accumulated experience of skilled labor, in our view we should specialize in the production of complex types of products while certain traditional types of production based on transshipped agricultural raw materials should either be discontinued all together or substantially curtailed.

In the Central Asian republics and other regions that utilize labor resources similarly, the acceleration of the growth of labor productivity may in turn be achieved on the basis of rapid industrial development. Intensification here essentially means the culmination of industrialization. Therefore, the size of the work force in industry, construction, and in the production infrastructure must grow—much more rapidly than before—based on the creation of new enterprises and the expansion of existing enterprises. It is important to overcome the existing tendency to copy the structure of industrial production in the [Soviet] Union as a whole or of individual republics with an advanced level of industrial development. Local managers are generally striving at all costs to build "prestigious" facilities for producing technically sophisticated types of products even though it is as yet extremely difficult to staff them with their own skilled personnel.

Experience suggests, and the interests of the intensification of production and social development of the nation demand, the widespread construction of food and light industry enterprises in these regions. They have the conditions, especially natural and climatic conditions, for this. As yet, however, most of the cotton, wool, and leather from these republics are processed in other regions. This situation must also be decisively altered. Second and third shifts can be a help here in such a situation. These branches are those in which the local population is most willing to work, especially if the enterprises are small and are situated in a nearby rural locality. Industrialization, understood in this sense, will help to change the mode of life of the indigenous population, will create a favorable climate for training skilled personnel, and, as successes are registered in this area, will make it possible to develop increasingly sophisticated production facilities.

Skepticism is generated by proposals to move "surplus" workers to other regions of the nation that have a greater need for working hands in the interest of providing them with employment. People are not raw materials or equipment that can be transferred willy-nilly from place to place. The uniqueness of the way of life that derives from ancient national traditions sharply limits the freedom to maneuver human resources. Associated therewith is the as yet insufficient mobility [of certain sections of the population] and the insufficient capacity to adapt to novel conditions. The local indigenous population is reluctant to change its rural address for an urban address even within its own republic. Thus, mass migration is a matter of the distant future.

To this it should be added that under the conditions of intensification the need everywhere is not merely for workers, but for skilled workers, which are in very short supply in the Central Asian and other republics with a similar manpower situation.

The steady and rapid growth of labor productivity, while comprising the main condition to the solution of the manpower problem, demands that each individually and all of us together work more intensively. But the greatest labor return will result not only from a conscientious and responsible attitude of every person toward his work. This means the creation of favorable conditions that ensure the rational employment of the population and the dramatic acceleration of the growth of labor productivity.

Note

1. There is the opinion, which is shared by the author, that psychology will occupy a dominant place among all sciences by the end of the twentieth century. The intensification of production will depend no less on its accomplishments and the ability to apply them in practical economic activity than on progress in technology and in the technological disciplines.

L. KOSTIN

Restructuring the System of Payment of Labor

The strategy of accelerating socioeconomic development requires a decisive turn to intensive methods of economic management, the increased effectiveness of production on the basis of scientific-technological progress, the mobilization of economic, organizational, and social factors, and the increased economic independence and responsibility of associations and enterprises. An important role in the realization of these objectives belongs to the restructuring of the existing system of labor remuneration. This restructuring is presently underway in the productive branches of the national economy, in science, in health care, and in higher education. The conversion of public education employees to the new conditions of labor remuneration has been completed.

Major changes in the payment of labor are taking place in the branches of material production. Based on the directives of the Twenty-Seventh CPSU Congress and the experience of the leading collectives, the CPSU Central Committee, USSR Council of Ministers, and All-Union Central Council of Trade Unions issued a decree "On Improving the Organization of Wages and On Introducing New Wage Rates and Salaries for Personnel in the Productive Branches of the National Economy." The contours of the present restructuring of wages in this sphere are determined by the need to resolve the following problems: (1) strengthening the stimulative role of

Russian text © 1987 by "Pravda" Publishers. "Perestroika sistemy oplaty truda," *Voprosy ekonomiki*, 1987, no. 11, pp. 41–51.

Professor Kostin holds a doctor's degree in economics and is first deputy chairman of the USSR State Committee for Labor and Social Problems.

wages; increasing their significance in the growth of labor productivity; decisively improving the quality of all output; securing the more complete utilization of equipment and other productive capital; and the all-around conservation of material resources; (2) the elimination of leveling; the realization of the principle of social justice; the organization of labor remuneration in strict accordance with the socialist principle of payment according to one's labor; and (3) the elimination of cumulative shortcomings in the system of wages.

The report at the January 1987 Plenum of the CPSU Central Committee noted that "production and work incentives are essentially oriented toward quantitative, extensive development." Now, however, primary emphasis is on the intensification of production, on increasing the effectiveness and improving the quality of labor. The last general reform of the labor remuneration system and increase in wage rates and salaries in the productive branches date back to 1972–75. In recent years, the average wage has risen almost 1.5-fold while rates and salaries have remained the same. As a result, the level of the wage rate has declined almost 50 percent. The quality of norming has deteriorated. The fulfillment of norms in 1986 was 128 percent, and in machine building—almost 130 percent. Differences in the remuneration of skilled and unskilled labor have diminished. In machine building, the difference in wage rates between the second wage-skill grade (almost no one is assigned to the first grade) and the sixth wage-skill grade was 48.5 rubles a month. Differences in the level of pay of workers and specialists have diminished. While in 1965, the wages of specialists in industry were 146 percent of the wages of workers, in 1986 the figure was just 110 percent. In construction and civil machine building, the average wage of specialists was below that of workers. The existing bonus system evoked much criticism. Over a long period of time, many different bonus systems and terms accumulated: in industry alone, there were 56 additional systems in operation.

The current wage reform and the introduction of new wage rates and salaries in the productive branches of the national economy are the most prominent measure in the social program of the Twelfth Five-Year Plan. Suffice it to say that the new rates and salaries apply to 75 million workers and employees, i.e., roughly two-thirds of the total work force in the public economy.

Major changes in wages are the equivalent of reform of the system of wages. They must accelerate the restructuring process in all spheres of our life in every way. Distinguishing features of this reform consist first and foremost in the fact that the restructuring of wages is comprehensive. For the first time, such a reform entirely encompasses the principal components of wage organization: the wage rate system, the norming of labor, the system of salaries for specialists and employees, the mechanism of additional payments [*doplaty*] and increments [*nadbavki*], and the bonus system, i.e., all elements of labor remuneration with the exception of regional coefficients.

What is more, while wage rates and salaries of low- and middle-income personnel were raised in the seventies, the current reform affects all personnel in associations, enterprises, and organizations. The wages of each member of the work collective—from worker to manager—will be made directly dependent on the final work indicators of the collective and the personal labor contribution.

A fundamentally new direction in the restructuring of wage system in the productive branches consists in the fact that the substantial broadening of the rights of enterprises and the introduction of new terms of labor remuneration are integrally connected with the reform of the economic mechanism. It is specifically through wages that the new economic mechanism can and should be conveyed to each subdivision, to every worker. This will make it possible to align the interests of the enterprise, shop, brigade, and every worker with the interests of society as a whole and to secure the material interest of one and all in raising the effectiveness of production.

Finally, the fact that the increases of wage rates and salaries in industry, construction, agriculture, transport, and communications will for the first time be financed, and within fall within the limits, of the enterprises' own earnings is a most important feature of this wage reform. As a result, a more active influence will be exerted on the effort to find reserves and to increase the effectiveness of production.

The decree on the system of wages is a natural aspect of the reform of one of the principal components of the economic mechanism and is the result of the large-scale collective effort of numerous specialists, organizations, institutions, and state agencies. Individual research and proposals by scholars at the Institute of Economics of the USSR Academy of Sciences, the Scientific Research Institute of Labor, and other research institutes, as well as publications in the journals *Sotsialisticheskii trud* [Socialist labor], *Voprosy ekonomiki* [Problems of economics], *Planovoe khoziaistvo* [The planned economy], and *Ekonomicheskaia gazeta* [Economic herald] and other press organs were utilized in its preparation. Nevertheless, the contribution of economists to proposals on the restructuring of wages was still not sufficient. For the most part it was necessary to use not scientific research but existing experience, experimental results, and the ideas and suggestions not so much of economists as of laymen. In the formulation of theoretical problems, much attention is unfortunately devoted to the criticism of shortcomings, and considerably less attention is given to the well-reasoned substantiation of proposals on improving the system of labor remuneration and its individual elements. Economic science has yet to give the nation a proper theoretical grounding for a system of labor remuneration that is optimally effective and socially just.

The correctness of labor remuneration depends not only on the reform of its system, but also to a great degree on the correct choice of sources and methods for forming wage funds. With the conversion of enterprises to the new methods of management, the base-increment principle [*bazisno-prirostnoi printsip*] has become the basic principle in determining funds for the payment of labor. In the process of generating proposals and discussions of this question, the majority of ministries and enterprises spoke out for just such a method. The practicality of such proposals is understandable—to provide a definite, quite stable system of payroll funds, even if the results of the work are not entirely successful. But this does not correspond to the current tasks of production and the principle of social justice. The drawbacks of planning based on the attained level are inherent in the base-increment method. There are great differences in the starting conditions of individual enterprises. The leading enterprises, who have already used many of their reserves today, find themselves in a worse situation than lagging enterprises. This has also proven to be the case today. The regulation of wage funds by personnel categories has also proven to be a failure.

Recent decrees on improving the economic mechanism defined from above the wage funds for five categories of personnel: industrial production personnel (according to norm); nonindustrial personnel; managers, engineering-technical personnel, and employees (according to norm); designers, technologists, and scientific personnel (according to norm); and quality control personnel. The idea was to prevent the shifting of resources for the payment of labor from one category to another. However, it is here that enterprises are frequently compelled to alter the existing relations, for example, to increase the wage fund for specialists in connection with scientific-technological progress. Therefore, the Law on the State Enterprise (Association) does not include this regulation.

The testing and introduction of the most effective methods of determining resources for labor remuneration remains an important theoretical and practical problem. What is more, as indicated in the guidelines on the radical restructuring of economic management, different methods of forming resources for labor remuneration obviously can and should be applied in different branches and under the conditions of different methods of management, in particular, under the conditions of full cost accounting.

Of late, the residual effect method [*ostatochno-rezul'tativnyi metod*] of forming resources for labor remuneration has become widespread in our country. It has been advanced and supported by individual Soviet economists. But in addition to its positive aspects, especially the fact that it is instrumental in linking labor remuneration more closely and rigidly to the final results, it also has its drawbacks, as indicated, in particular, by its practical application in the last few years in the People's Republic of Bulgaria.

In planning, there is the very important problem of establishing a correlation between the growth of labor productivity and the average wage. Each year, USSR Gosplan [State Planning Committee] together with the USSR State Committee for Labor and Social Problems assigns such correlations to ministries with due regard to the factors underlying the growth of labor productivity. Neverthe-less, there is not sufficient scientific substantiation for these correla-tions, even though the methods for making such calculations do exist. Here it is necessary to improve both the methods themselves, based on more flexible theoretical formulations, and the practice. Most ministries today assign enterprises the same correlations be-tween these indicators, which is of course theoretically and practi-cally unjustified. What is more, in connection with the rise of wage rates and salaries and the growth of the average wage of enterprise personnel on the basis of the enterprises' own funds, especially where this is a result of reductions in force, there arises the problem of observing this correlation in the course of each year.

When the size of the work force drops, labor productivity rises and resources accumulate, but the growth of wages lags. The re-verse may be the case in the following year. All this requires deter-mining and observing the correlation between the growth of labor productivity and the average wage in an ascending total from the beginning of the five-year plan, which is once again also dictated and suggested by practice. This question has thus now been re-solved.

The comparison and accounting of the quality of labor is a very important and complex problem. And even though a great deal of practical experience has been amassed here, the kind of correlation that should exist between the eighth and first wage-skill grades in machine building, for example (it was previously 3.6 and 3.2 and is presently 2.0), has not yet been theoretically proven. What is the most substantiated and optimal correlation?

It cannot be said that all problems involved in measuring the quantity of labor have been solved, especially in the nonproductive sphere, even though the normative base is increasing and improving with each passing year and computers are being increasingly used to calculate work norms. Issues of labor intensiveness are closely asso-ciated with this problem. Formulating the problems involved in labor intensiveness is of course required not only for labor remu-neration but also for the organization of labor, in particular, for determining the length of the work day, work and rest schedules, etc. But without an in-depth analysis of this problem and its quantitative expression, it will also be impossible to organize labor remuneration correctly.

At the present time, the application of contract forms of labor organization and payment for labor is taking great significance in connection with the conversion of enterprises and whole branches to full cost accounting and self-financing. These forms are being developed in construction, agriculture, and industry. At the same time, we are assessing the need to extend contract forms not only and not so much to the brigade as to larger structural subdivisions (enterprises and shops, for example). This work is encountering considerable difficulties in practice, and one of the reasons for this is the still deficient theoretical formulation of questions relating to the contract organization of labor and the place of the contract in the system of self-financing.

There are also a number of problems involved in the regional regulation of wages. There are any number of formulas here, but most of them are obsolete. The new tasks and the greater social orientation of plans and of all our work demand new approaches. The significance of these questions grows in connection with the need for the accelerated development of the eastern regions of the nation.

The problem of combining short-term work incentives through the wage system, increments, additional payments, bonuses with long-term incentives through pensions, length of service payments, and other social benefits is also of no little importance. The experience of a number of foreign countries, Japan in particular, attests to the expedience and effectiveness of their proper combination.

Many problems have also arisen in the bonus system. Here, in addition to the common approaches, it is evidently necessary to consider the particular features of individual branches, types of production, and the specific tasks in a given period.

There are still other important problems requiring research and development, but as yet the theory and practice of labor remuneration are unfortunately frequently empirical and based predominantly on experience. A number of economists are now saying that with the transition to self-financing there is no need for a wage system or for various forms and systems of payments. This is a vivid example of how we sometimes go from one extreme to another not only in practice but also in theory. Renunciation of the wage system in our view is an anarchistic, antiscientific position. Without the wage system it is impossible to measure labor correctly, to take qualitative differences in labor, and hence its compensation, into account. Theoretical research on the remuneration of labor must provide increased and improved scientific substantiation of published statistical data on labor remuneration and other questions pertaining to labor and social development.

*   *   *

In restructuring the base system of wages, the wage system and its decisive role will be preserved. One of the most important tasks posited in the decree on wage reform is returning to the wage system the role of principal regulator of wages and raising the share of the wage rate within the system to 70–75 percent. It is assumed that the wage payment will more fully take into account the skill level of the worker, the difficulty level of the work, and production conditions; in a word, the wage rate must be directly tied to the labor contribution.

It is no exaggeration to say that the introduction of the new conditions of payment of labor, including additional payment for work performed with a smaller work force financed by in-house resources, essentially amounts to the use of the Shchekino method on a nationwide scale.

One of the most important tasks to be realized in the course of the projected restructuring of wages is to increase the motivation of managers, specialists, and employees to accelerate scientific-technological progress, to improve product quality, to increase labor productivity and the effectiveness of production. The salaries of managers and other enterprise executive personnel have not changed in more than twenty-five years. The decree calls for a considerable increase in the salary of this category of personnel as well.

The system of increments is being put in order: increments will henceforth be awarded only for high achievements in labor or for the time in which especially important work is performed.

A fundamental innovation is being introduced into the system of indicators for categorizing enterprises, shops, and sectors for the purpose of assigning executive personnel to pay groups. Most branches are planning to reduce the number of groups in which enterprises are categorized and also to reduce the number of such groups for shops and sectors. The principal goal here is to reduce the number of small, ineffective enterprises that are unable to address modern problems and to secure the concentration and specialization of production.

The categorization indicators have been made significantly stricter. These indicators are now oriented primarily toward raising the technical level of production, improving product quality, increasing labor productivity, and fulfilling volume production plans. The work-force-size indicator, which has justifiably been criticized, is not included in the new categorization procedure at all.

The task of accelerating economic growth rates in combination with the policy of expanding the rights and independence and raising the responsibility of associations and enterprises requires the introduction of a fundamentally new system of bonuses. The primary aim is to raise the role of bonuses in stimulating the fulfillment of plans and contractual delivery obligations, in raising the technical level and quality of production (work), in increasing labor productivity, in lowering the enterprise cost of production, and in conserving material resources of all types. The task is to secure a direct relationship between bonuses and the performance of each worker and of brigade and subdivision collectives. The rights of associations, enterprises, and organizations in this area are being substantially expanded. They have been granted the right to create a single material incentive fund, to incorporate in it all resources from special systems, and to decide questions pertaining to the awarding of bonuses to their personnel independently.

The system of bonuses for managerial personnel is being radically restructured. Instead of centrally assigned basic indicators for awarding bonuses to managers, starting in 1987 these indicators (with the exception of agriculture) will be established each year by ministries and departments of the USSR and union republics in agreement with the respective trade union organs. The result of economic activity in one or another branch must necessarily be among the basic bonus indicators.

The most difficult problem in making the transition to the new conditions of labor remuneration is the mobilization of the necessary resources. Preliminary calculations and existing practice show that the accumulation of resources will proceed in the following basic directions: (1) through technical reconstruction; improvement in the organization of labor and production, and in the performance of the planned volume of work with a smaller labor force on this basis; (2) as a result of the increase in the volume of production (work) and improvement in product quality (in the event of above-plan output, the wage fund will grow accordingly and improved quality will result in higher profit and higher payments to the material incentive fund); (3) on the basis of improvements in the structure of wages, including the elimination of relatively ineffective bonuses, additional payments, and increments; the substantial reform of output norms and other labor expenditure norms in every workplace; (4) in certain cases, part of the material incentive fund may be used, with the consent of the work collectives, to introduce the new terms of payment of labor. Certainly, the stimulative role of bonuses and rewards paid from this fund must not be lost in the process.

Notwithstanding the complexity of the task before us, the experience of the Belorussian Railroad, which received high marks at the Twenty-Seventh CPSU Congress, and that of many other collectives convincingly attests to the possibility and effectiveness of converting to the new conditions of payment of labor from in-house resources.

The groundwork for making the conversion to the new conditions of remuneration of labor began in 1987. As of October 1, 1987, the new wage rates and salaries were introduced in all production branches with a work force of approximately 10 million persons. The conversion is being actively carried through in the USSR Ministry of Railways, the USSR Ministry of the Petroleum Industry, the USSR Ministry of the Shipbuilding Industry, the Belorussian SSR Ministry of Automotive Transport, and a number of ministries in the construction complex.

On the basis of the conversion experience, it can be said that the new principles of organization of wages and bonuses make a worker's earnings directly dependent on performance and increase the interest of work collectives in the acceleration of scientific-technological progress, in increasing labor productivity, in raising product quality, and in resource conservation. Collective forms of labor organization and work incentives are being more broadly developed. Almost all enterprises are releasing a substantial number of workers (from 4 to 10 percent). By July 1, 1987, the conversion of all of the nation's railroads to the new conditions of payment of labor was complete. As a result, 280,000 persons were released and labor productivity during that time increased by 14–15 percent, or 3.7 percent higher than the target for the entire five-year plan.

The oil-refining industry, which is chronically short of workers, released more than 70,000 persons. As a result of the improvement of labor remuneration, the majority of enterprises achieved above-plan growth of labor productivity and substantially improved other indicators of their production activity. Many of them for the first time in recent years fulfilled their delivery obligations, reduced production costs, increased profitability, and strengthened labor discipline.

Nevertheless, there are also serious shortcomings in this work. As sociological studies have shown, the principal reason is that a considerable number of managers and workers in the economic and especially the technical services have little knowledge of the essence of the new mechanism of payment of labor and are ineptly and timidly using the broad rights granted to enterprises in this area.

The introduction of new conditions of payment of labor is not always accompanied by radical improvement in the norming of labor. In the Khar'kov Hammer and Sickle Production Association and at a model footwear factory in Rostov-on-Don, output norms were revised and increased by the same percent without analyzing the intensiveness and substantiation of existing norms. At a number of surveyed enterprises, only between 20 and 40 percent of the existing norms were revised. As a result, even after the transition to the new conditions of labor remuneration, the overfulfillment of norms at such enterprises is in excess of 30 percent. Included in this number is Wood-Processing Combine No. 3 of *Mospromstroimaterialy*, the "Pioneer" plant of the Estonian SSR Ministry of Local Industry, and others.

Enterprises have been given broad rights in differentiating the size of additional payments for working conditions depending on the actual conditions in the work place. Nevertheless, many enterprises assign the same additional payments for all workers. This has been seen to be the case at the Azovkabel' plant and at the Minsk October Revolution Machine-Tool Building Association.

The decree on improving the organization of wages calls for raising the wage rates of workers by 20–25 percent and the salaries of specialists by 30–35 percent, in order to increase the pay of specialists—which as already noted is frequently lower than the pay of workers—to a greater degree. Nevertheless, in a number of construction organizations and at enterprises of the RSFSR Ministry of the Textile Industry, the level of wage increases for specialists is lower than that of workers. At the same time, there are instances of mechanical, unsubstantiated, mass lowering of the wage grades of workers without the individual evaluation of the difficulty of the work performed in each work place and their skill levels. The certification of specialists for the purpose of raising the pay of highly qualified, talented specialists and managers is frequently only formal.

A special word should be said about the restructuring of the bonus system. In all productive branches from this January on, enterprises and organizations themselves must define the indicators, amounts, and conditions of bonuses and must focus their attention on stimulating the intensification and increased effectiveness of production. However, many enterprises that were accustomed to receiving standard statutes from above, proved to be unprepared to revise and establish bonus systems that were the most effective for them.

Many of the surveyed enterprises made no changes whatsoever in the organization of the workers' bonus system. And where the changes have been made, the bonuses frequently do little to stimulate such key indicators as contractual deliveries, raising labor productivity, and lowering material and labor expenditures. It continues to be the practice to award bonuses to designers, technologists, and other specialists not for the development of new equipment and technology but for general production indicators. Quality control inspectors frequently receive bonuses not for product quality but for the volume of production and profit. Many different bonus indicators that have little relationship to workers' activity continue to be applied. Instead of creating a system for earning bonuses and nominating workers for bonuses, enterprises continue to widely use a system that strips workers of bonuses.

The transition from individual bonuses to bonuses for collectives of brigades and other structural subdivisions is proceeding slowly. There have been practically no substantive changes in incentives for workers to promote economization of material and fuel-energy resources.

There are serious shortcomings in the planning of resources for labor remuneration. For example, a number of ministries have instituted in all subordinate enterprises a single norm governing the increase in the wage fund that does not take into account the level of utilization of reserves at enterprises, the state of establishment of work norms, and the structure of factors underlying the growth of labor productivity. Such an approach reduces the effectiveness of normative planning and places enterprise collectives in unequal starting conditions when they are converted to the new system of payment of labor and work incentives.

Thus, there are numerous shortcomings in work on reforming labor remuneration in branches of material production. The USSR Council of Ministers, after discussing the results of the fulfillment of the State Plan for the Economic and Social Development of the USSR in the first half of 1987, expressed concern about the state of the effort to introduce new wage rates and salaries in the productive branches of the national economy. It noted that while there were positive results in this regard, many ministries were allowing the realization of this most important social task to take its own course.

Now that the transition to the new conditions of payment of labor is increasingly taking place on a mass scale, we should take into account progressive experience, avoid shortcomings in the given work, and make the most effective use of the existing potential for radically improving the system of wages and for increasing the effectiveness of production.

*   *   *

The restructuring of labor remuneration is also being carried out in the nonproductive sphere. Its main direction is to establish a closer dependence between wages and the quality of labor, the results of labor, and the skill level and experience of the worker. The introduction of the new conditions of payment of the labor of education personnel, whose pay has increased by an average of 35 percent, is now complete. Efforts regarding labor remuneration in the scientific establishment, a complex matter, are underway. Pay increases and reforms for public health and social security employees have begun. A decree has been adopted that introduces new conditions of the remuneration of labor of personnel at institutions of higher learning. All these measures affect the interests of approximately ten million persons.

In the health care field, the salaries of surgeons and anesthesiologists are being raised to a higher degree. The salaries of highly qualified physicians and pharmaceutical chemists who are certified in the highest, first, or second qualification category have been raised by fifty, thirty, and fifteen rubles, respectively, while the salaries of surgeons have been raised by seventy-five, fifty, and twenty-five rubles a month.

With the consent of trade union committees, heads of institutions are authorized to pay increments from savings on wages to physicians, pharmaceutical chemists, other medical personnel, specialists, and employees up to 30 percent of their salary for applying advances in medical science and progressive work methods, for the complexity, intensiveness, and high quality of their work. These increments may be paid for a period of one year. The increment may then be confirmed for a new period, may be assigned in a different amount, or may be terminated depending on performance in the preceding period.

New additional payments have been introduced for medical personnel holding the academic degree of candidate of science (thirty rubles) and doctor of science (fifty rubles). The salaries of physicians awarded the honorary title "People's Physician of the USSR" are being raised by fifty rubles. The salaries of physicians and pharmaceutical chemists that have been awarded republic honorary titles have been increased by thirty rubles.

Health care and social security institutions have been authorized to introduce the brigade form of labor organization and wages for paramedical and junior medical personnel, specialists, employees, and workers. Brigade members who increase the volume of work performed over existing norms and who perform high quality work may receive an additional payment of up to 75 percent of their salary (in the case of secondary and junior service personnel) and up to 50 percent (in the case of specialists, employees, and workers).

The personnel of these institutions will receive bonuses for attaining the best results in their work and for improving the quality of services to the population with the condition that they fulfill all the indicators included in the plan. Up to 2 percent of the planned wage fund, as well as savings on the fund, may be expended on bonuses. Additional pay for night work and a number of other additional payments have been established.

Raising and reforming the pay of health care and social security personnel will require 3.7 billion rubles, including 3.4 billion rubles from the state budget. Work on the introduction of the new conditions of payment of labor in this sphere must be completed in 1991.

Restructuring the system of labor remuneration for scientific and research workers is very important. It has been in progress since 1985, following the adoption of the decree of the CPSU Central Committee, USSR Council of Ministers, and AUCCTU "On Improving the Pay of Scientific Workers, Designers, and Technologists in Industry" (1985). The main task of this restructuring is to increase the interest of personnel in the acceleration of scientific-technological progress, to raise their responsibility for the scientific and technical level of research and development, and to increase the volume and improve the quality of work with a smaller labor force. This decree contains the fundamentally new principles of wage organization that were more fully developed in the decree on pay in the productive branches.

The transition to the new conditions of payment of labor in science and research was for the most part formally complete in early 1987. They have been introduced in almost 3,800 scientific, design, and technological collectives of industrial ministries and departments, in the USSR Academy of Sciences and academies of sciences of the union republics, and in collectives at 130 institutions of higher learning.

Industry as a whole, the USSR Academy of Sciences, academies of sciences of the union republics, and the USSR Ministry of Higher Education where the new conditions of labor remuneration have been instituted number more than 1.1 million scientists, designers, and technologists. The results of checks conducted in more than three hundred collectives attest to the positive influence of the new principles of remuneration of labor for scientific and research personnel, designers, and technologists on the growth of their creative activism and on their reinforcement with promising young cadres. The expansion of the rights of creative collectives in the payment of scientific and engineering work has increased the responsibility of personnel for the timeliness and quality of their research and development efforts. There has been a considerable reduction in the time invested in this work and in the number of errors in design and technological documentation. The introduction of the new wage system has been accompanied by revisions of work plans from which topics of secondary importance have been deleted, and by additional targets for the most effective directions of scientific-technological progress.

Of course, a general characterization of the influence of the new conditions on the scientific and technical level of research and development on product quality and on the economic effectiveness of production can only be made after a sufficiently long period of time. Nevertheless, even now it can be said that, on the whole, the relationship between wages and the personal contribution of personnel to the acceleration of scientific-technological progress has grown stronger. This is particularly evident in collectives where the new conditions of labor remuneration are being skillfully applied.

On the whole, the number of scientific and research workers, designers, and technologists has been reduced by almost sixty thousand. This includes a 7.3 percent reduction in industry. This number has been reduced to approximately the same degree in the USSR Academy of Sciences and the academies of sciences of the union republics.

Work has begun on eliminating wage leveling. Promising young personnel have received very considerable salary increases. The salaries of the best of them have frequently been raised by 50, 100 and even 150 rubles a month. At the same time, as a result of certification, the salaries of approximately twenty thousand persons have been lowered, and approximately the same number have been demoted to lower positions. The reduction of the salaries of certain scientific workers with an academic degree was very appreciable—up to 100–120 rubles a month.

However, the basic restructuring of the organization of labor and wages in scientific, design, and technological collectives is still not being carried out. The impact of the wage system on the scientific and technical level of research and development and the introduction of their results in production is still faint. In the majority of surveyed institutions, organizations, associations, and enterprises, the certification of personnel was a liberal process that did not take into account the new high demands on the technical level and quality of the product. Thus, while in eleven civil machine-building ministries in general, only 3 percent of the persons certified were declared to be unfit for the positions they occupied, the targets of state plans for new technology and scientific-technological programs in this branch are not being fulfilled and the share of products in the highest quality category is growing slowly.

The mechanism of applying increments for the performance of most important projects directed toward bringing newly assimilated products up to world levels has not yet been activated in full measure. In a number of industrial ministries (the Ministry of Chemical Machine Building, the Ministry of Machine Building for Light and Food Industry and Household Appliances, and the Ministry of the Chemical Industry), allocations for this purpose have been insufficient, and no more than 15 percent of the work force is involved therein. Increments are for all intents and purposes not offered in most collectives of the academies of sciences and institutions of higher learning.

Trends toward the egalitarian distribution of economies gained persist. Thus, in the Ministry of Light Industry, the Ministry of Instrument Making, Automation Equipment, and Control Systems, and the Ministry of the Chemical Industry, there are many instances where salaries are raised by 5–10 rubles a month and increments in the same amount are awarded. In particular, the savings resulting from the elimination of six vacant positions at the Scientific Research Institute of the Wool Industry (Ministry of Light Industry) were mechanically divided among eighty-eight persons, half of whom had 5–10 rubles added to their pay.

There are instances of irresponsible attitudes being taken toward the application of the new conditions. Thus, the Ministry of the Chemical Industry converted the Scientific Research Institute of Cotton Cellulose Chemistry (Tashkent) to the new conditions of labor remuneration without introducing any changes or improvements in its activity, in its work profiles, or in the structure and size of the pay of research workers. The Scientific Research Institute of Chemical Machine Building (of the Ministry of Chemical Machine Building) reported the completion of work having resources comprising 1 ruble 80 kopecks a month per person.

The passive attitude toward the use of progressive knowhow amassed in the process of conducting the Leningrad experiment is a source of great concern. The norming of their labor is at a low level, particularly in the Ministry of Power and Electrification, the Ministry of Petroleum Refining and the Petrochemical Industry, the Ministry of the Medical and Microbiological Industry, and the Ministry of Machine Building for Light and Food Industry and Household Appliances. Slow progress is being made in introducing the payment of wages for the end results of work performed; in forming temporary subdivisions and task forces for solving key scientific and technical problems directly in production; and in awarding bosunes for attaining indicators at the world level.

Inertia is evident in reforming the structure of management. Measures are not being taken to close down unproductive scientific institutes, design and technological organizations and subdivisions.

Normative planning of the wage fund still does not take into account the role of scientific, design, and technological cadres in increasing the effectiveness of production.

The supply of scientific, design, and technological collectives with technical hardware is low. Their need for equipment and for computer-aided design systems will be satisfied by less than 5 percent under the current five-year plan. Nor is the experimental base being properly developed.

The effort to reform labor remuneration in science and research cannot be considered complete. Much remains to be done in this area in connection with the adoption of the decree of the CPSU Central Committee and USSR Council of Ministers "On the Conversion of Scientific Organizations to Full Cost Accounting and Self-Financing" (1987). In order to strengthen the dependence between the results of scientific labor and the payment for this labor, work will be continued on reforming existing forms and searching for new forms of labor organization and work incentives. In particular, a system for concluding contracts between the administration of a research organization and groups of scientists or individual specialists for the performance of research and design work will be introduced into the institutes' work practice.

*   *   *

Thus, the restructuring of the system of labor remuneration in both the sphere of material production and in the nonproductive sphere is not a simple task and is not without interruptions and shortcomings. Therefore, the highly skilled and effective aid of economists is required to ensure its implementation at enterprises. Without resolving in full measure the questions relating to the radical restructuring of wages, it will be impossible to secure fulfillment of the targets of the Twelfth Five-Year Plan and the accelerated socioeconomic development of our country.

S. Shatalin

Social Development and Economic Growth

Issue no. 13 of Kommunist *published an article by Academician T. Zaslavskaia which examined a number of little-investigated and much-debated problems concerning the interaction of social policy and the human factor in production.† This article by S. Shatalin, corresponding member of the USSR Academy of Sciences, continues the discussion.*

In formulating the concept of the acceleration of the nation's socioeconomic development and in providing a deep and comprehensive analysis of its determining factors together with the methods of its constructive implementation, the CPSU has made an enormous creative contribution to the treasury of Marxist-Leninist social thought and to the practice of building communism. The party has pointed to the growing reciprocal influence in modern society of economic, social, ecological, and scientific-technological factors that are of a dialectical, contradictory character. This applies to a particularly great degree to the interaction of economic and social factors (we somewhat tentatively classify ecological factors under the latter) of national economic development, an interaction that is variously manifested over time.

We shall examine the influence exerted on economic growth by

Russian text © 1986 by "Pravda" Publishers. "Sotsial'noe razvitie i ekonomicheskii rost," *Kommunist*, 1986, no. 14, pp. 59–70.

The author is a corresponding member of the USSR Academy of Sciences.

†For the English translation of this article, see Tat'iana Zaslavskaia, "Social Justice and the Human Factor in Economic Development," *Problems of Economics*, vol. 30, no. 1 (May 1987).

processes associated with the betterment of the people's well-being and the improvement of the system of income distribution in a socialist society. [We will also examine] the creation of a powerful motivational mechanism that would stimulate all workers to attain maximum economic effectiveness by actually involving the working people in the management of social property, and to participate in making strategic economic planning decisions on the distribution of social resources at all levels of the national economic hierarchy.

The causes of negative trends and certain conclusions

As noted at the Twenty-seventh Congress, our country's economic growth and, consequently, the rise of the population's standard of living have not been sufficiently favorable in recent years. The growth rates of national income used for consumption and accumulation have clearly shown a downward trend. In 1961–65 the average annual increase in the physical volume of national income was 5.7%; in 1966–70—7.2; 1971–75—5.1; 1976–80—3.8; and 1981–85—3.1%. The growth rate of the productivity of social labor calculated on the basis of the physical volume of produced national income has also continuously declined (after 1970).

The average annual growth rate of real per capita income—the best general indicator of the dynamics of the population's standard of living—has also waned: 1961–65—3.6%; 1966–70—5.9%; 1971–75—4.4; 1976–80—3.4; and 1981–85—2.1%. Thus, during the Eleventh Five-Year Plan the average annual growth rate of the physical volume of national income and real per capita income, like other indicators, proved to be very low.

The party has already evaluated these negative trends. What have been their principal causes?

The reduced potential for extensive economic growth (primarily in the form of natural and labor resources) as a result of objective circumstances has not only not been compensated but has been intensified by the decline in the average annual rate of increase in the aggregate effectiveness of utilization of production resources. According to our calculations, the rate of increase was 2% in 1971–75, 1% in 1976–80, and 0.6% in 1981–85. As a result, the share of intensive factors in the nation's economic growth has not shown any upward trend: in 1971–75 it was 43%; 1976–80—28; and in 1981–85—22%.[1]

The "gross output" [*val*] economic mechanism and errors in the structural resource distribution policy, particularly the clearly low rate of investment in machine building, which sharply decelerated the saving of fuel-energy resources and metal in the national economy, have had a most negative impact on the lowering of the growth rate of effectiveness of the use of production resources. The same role has been played by the lag in the development of the production and social infrastructure, especially in rural areas where losses of output (in all stages before it reaches the consumer) have amounted to almost one-fifth.

The relaxation of the system of material incentives for workers, the growth of egalitarian trends in the remuneration of labor, and the boosting of wages through higher job classifications and overreporting of hours are an important cause of the deceleration of the country's socioeconomic development. The imbalance in the consumer sector of the economy has led to an increase in profiteering and corruption, to the devaluation of the ruble, to the intensification of inflationary processes, and to the growth of the population's unearned income. All this has constantly lowered the social and moral prestige of honest labor for the good of all society, has deformed the socialist way of life, and has often grossly violated socialist social justice.

The essentially residual principle of resource allocation for the development of the social sphere of the national economy, which was sharply condemned in the decisions of Twenty-seventh CPSU Congress, has been highly detrimental to economic growth rates, to increasing the aggregate effectiveness of social production, and to the resolving a number of key social problems in the development of our society. The share of capital investment in nonproductive construction was 27.7% of total investment in 1985; this was a decline of almost 8 points compared with 1960. Wage increases for workers in the nonproductive branches during those years were smaller than in the productive branches and in the national economy as a whole.

Two erroneous methodological principles were the main reasons for such an ineffective structural policy on the distribution of society's resources. First, the resources allocated for the development of the social sphere were thought of as being aimed at the solution of purely social problems, frequently in terms of social philanthropy, as a direct brake on the country's economic growth rates. Second, there has been an extremely metaphysical, persistent conviction that social problems become less urgent as the population's living standard rises. It is a direct negation of the dialectical approach to the investigation and control of the development of socioeconomic processes in our society, because the very needs of the population are continuously growing both quantitatively and qualitatively; [existing problems] are increasing in complexity and new problems are emerging. In other words, as Lenin noted, the objective process of constantly increasing needs is in motion.

At the same time, we must bear in mind the unfavorable influence on the USSR's economic growth rates exerted by the arms race forced on us by Western capitalist countries.

All this can be summed up in the words of M. S. Gorbachev: "The most important thing was that we failed to make a prompt political assessment of the change in the economic situation, that we did not appreciate the urgency of converting the economy to intensive methods of development and the importance of making active use of the attainments of scientific-technological progress in the national economy. While there has been no shortage of appeals and discussion in this regard, practical efforts have been at a virtual standstill."

These are bitter but just words from which constructive economic conclusions must be drawn. The acceleration of the country's socioeconomic development is a concept that is based on the premise that the average annual rate of increase in the physical volume of national income used for consumption and accumulation must be approximately 4.7% in 1986–2000, 4.1% during the Twelfth Five-Year Plan, and 5% in 1991–2000. In other words, we will have to "speed up the acceleration" of the country's socioeconomic development.

We estimate that in order to secure the planned economic growth rates, it will be necessary to raise the average annual growth rate of the aggregate effectiveness of utilization of production resources in the time ahead to 3–3.5% and to increase the share of intensive factors in the growth of national income to 65–75%. Under the Twelfth Five-Year Plan, the increase in the aggregate effectiveness of resources will be approximately 2%, while the share of intensive factors will be approximately 50%. In order to make an objective assessment of the grandiose scale and extraordinary complexity of the realization of this objective, upon which the fate of world socialism largely depends, it is necessary to consider at least the following factors:

—We cannot count on any acceleration in the rate of introduction of additional material, labor, and natural resources in social production or appreciable improvement in the fuel, energy, minerals, and raw materials situation in the world market. The only real alternative here is the all-out conservation of all resources as a result of a dramatic improvement in structural, especially investment, policy and radical reform of the economic mechanism.

—The social and ecological strain on the economy will continue to grow in the future. In productive capital investments allocated for the Twelfth Five-Year Plan and the period up to the year 2000, there must objectively be an increase not for increasing production capacities, but for preserving and improving the state of the environment, for creating modern, comfortable workplaces, and for eliminating manual labor, especially semiskilled, strenuous manual labor that is often injurious to health. However, from the long-range point of view, all this should also be regarded as a real factor in increasing the effectiveness of the use of society's material, labor, and natural resources, and consequently, in the acceleration of economic growth rates.

—By definition, the planned growth rates of the physical volume of national income and the population's standard of living do not include the inflationary component; hence, there is need for a greater increase in economic growth rates compared with the level in the past period. It should also be taken into account that the absolute reduction in the production of alcoholic beverages will in a formal sense have a ''negative'' impact on the projected rates of economic development. However, the most important consideration here is the favorable economic perspective: the sharp reduction in the incidence of drunkenness, in addition to everything else, is the direct path to increasing the effectiveness of the utilization of all production resources, to reducing flaws in production, and to improving product quality.

—The aging of our country's population and the objective need to raise the average size of pensions will require a considerable increase in the investment of resources in the social security sphere. The same will be true of party and state measures to bolster certain low-income families.

We will not go into greater detail here on the problem of improving resource and investment policy and the entire complex of problems involved in the radical reform of the economic mechanism. But let us discuss certain key questions of social policy which—in addition to the fact that they have great social import of their own—must become a powerful factor in the effective acceleration of the nation's socioeconomic development based on scientific-technological progress and a dramatic rise in the level of effectiveness of social production. Here we must also objectively examine the problems that were poignantly raised by Academician T. I. Zaslavskaia in her article (*Kommunist*, no. 13).

In our view, socialism is now directly confronted with the need to resolve the basic, global problem of creating a powerful, all-around mechanism for motivating the economically effective utilization of production resources—a mechanism more powerful than that created by the capitalist West in the hundreds of years its existence. Only on this basis can socialism meet its primary objective of creating the highest level of public well-being in the world, of ensuring the genuinely all-around, harmonious development of the individual, and presenting the most attractive socialist way of life as the goal of worldwide socioeconomic and moral and ethical progress.

The motivational mechanism, which stimulates workers to perform highly effective labor, is an extremely capacious and many-sided concept. Let us dwell on what we consider to be its key aspects.

On two types of real income

It is necessary to create in the shortest possible time an effective, flexible system of material incentives for workers that unequivocally links the remuneration of their labor with their real contribution to social production without restrictions on the scale of its differentiation. A special role in the effective solution of this problem must belong to collective team forms of labor organization and wages within the framework of radical economic reform, and to the sharp expansion of the economic rights and economic responsibility of production associations and enterprises in the disposition of resources and in the adoption of economic planning decisions, including decisions regarding remuneration of labor. The socialist state has sufficiently powerful socioeconomic instruments to ensure that the differentiation of workers in accordance with actual differences in their labor contribution would not lead to social tension in society. What is more, as the Twenty-seventh Congress emphasized, the remuneration of labor on the basis of its actual results is one of the main formulas of socialist social justice.

As we know, the increase in teachers' pay, which began under the Eleventh Five-Year Plan, is now nearing completion. The wages of health care workers, certain categories of cultural workers, and higher education workers will be raised under the Twelfth Five-Year Plan. The interests of acceleration of socioeconomic development demand that future average wages in the leading branches of the nonproductive sphere be on a par with wages in material production. In our view, this is one of the fundamental issues of economic policy. Let us suggest once again that it would be a serious mistake to approach this question one-sidedly from the standpoint of the development of material production without regard to the latter's relationship to the social sphere.

But realizing the principle of remuneration based on labor still does not solve the problem of creating an effective system of material incentives for workers. Socialism will have to create not only a mechanism for full employment (this was already accomplished in the stage of extensive development), but a mechanism for socially and economically effective and rational full employment. The principles of socialism are not philanthropic principles that automatically guarantee everyone a job regardless of his capacity to fill it. Man must engage in daily economic struggle to maintain an adequate workplace for himself. Even now, in our view, serious thought should be given to the creation of a hierarchically organized state system for the training and retraining of cadres released from social production under the influence of scientific-technological progress, structural technological changes in the economy, and changes in the demands on skills. This system could be financed through the introduction of payments for the use of labor power by associations, enterprises, and organizations. Economists have written about this measure for many years, and there would seem to be no grounds for failing to realize it in the course of a radical economic reform. Enterprises, production associations, and organizations must be given significantly more rights in planning the size of their work force, and in determining the wage fund and its average level, naturally within the framework of the centralized regulation of these processes. A number of real problems that objectively arise in connection with the realization of the principle of rational employment were examined by T. I. Zaslavskaia in her article, the basic conclusions of which we support entirely.

The time has long been ripe for the optimal combination of wages and social consumption funds. They are the two basic types of income in socialist society. At the same time, the historical trend is such that payments and benefits from the social consumption funds are continuously growing. They will increase by 25% during the Twelfth Five-Year Plan, and in the period between 1986 and 2000 they will roughly double.

Wages are the principal mechanism for the distribution of income as well as material goods and services in socialist society. Payment based on labor is socialism's objective economic law, deviation from the demands of which, as the Twenty-seventh Congress emphasized, has been and continues to be highly detrimental to the Soviet economy. The main task of earned income is to stimulate the growth of social production and to increase the effectiveness of the utilization of production resources. Only on this basis can there be high and stable growth of the population's standard of living. But it is specifically wages that perform the basic stimulative function in the distribution system.

Social consumption funds are distributed directly to members of socialist society regardless of the quantity and quality of expended labor even though the size of pensions (and in part, scholarships) depends on the past or future labor contribution. This makes it possible to say that they for the most part perform the socially guaranteed function of income distribution under socialism. But as we know, social consumption funds are not a homogeneous socioeconomic category. One part of these funds provides for the population's social security (pensions, grants, scholarships); another part satisfies the needs of members of socialist society with the highest social priorities: medical care, education, part of the services of cultural institutions, subsidies for the maintenance of housing, etc. The fact that society makes these goods and services available to all members of society free of charge or at a nominal price means that society exercises social guardianship over these needs. It does not consider it possible to make their satisfaction the prerogative of individual choice dependent on each individual's means. This gives all members of society social guarantees of their access to the material basis of man's harmonious development, which is also "advantageous" for the development of socialist society as a whole.

Thus, wages and social consumption funds dialectically complement one another. As emphasized at the congress, they make it possible to realize in full measure one of the main principles of socialism—the principle of combination of the economic effectiveness of the utilization of resources with socialist social justice.

Naturally, the border between the economic and social functions of income distribution is determined by many circumstances: the level of economic development of society, its wealth, the character of existing needs and the population's preferences, the character of labor, and the entire system of socialist values. But its objective conditionality emphasizes the need for the strict differentiation of the role of wages and social consumption funds for each stage in the country's socioeconomic development, and the need to differentiate the economic and social functions of redistribution relations in order to implement effective socioeconomic policy. This differentiation is the basis for determining the range of the tasks of socioeconomic development that can be most effectively resolved by improving the wage system, and those that require the effective use of social consumption funds.

Confusing the functions of distribution relations only leads to social and economic costs. They arise when wages are used in the attempt to solve purely social problems and when social consumptions funds are wrongfully assigned a material incentive function. Typical manifestations of this function are wage leveling, boosting wages with accounting tricks, etc., which greatly deform the main principle of socialist distribution according to one's labor. At the same time, the economic basis for stimulating the effective use of production resources naturally deteriorates sharply, and the principles of socialist social justice are violated.

The policy of strengthening the departmental component of social consumption funds, and the attempt to create a more effective system of material incentives on the basis of departmental social consumption funds, lead to equally negative consequences.

Naturally, it is not a question of denying altogether the possibility of using the social and cultural funds of productive associations and enterprises for the material stimulation of people in the interest of increasing the effectiveness of social production and of accelerating scientific-technological progress, i.e., for solving purely economic problems. However, the realization of such a possibility requires serious theoretical study of the question without which socioeconomic policy will inevitably be biased.

Wages express economic relationships between society, work collectives, and workers in social production that characterize the integral dependence of the amount of remuneration on performance. Social consumption funds, on the other hand, are the essence of social production relationships between socialist society and its members. They characterize income distribution regardless of the quality and quantity of the workers' labor inputs.

Therefore, in principle the present social and cultural funds of production associations and enterprises are not, in a political economy sense, social consumption funds even though they bear an outward resemblance to them. Social and cultural funds formed from enterprise profits are essentially a type of earned income that is paid out in kind. Only in the latter respect are they similar to social consumption funds (more precisely, the part of them that is represented by goods and services provided free of charge or at a nominal price). Social and cultural funds are available not to *members* of socialist society, but to *workers* of associations and enterprises that earn them through their own economic efforts. Social consumption funds, as already noted, secure social guarantees and social standards of satisfaction of the needs of all members of socialist society that it considers to be most important based on the demands for the development of the individual and social progress in general. Production associations and enterprises may use their own social and cultural funds to ensure the more complete satisfaction of deserving shock workers' needs for medical care, education, culture, etc., than society guarantees all its members whereever they may live or work. We believe that these funds in the future should be used to a greater degree for improving working conditions and the nature of labor, for creating modern, comfortable workplaces.

It should be noted that there are still a number of unresolved problems here. For example, why should people who are doing a good job at malfunctioning enterprises suffer? What should be done when medium-size and small enterprises lack the resources required to form adequate social and cultural funds? There is evidently promise in such forms as the cooperative use of social and cultural funds by enterprises and associations, additional benefits for workers who are doing a good job, etc. These questions merit careful theoretical interpretation and require a practical solution from the standpoint of social justice.

Attention to all aspects of the motivational mechanism

Labor as such, i.e., working conditions, the nature of the labor, the challenge, elements of creativity and attractiveness, the potential for self-affirmation, is the most important source of interest in highly skilled, highly productive labor. However, at the present time there are still millions of workers engaged in strenuous, manual, semiskilled labor. While the number of uncomfortable workplaces is declining in relative terms at individual enterprises, their absolute number is on the rise. And this leads to serious social and economic losses, because with the Soviet people's present living standard and the objectively formed system of their socioeconomic, moral, and ethical needs, our obvious shortcomings in such a form of incentives as the "stimulation of labor through labor" frequently cannot be compensated by any manner of wage hike. Our party is now steering a steady course to radically altering working conditions and the nature of labor in the nation's economy. The share of manual labor in the productive sphere is slated to be reduced to 15–20% by the year 2000. This course (especially in the long view) not only "works" for the purely social attainments of socialism, but also has the most beneficial influence on maintaining high, stable national economic growth rates.

We must see to it that the social and ecological parameters of newly commissioned workplaces fully accord with modern demands [and that these parameters] are not violated under any circumstances. Nevertheless, even today priority is frequently given to technical and economic indicators of new projects, which are essentially a continuation of the residual principle (which was condemned by the congress) of allocation of resources for the development of the social sphere of the national economy. Attempts to realize instantaneous economies at its expense are ultimately negatively reflected in the level of economic effectiveness of the utilization of production potential, and consequently, in economic growth rates as well.

The creation of a powerful motivational mechanism requires a thoroughly developed system of social guarantees first and foremost on the basis of the expansion and more effective use of social consumption funds. The connection between effectiveness and economic growth here is direct. When socialist society can rely on social consumption funds to satisfy vitally important needs, it can more decisively maneuver economic levers for the material stimulation of workers and differentiate their wages in accordance with their actual labor contribution without the least detriment to true socialist social justice.

The real participation of the working people themselves in the disposition of socialist property, in the distribution of resources, and in the establishment of wage levels is without a doubt one of the most important conditions to a highly effective mechanism for stimulating highly productive labor at all levels. Only by creating a system of genuine proprietary motivations is it possible to put an end to the very typical situation with the subjects of public and cooperative ownership where "too many cooks spoil the broth" and to widespread social apathy and indifference. For the sake of objectivity, it must be said that socialism is in large measure only beginning the creation of such a self-governing system, and that this is to a considerable degree the direction of the radical economic reform and of the development of the entire intricate complex of socialist property relations, because it is specifically here that socialism enjoys the main historical advantage, toward the realization of which all our efforts must be oriented. The Twenty-seventh Congress posed the basic task of revealing the potential of public ownership, of widely using the cooperative and individual labor activity of the working people in the production of consumer goods and services, and of making this activity an integral part of the social system of socialist management. However, it must be said that this course is being realized very slowly in practice even though it clearly promises improvements in the consumer sector of the economy, the creation of more flexible mechanisms in the employment of the population, and the inclusion of resources in economic circulation that are practically inaccessible to large-scale production.

As the experience of many years shows, it is impossible to create an effective system of material incentives and to increase the effectiveness of resource utilization dramatically without resolving the problem of global and structural balance in the consumer sector of the nation's economy. Economists estimate current unsatisfied effective demand of the population at several tens of billions of rubles. The fact that there are frequently too few commodities on which to spend an honestly earned ruble naturally undermines material incentives for raising labor productivity. The party firmly intends to correct the situation in this area in the shortest possible time. The USSR Food Program, the Comprehensive Program for the Development of the Production of Consumer Goods and the Service Sphere in 1986–2000, and the entire aggregate of measures to raise the Soviet people's living standard are intended to address this problem.

The principal avenue here is the acceleration of the growth rates of consumer goods production and paid services, the improvement of their quality, and the expansion of their mix. But this is only part of the problem. There must be strict planned monitoring of the growth of the population's money incomes so that their rise would be strictly proportionate to the growth of social labor productivity and the actually available mass of goods and services. The disproportions that have arisen here have to a considerable degree been the consequence of the fact that these objective demands were simply ignored in the past, exacerbating inflationary trends in our economy. Here, too, we concur with Zaslavakaia and other economists: the question of basically rectifying retail prices on material consumer goods and rates on paid services rendered the population by branches of the nonproductive sphere of the national economy is long overdue. The present system of retail prices is largely out of date and does not correspond to modern conditions of production or supply and demand for goods and services. This has particular application to the production and sale of highly state-subsidized meat products which, as calculations show, are for the most part consumed by the population in the relatively higher income brackets. In our view, the raising of prices on meat products—of course, with appropriate adjustments for low-income groups in the population—would substantially improve the situation in the consumer market, would create more highly substantiated demand for various types of commodities, and would establish normal conditions of operation for the producers. It is important to emphasize that the raising of prices should not be a purely static financial act in the consumer market that cuts "ineffective," low-income consumers off from the consumption of a number of goods and that leaves the producers of scarce goods and services unaffected. We believe that consideration should be given to ensuring that some of the income resulting from the raising of retail prices goes to the producers of goods and services and helps to eliminate bottlenecks. In other words, an ever larger part of the capital investments would be regulated by the mechanism of socialist commodity-monetary relations. The possible "monopolistic effects" that might arise here could be compensated by a well-conceived tax policy.

Considering the present economic situation, the comprehensive reform of retail prices would have to be carried out on the basis of an increase in their average level, which requires careful consideration of mechanisms that will compensate this rise with respect to different social income groups. Current income can be compensated in full measure, but a certain degree of devaluation of the population's savings is inevitable. And as Zaslavskaia correctly notes, price reform will naturally also require the substantial reform [*uporiadochenie*] of the population's incomes, their redistribution, etc. The reform of the system of income (wages in the productive and nonproductive spheres, pensions, scholarships) is also an urgent economic act today. If we strive for a comprehensive solution to the problem—and this is essential— we should also carry out monetary reform in addition to the reform of retail prices and the population's incomes. Active policy in this area must promote the integral combination of the principle of increasing the economic effectiveness of resource utilization with the attainment of genuine socialist social equality.

The Twenty-seventh CPSU Congress advanced numerous key social issues that we must resolve by the year 2000. One of the first places here belongs to the housing problem. At least two billion square meters of housing are scheduled to be commissioned in 1986–2000, thereby making it possible for our country to realize its basic task of providing every family with a separate apartment or house. This will be a qualitative jump on the road to providing the entire USSR population with housing. By way of implementing their policy of increasing the share of resources allocated for the development of the social sphere, the party and the state called for a sharp increase in the volume of housing construction already under the Twelfth Five-Year Plan, raising it to 595 million square meters.

This is unquestionably the main direction in solving the housing problem. In accordance with the new conditions of the country's socioeconomic progress and the substantially higher living standard of the population, it is necessary to improve the principles of financing housing construction, its distribution, and payment for utilized housing. Future plans call for increasing the share of cooperative and individual construction, thus utilizing the population's resources to a greater degree. The question of changing apartment rent in order to take into account total housing area, its quality, location, etc., is under discussion.

But in our view, even the realization of these measures will not resolve many complex problems in this area. The question of introducing socially guaranteed minimum housing for the population free of charge, which is akin to social consumption funds, is long overdue. This idea is also supported by Zaslavskaia, although we do not entirely agree with her that the criterion of dividing goods into those that are free and those that must be paid for has been supplanted by their material-physical type. The state state must socially guarantee and protect the basic level, the social standard of satisfaction of the need for housing. Within these limits, housing is a social good, a certain amount of which (differentiated by territory, sex-age and social income groups in the population, etc.) must be made available to every member of society free of charge. Beyond this socially guaranteed minimum and social standard, housing becomes a good that must be fully paid for. The difference between economic and social need, between economic and social goods determines the boundaries between the satisfaction of needs free of charge or at a price, boundaries that are measured according to the growth of society's wealth, the level of its economic development, change in socialism's system of social, economic, moral, and ethical values, and the rise in the cultural and educational level of its members.

This complex of measures in the realm of housing policy will make it possible to draw considerably more housing into the orbit of the law of distribution according to labor and will make possible the healthy use of commodity-monetary relations on a socialist basis. This will substantially increase their stimulating influence on the material motivation of the workers, and consequently, on raising the economic effectiveness of social production, and on maintaining high and stable rates of economic growth. This circumstance is all the more important because housing is a socioeconomic good, the need for which objectively grows as the standard of living rises, and it is extremely difficult to saturate.

The task of radically restructuring the material-technological base of the USSR's sociocultural complex, which must correspond to the highest standards in the world, is now on the agenda. The Twenty-seventh Congress took note of the harm that has been inflicted on the country's socioeconomic progress in general by the lag in the development of this complex.

Presently there is a need to improve the situation in health care, education, etc. An unsubstantiated differentiation has developed between various cities, rural areas, and economic regions, as well as various strata of the population in the enjoyment of culture. The most important social task and one of the avenues to the attainment of genuine socialist social justice is to sharply expand the volume of services provided by the sociocultural complex, to improve their quality, and to equalize access to them by people living in large, medium-size, and small cities and towns, rural areas, and different economic regions in the nation. This is at the same time a necessary prerequisite to increasing the effectiveness of economic growth. "Investments" in man, which are largely realized through the development of the country's sociocultural complex, sharply raise the quality of labor power and promote its continuous improvement, without which the acceleration of socioeconomic progress is inconceivable. Also manifested therein is the true, economically stimulative function of social consumption funds, because the services of branches belonging to the sociocultural complex are to a considerable degree provided free of charge or at a nominal price. Measures that are taken in connection with the reform of the entire system of education must also become part of the strategy of development of the USSR's sociocultural complex.

Large-scale measures in the realm of social security must also be carried out in the period that lies ahead. Total reform of the pension system is extremely urgent. As is known, the last pension reform was in 1956, and the procedures it introduced are largely obsolete. The economic plight of pensioners is continuously worsening compared with the working population. Considering the real growth of retail prices over the last 25–30 years, it can be said that their living standard has also declined in absolute terms.

The party and the state have already begun implementing measures to raise the living standard of pensioners. The Twelfth Five-Year Plan will continue raising minimum old-age and disability pensions for workers and employees as well as loss-of-breadwinner pensions and will begin raising previously instituted pensions for collective farmers. The size of this increase will naturally be associated with the volume of actual resources that our country will have at its disposal in 1986–90. With the growth of national income, it may be possible to commence overall pension reform. According to the calculations of a number of economists, pensions should amount to approximately 67–70% of workers' wages. We propose the introduction of the following socioeconomic mechanism for changing the size of pensions as a result of fluctuations in the average index of retail prices on material goods and services: raising the former if the given index rises and stabilizing them even if it declines. It must also be remembered that an increase in the size of pensions as a result of the increased effectiveness and volume of social production will have a positive impact on the level of economic effectiveness of the utilization of production resources. In other words, pensions for the population perform not only a purely social function but also an important economic function that ensures the country's high economic growth rates.

One of the demands of our party's program is to use social consumption funds to bolster certain low-income groups in socialist society's population. As calculations show, the presence of pensioners and children in families continues to be one of the most important reasons why families remain in the low-income category. This also determines the strategy for bolstering these families and for using social consumption funds correctly. We have already discussed pensions. Next on the agenda is increased social assistance to families with children. The Twelfth Five-Year Plan will raise the age of children for whom grants will be paid to low-income families; medicines will be supplied free of charge for children up to the age of three years; partially paid child care leave is being increased to 1.5 years for working mothers, etc.

Naturally, all these processes will grow intensively in 1991–2000. At the same time, it must be remembered that the low-income boundary permitting families to receive various types of social assistance from the socialist state will be expanded with the growth of the physical volume of national income and the rise in the standard of living. The indicated measures are essentially also elements of an active demographic policy directed toward correcting the country's very unfavorable situation. The correction of the situation will be an additional factor in sustaining high, stable economic growth rates.

Only some of the questions in the interrelationship between social development and economic growth have been treated in this article. This is an extremely multifaceted problem. Its investigation, as already noted in the article by Zaslavakaia, must be greatly intensified. Taking into account the interaction of economic, social, ecological, and other factors, it will ultimately be necessary to provide scientific substantiation of the optimal distribution of resources in the national economy at all levels of the planned management hierarchy.

Note

1. These calculations were performed together with V. G. Grebennikov, the holder of a candidate's degree in economics.

Property
and
Social
Justice

V. V. KULIKOV

The Structure and Forms of Socialist Property

The Twenty-Seventh CPSU Congress advanced the problem of reforming property relations to the forefront. The new edition of the CPSU Program adopted at that Congress emphasizes: *"the strengthening and enhancement of public ownership of the means of production*, which is the basis of the socialist economic system, is now and will continue to be the focus of the party's attention. In the future as well it will be necessary to raise the level of socialization of production, its planned organization, and to steadily improve the forms and methods of realization of the advantages and potential of public property" (1). What occasions such a formulation of the question? It is predetermined primarily by the fact that ownership of the means of production forms the basis of any society's economic system. It is this that permeates all production relations and acts as the "clamp" that unites them into a unified whole. For bourgeois society, this is private capitalist ownership. For socialist society, it is public ownership. The basic advantages of socialism and all its historic attainments are specifically associated with public ownership of the means of production.

In conformity with the directives of the Twenty-Seventh CPSU Congress, which accorded top priority to reforming property relations, the materials of the June 1987 Plenum of the CPSU Central Committee indicate the need to develop new conceptions of such a key issue as socialist property.

As is known, in the seventies and early eighties economic growth

Russian text © 1987 by "Progress" Publishers. "Struktura i formy realizatsii sotsialisticheskoi sobstvennosti," *Rabochii klass i sovremennyi mir*, 1987, no. 5, pp. 16–25.

Prof. Vsevolod Vsevolodovich Kulikov holds a doctor's degree in economics and heads the Department of Political Economy of the Academy of Social Sciences under the CPSU Central Committee.

rates declined, and the quality of this growth worsened. Negative trends that became clearly apparent during that period indicated that the working people's feeling of proprietorship had diminished: this was also reflected in their attitude toward work. How can the sense of proprietorship of each worker, collective, and all society as a whole toward public property be strengthened, how can the disharmony of personal, collective, and social interests that rendered impossible the acceleration of the nation's socioeconomic development be corrected? Such are the basic issues in the restructuring and modernization of socialism's economic system. It is from this point of view that we shall examine the problem of the structure and forms of realization of socialist property.

I

In examining the structure of property relations, it is fundamentally important to determine whether this structure is becoming simpler or whether it is becoming increasingly complex and diverse. The practical significance of such a formulation of the question is connected with the fact that its solution also primarily depends on forms of management that are legitimate for socialist society.

Theory and practice for a long time proceeded (even though this has by no means always been clearly recognized) from the idea that the structure of both property and forms of management under socialism is quite simple: state and cooperative forms of ownership and management, as well as personal property, with which the personal household plot and the household were also connected in one way or another. It was believed that this structure was in large measure static, and that if it changed it did so in the direction of greater simplicity. In accordance with these ideas, from time to time there were attempts to artificially force the reduction of distinctions between cooperative property and state property and to eliminate personal household plots (PHPs). There were unrealistic plans to curtail work at home, which were reinforced, in particular, by real steps to draw women into social production in unduly large numbers. The latter had a negative impact on the dynamics of infant morbidity and mortality, on care for the ill and the aged in the family setting, on child-rearing, and led to moral and material losses in society (paid sick leave, legal and illegal absenteeism for valid reasons, etc.). The feminization of a number of spheres led to the lowering of their effectiveness (this applies to both material and nonmaterial production and especially to public health and education). Public and personal property were sharply differentiated by sphere, as a result of which personal property acquired a markedly consumerist nature and its relationship to production became single-valued and unidirectional—through distribution of part of the created product to personal disposal. Did such single-valuedness and unidirectionality of the relationship between public and personal forms of property develop a sense of proprietorship in each worker? Evidently, they did not.

From time to time there was a clearly discernible policy of confiscating all personal property that did not come under the heading of personal consumption in the narrow interpretation of the term. Such confiscation also applied to housing (and therein lies one of the reasons why the cooperative housing system did not develop appreciably for a long time, and why it has still not become the practice to purchase apartments from the state), garden plots, and cottage as well as agricultural equipment.

Relations directly between enterprises became increasingly confined to commodity exchange of a predetermined range of products. Competition between work collectives was largely reduced to the statistical (paper) comparison of performance for a certain period of time and began to lose the character of a real economic relation. Evidently according to the logic of "the rule of opposites," there began a flow of literature and dissertations during that period that were designed to prove the basically correct principle that socialist competition is an economic relation and that there is a special objective economic law— the law of competitiveness. Since the actual practice of economic management attested to the contrary, there was need for special proof "from science" that contrary to appearances, this was truly the case.

Of course, the actual events did not fit into the theoretical scheme which maintained that with the transition to socialism, the structures of relations of property and forms of economic management would be simplified; indeed, the events occasionally punched holes in this scheme. So it was that mixed inter-collective and state-collective farm facilities came into being. In various forms, some of the enterprise's resources were unified and used jointly to resolve a number of social issues; the property of public organizations was affirmed; the cooperative form of housing construction became widespread; and certain forms of secondary employment, for example, student and nonstudent construction detachments, came into being.

Theory, however, demonstrating a kind of snobbism, avoided these holes, considering them to be short-lived and not immanent to socialism. If any of these phenomena came within the field of vision of theoretical analysis, they were viewed primarily on the basis of the affirmed views of the dynamics of the structure of forms of property and economic management. Such, at a time, were the discussions of the socioeconomic nature of mixed inter-collective and state-collective farm formations. But for all the differences between the participants in the discussions, there was one dominant approach—the characterization of these formations from the standpoint of reducing the distinctions between collective farm and cooperative property and state property.

In addition to this, a number of forms of economic life were forbidden, which led to underutilization of the potential for the development of production, and consequently to interruptions in supply and services for the population. When any of the forbidden or formally unauthorized types of economic activity came into being nevertheless, by virtue of their quasi-legal or even illegal status, they invariably acquired distorted forms. As a result, they did more harm than good, even though they could have had a positive effect under other conditions.

It is here that the roots of the so-called second or shadow economy with all its pluses and minuses lie. The point at issue here is not only the individual form of economic activity but also relations between enterprises, institutions, and departments (covert performance of services for one another, covert exchange of scarce goods, etc.). Without such nonlegalized relations, the economy could not have functioned under the existing conditions, but the deformation of relations in the process created favorable soil for abuses and criminally punishable actions. Here, the logic of degeneration of one into the other is quite simple. Initially, an illegal action may be committed in the interests of the cause, but due to the immunity and decorum involved with this type of action, the actions are no longer in the interests of the cause but are performed for selfish interests. Therefore, economic abuses cannot be reduced to a minimum until the grounds for them is removed.

When addressing the question of the dynamics and structure of forms of property and economic management, it is also useful to consider the lessons of development of the capitalist countries. The sharp polemic that V. I. Lenin conducted against the Kautskian theory of ultra-imperialism at the beginning of the century is known. One of his conclusions was: "There is no doubt that the trend of development is *towards* a single world trust absorbing all enterprises without exception and all states without exception. But this development proceeds in such circumstances, at such a pace, through such contradictions, conflicts and upheavals—not only economic but political, national, etc.— that inevitably imperialism will burst and capitalism will be transformed into its opposite *long before* one world trust materializes, before the 'ultraimperialist,' world-wide amalgamation of national finance capital takes place" (2).

Real life at that time had not yet provided the economic data required to solve the question, and therefore the answer was of a predominantly political nature (before "capitalism will be transformed into its opposite," i.e., before the socialist revolution occurs). Now that more than seventy years have passed since these lines were written (1915), there is sufficient material for concluding what in reality is happening. Life has shown that the diversity of forms of management in the developed capitalist countries since the beginning of the century has not only not diminished but has even increased. There has been a certain rebirth of small-scale production on a new foundation, which also requires revisions in the idea of the obligatory limitation to two forms of ownership for all (or a number) of countries embarking on the path of socialist development. Incorporating not only peasant farms but small urban farms as well as farm production of a new type, cooperative property thereby obtains additional foundations after the socialist revolution.

On the whole, it can be said that in developed capitalist countries under present conditions there is a large set of forms that differ in their nature, and that this diversity is increasing rather than diminishing. What does the bourgeoisie gain from such diversity and its intensification? It makes it possible for the bourgeoisie to assimilate and utilize the smallest possibility for the development of production and on this basis to expand the scale and diversify the forms of capitalist appropriation.

Such is one of the lessons of historical development, and it must obviously be taken into account under the new social conditions.

The policy of accelerating economic growth presupposes the mobilization of all potential and reserves, and the use of all those forms of economic activity for which there is an objective basis and that are not in conflict with the social nature of the socialist system. But this line will inevitably complicate the structure of property relations and intensify the diversity of forms of economic life. It is in this context that we must view the development, envisaged by the USSR Law on the State

Enterprise (Association), of economic competition between enterprises and the conferral on them of the right to use funds at their disposal for the creation of joint productive as well as nonproductive facilities, and to relinquish part of the incentive funds to allied enterprises that helped to achieve the additional effect (see Art. 2, paragraph 4; Art. 4, paragraph 4; and Art. 21 of the Law) and to form mixed enterprises (including enterprises with the participation of foreign capital).

Various forms that strengthen direct ties and feedback between public and personal property can play a substantial part in strengthening the feeling of proprietorship and in unleashing the initiative of the working people. The potential range of these forms is extremely varied. They include the development of property of public organizations, the number of which will grow; the use of personal savings on a cooperative and noncooperative basis for the solution of a number of social problems (not only housing but also the problem of providing the population with telephone communications, child care institutions, and sports and other facilities); and even for the development of existing enterprises.

Also included under this heading are: the introduction of the family contract; the use, e.g., of personal transportation in the activity of certain organizations and institutions on a contract basis; the development of various forms of secondary employment, including the amalgamation of working people into groups for the purpose of resolving individual production questions (small-scale construction, in the consumer service sphere, in trade, etc.). The final point is the intensification of various forms of individual labor activity envisaged in the recently adopted Law. This question merits special examination by virtue of the fact that it has generated much interest both at home and abroad.

II

In the course of public discussion of the Law on Individual [Labor] Activity, the impression may be created that this activity is being introduced in our country for the first time. However, it not only existed to a certain degree previously, but it was basically constitutional. It was permitted by the 1936 Constitution of the USSR. It is also provided for in Art. 17 of the present Constitution, which states: ''in the USSR, the law permits individual labor in handicrafts, farming, the provision of services for the public, and other forms of activity based exclusively on the personal work of individual citizens and members of their families.'' Nevertheless, the given article has not been properly supported by normative acts. They have not always been coordinated with one another and have not encompassed many types of individual labor activity that actually existed and (what is very important) were recognized by public opinion. Each of us can cite hundreds of examples of our use of individual services not provided for by existing normative acts. The formal right thus contradicted the real situation, which in itself cannot be deemed normal. Such a state of affairs has artificially restricted individual labor activity and has led to the underutilization of the labor and creative potential of our people. Nevertheless, the existing potential here is very significant. The country numbers 55 million pensioners and 5.5 million students in institutions of higher learning and trainees attending technicums. Not all of them are able or willing to engage in labor activity. But it is clear that under the proper conditions, a considerable percentage of them would do so. Moreover, as the polls indicate, approximately 40 percent of the workers and employees (and they number approximately 130 million in our country) have expressed the desire to engage in individual labor activity. It is once again clear that not all of these 40 percent will do so. An abstract wish is one thing, the realization of the wish another. Nevertheless, it is also clear that the reserves here are enormous.

There is yet another side to the question under review. Up until now, we have often refused to make it possible for people to realize additional income lawfully. This has resulted not only in the underutilization of labor resources but has also prompted some people to seek devious ways of applying their knowledge and experience. Of course, the possibility of obtaining additional income must be sought and made available primarily in socialized production, but to ignore individual labor activity for the good of society is a luxury we cannot permit ourselves. The adopted law lifts artificial constraints on individual labor activity and substantially expands the list of legislatively authorized forms of such activity (by more than thirty), which will unquestionably help to overcome the shortage of a number of consumer goods and services and to improve their quality. The law brings formal rights into accordance with practical demands, which is entirely in keeping with the spirit of realism that permeates all the decisions of the Twenty-Seventh CPSU Congress.

The result of the imposition of artificial restrictions on individual activity was that some of its forms existed only on a quasi-legal basis.

This created an environment that encouraged abuses, that gave part of the population access to unearned income, and that promoted private property aspirations that are alien to our system.

The adopted law puts everything in the sphere of individual activity in its place. Everyone is given his due. First, while it strengthens and develops respect for honest labor for the people's good, the law does not remove all restrictions on individual labor activity. Still banned are all forms of individual labor activity that conflict with the nature of socialism and that contradict society's interests. Only labor activity that is based exclusively on the personal work of individual citizens and members of their families is permitted. Such antisocial forms of individual labor activity as the production and repair of all types of weapons, the production of poisonous and narcotic substances, and the organization of games of chance are still prohibited.

Second, the law strengthens public oversight aimed at thwarting private property aspirations and the extraction of unearned income, and imposes stiffer punishments for these actions. In this regard, the Law on Individual Labor Activity has been closely coordinated with the previously adopted Law on Unearned Income.

As is known, this law has occasionally been misapplied, thereby evoking the natural dissatisfaction of our people. Such encroachments on people's lawful rights were inevitable before order was brought to the issue of individual labor activity. Today, however, additional legal principles have been created for the purposeful and effective exercise of the Law on Unearned Income.

From the standpoint of strengthening public oversight, it is also important that the adopted law provides that the state shall encourage citizens engaged in individual labor activity to enter into contractual relations with state, cooperative, and public enterprises, institutions and organizations and shall also encourage their amalgamation into cooperatives, voluntary societies, and companies. This will facilitate the ever greater integration of individual forms of labor activity with socialized production: in such a case, they will become not only a supplement but also a continuation of the latter.

Such activity is sometimes regarded as private, and in some countries the word "individual" is even translated as "private," which provides grounds for speculation regarding the rebirth of the private sector in the Soviet Union. Individual labor activity was also characterized as private in the 1936 Constitution of the USSR, Art. 9 of which states: "In addition to the socialist system of economy, which is the predominant form of economy in the USSR, the law permits the small private undertakings of individual peasants and handicraftsmen based on their own labor and precluding the exploitation of the labor of others.'' In the official documents of today, however, the term "private" is not used in reference to individual labor activity. What is this—an altered phraseology or a reflection of the new state of affairs?

In the late thirties, the small individual farms remaining in the nation were indeed the remnants of the private sector that had existed in the transitional period. What is more, they were practically the sole source of livelihood of their owners. Individual activity today, however, originates under different conditions and with different goals. It also has a different subject. In most cases, it serves as a form of secondary employment and is intended to provide supplemental rather than basic income. The potential of socialized production today is also different: all the necessary objective conditions are at hand for securing the real integration of individual labor activity with this type of production.

In order to clarify matters, let us draw an analogy with certain phenomena from the practice of capitalism. As has repeatedly been shown in the works of the founders of Marxism-Leninism, with the advent of the speculative trader [*skupshchik*], homework was transformed from (medieval) craft work into the capitalist economic form. In precisely the same way, small producers in developed capitalist countries are for the most part "tied" to large firms, and it would be a mistake to view them outside of this relationship. The same approach must also be applied in deciding the question of the socioeconomic nature of individual labor activity in socialist society.

Of course, the possibility that individual labor activity will degenerate into private activity cannot be excluded. But socialist society today has sufficient economic and noneconomic means to prevent such degeneration. The future of individual labor activity is clear—increasing integration with socialized production. Naturally, this does not exclude competition between socialized and individual forms of activity. To a certain extent, such competition is beneficial. What is more, examples of more effective work will be instrumental in discouraging managers from finding excuses to justify the low quality of work performed at institutions entrusted to them. On the whole, the search for effective work techniques is expanding.

Summing up the foregoing, we should emphasize that there are at least three important circumstances regarding the question of lawful forms of economic life under socialism.

First, it must be considered that the level of the productive forces and of the socialization of production in various sectors of the national economy is still not uniform. Stable and considerable gaps in technical levels persist at different enterprises and in different branches and regions. There are substantial differences in the content of labor and working conditions, and the attachment of workers to certain types of labor is quite stable. It is not for nothing that people speak of the technologically mixed modern economy. Failure to give full consideration to this circumstance nurtures two opposing but nonetheless very real tendencies: on the one hand, the tendency to go too fast in introducing higher socialized forms of management, and on the other hand, the tendency to delay in instituting overdue reforms. The stereotypical approach and leveling in either direction are harmful, deprive management forms and methods of their proper flexibility, and in some cases result in production relations that are too premature for the existing level and potential of development of the productive forces or that conversely lag behind them. The result in either case is the same: the inhibition of economic growth. The very fact that appreciable differences exist in technical levels and in the level of socialization of different economic links necessarily predetermines the diversity of forms of economic activity and complicates the structure of property relations.

Second, it is necessary to distinguish between the basic (substantive) forms of public ownership (state and cooperative forms of ownership of the means of production are included among them) and the derivative, secondary forms that originate on their basis. What is more, each of these series has its own system of subordination. Thus, the establishment and strengthening of state ownership of the most important means of production play a decisive role in imparting a socialist nature to cooperative property resulting from the socialization of small private farms. As regards the derivative forms, on the other hand, some of them arise within the framework of the social form of ownership, including public ownership, expressing the enrichment of the forms of its movement, while others serve as its unique continuation. Individual forms of labor activity should be regarded specifically from the latter standpoint. Also included here is one of the objective criteria of their selection: the possible use of all those forms of individual labor activity that demonstrate effectiveness in various sectors of the economy and that are not in conflict with the social nature of our system. "Naturally, such types of labor," it was emphasized at the Twenty-Seventh CPSU Congress, "must be fully combined with socialist management principles, and must be based either on cooperative principles or on contracts with socialist enterprises'' (3).

The integration of individual forms of activity with socialized forms serves to makes them the continuation of the latter while its forms, as shown by the experience of a number of socialist countries, may vary to a great degree.

Third, it is necessary to distinguish between general and secondary directions of economic development without contrasting one to the other. It would be at the very least naive to think—and one occasionally encounters such assertions—that the intensification of individual forms of labor activity is the panacea for virtually all economic ailments. The general problem continues to be the reform of public forms of management, and nothing or no one can free us of this problem.

At the same time, it is wrong to think that under the real conditions of socialist management it is possible to get by without actively using individual forms of labor activity, that the general line of all-around strengthening of socialized forms of management virtually excludes such use. What is more, it is connected not with circumstances of the moment but rather stems from the essence of the policy of using all forms that promote the development of production and that do not conflict with the social nature of our system.

The increasing structural complexity of socialist property relations and forms of economic activity means at the same time that the structure of economic work incentives and motivations is not only not leveling out but is becoming increasingly multifaceted. Socialism here not only does not eliminate diversity but even develops a need for it.

III

''It would be naive to think,'' it was stated at the Twenty-Seventh CPSU Congress, ''that a sense of proprietorship can be instilled with mere words. The attitude toward property is formed first and foremost by the actual conditions into which a person is placed, by his possibility to influence the organization of production and the distribution and utilization of the results of labor'' (4). The question of in which directions and on the basis of which principles socialist ownership of the means of production realizes itself in the capacity of public ownership acquires decisive significance. And no small number of problems have accumulated here both in theory and in practice. At the same time, it should be emphasized that not enough attention has been devoted up to now to the question of economic forms of realizing socialist ownership of the means of production. It has not even been clearly formulated and subjected to special research. In those rare instances where there has been discussion of the forms of realization of public ownership of the means of production, everything has usually been reduced to the incomes of enterprises and the working people, to the question of their well-being. And, of course, the incomes of the population and of economic units and the question of their well-being and its growth have a direct bearing on the forms of realization of public ownership of the means of production. But incomes and well-being are only a manifestation of the realization of public ownership. It is necessary to investigate the actual process of realization, the forms under which it occurs, the principles of this realization, and its methods and mechanism.

One of the main shortcomings of the existing system of management in our view is that it cultivates a feeling of dependency in a number of directions. The latter has begun to appreciably inhibit the growth of the effectiveness of production and the development of society in general. Wages have increasingly been assigned compensatory functions that are not basically inherent in their nature: in determining wages, the worker's labor contribution has been relegated to second place while social considerations (the need to ensure everyone a minimum level of consumption, the need to consider the number of dependents a worker has, etc.) have been moved into first place. The connection of distribution through public consumption funds with [a worker's] labor contribution has been broken. The state has redistributed resources between enterprises, departments, and regions regardless of their labor contribution, which has led to the maintenance of those who function poorly or those who work in branches for which society no longer has a need at the expense of those whose performance is good.

It has become the norm in management practice to grant across-the-board wage increases to entire strata of working people regardless of individual performance or of whether their performance improves after the increase. It has also become standard practice to compensate enterprises and branches for their costs regardless of whether or not they are within the social norms. An elemental truth is fading from view: every wage increase and all funds for the development of production must be earned and backed by a higher labor contribution.

Experience shows that universal employment does not by any means always go hand in hand with rational employment. A paradoxical situation develops as a result: a manpower shortage in the national economy at the same time that there is a manpower surplus at a number of existing enterprises, which necessarily reduces the effectiveness of social production and results in paying out money that has not been earned.

The cultivation of a feeling of dependency leads to *egalitarianism*, and one and the other combined result in *unearned income*. The latter is usually equated with speculative income, bribes, theft, and other similar types of antisocial phenomena. But for all the urgency of the problems associated with these phenomena and the need for the most resolute struggle against them, unearned income must not be reduced to them. It would be just as wrong to connect the latter exclusively with large income.

Another stereotypical but incorrect notion is that unearned income is formed chiefly on the basis of individual types of activity. Without diminishing the possibility of forming such income in this sphere, we must emphasize that social production is the principal sphere from which unearned income derives. In other words, unearned income is much more varied and widespread than commonly believed, because any income, regardless of the amount or how it is formed, is unearned if it has not been entirely worked for. In all these cases, and this must be said frankly, one exists at another's expense.

But the most important point here is not even the income itself but the belief that social guarantees and goods should come automatically: people in socialist society have a right to them simply by virtue of the fact of their birth. The deeper relationship between these guarantees and the first part of the fundamental socialist principle (from each according to his abilities, to each according to his labor) is lost. Things have reached the point where a banner with the slogan "The working day is labor's gift to the Soviet people," i.e., it is a gift that I may or may not bestow, was displayed in a large industrial city. Such is the inevitable result of simplistic ideas regarding social guarantees, regarding the attitude "at society's expense," and of actions in accordance with these ideas. At the same time, socialist society is by its nature a laboring society and, while ensuring conditions for wholehearted labor and full employment, it can and should extend these guarantees only to those who work conscientiously. It is precisely the deviation from this principle that lays the ground for a feeling of dependency, for slipshod work, for legal but essentially unearned income. It is on this basis that the individual becomes alienated from public property.

On the whole, it can be said that the ideology of dependency leads to the lowering of the labor and social activism of the working people with all the attendant negative consequences.

The principle enunciated at the Twenty-Seventh Congress regarding the necessity of creatively using Lenin's idea on the tax-in-kind [in the form of foodstuffs] (5) in its application to modern conditions is of exceptionally great importance for the solution of all these questions. One might ask what relationship does a form that was generated by the socialist government's ties with individual peasant farms have to developed socialist society? This form essentially expresses an approach that is important to socialist management: the centralized share of the created product, like the share of the worker and work collectives, may not be arbitrary. These shares have their own objectively determined boundaries. Thus, the point at issue is the share of participation in the created product and the shared distribution of the product. This formulation of the question is fundamentally new and must be analyzed. For this, we can turn to Marx's *Capital*. In his revelation of the essence of relations between hired labor and capital, Marx called decisive the circumstance under which, in accordance with the nature of the given relation, ". . . the worker has no share in the product whatsoever. . . ." (6) This is expressed in the fact that the entire product belongs to the capitalist.

With the establishment of public ownership of the means of production, every working person becomes an associated owner both of the material and physical factors of production and of the created product. And this means that every working person and collective has its own share in the gross product that is determined by their labor contribution. In Marx's words, this is the decisive point. Determination of the share at every level of management, whether this involves the work place or work collectives at lower levels, regions, branches, or the unified national economic level, makes it fundamentally possible to coordinate opposing interests, to ensure their reciprocal realization, to introduce guarantees and automatic increases or decreases of everyone's income depending on changes in the magnitude of the end result. After all, it seems to us that it is in this channel that we should view the assimilation of economic methods of management at all levels of the national economy, the broad use of economic norms, and the conversion of enterprises to full cost accounting, self-recoupment, and self-financing. The share approach in the distribution of the product also provides a real material foundation for socialist self-management, which itself is one of the most important forms of realization of property. The one who has the means of production in his hands is the one who manages. The actual maturity of public property can be judged according to the degree to which the working people participate in management as well as according to the level of their labor activism.

It was not by chance that Marx called self-management ". . . our best instrument for transforming the mode of production" (7).

The affirmation of public ownership of the means of production must be accompanied by the development of the self-management of the workers themselves. At the same time, it must be considered that in order that management be not only for the working people but also by the working people, it is not enough to give them the right to participate in management. The possibility and necessity of self-management that originated as a result of the establishment of public ownership of the decisive means of production are not automatically realized. Discrepancies in the practical implementation of the Law on Work Collectives are known. The essential feature here is the need to coordinate the self-management of the working people with their material interests. The share approach to distribution will make it possible to secure this coordination: if a given decision influences the end results, and if its amendment influences the incomes of the working people and their collective, every worker will have a real material interest in increasing labor activism.

The formulation of problems of restructuring and renovation of socialism's economic system has brought the following question to the fore: Does restructuring extend to the depths of production relations or does it only embrace their more superficial forms and the economic mechanism?

For all the importance that the radical reform of the economic mechanism that has been launched in the nation holds for the acceleration of economic growth, the reform cannot be restricted just to this. What is more, such a reform cannot be made without introducing fundamental, deep-seated changes in production relations—in public ownership of the means of production; restructuring of the economic mechanism is based on and reinforced by changes in its objective principles. It is precisely because restructuring encompasses all strata in the system and changes them qualitatively that it is acquiring a revolutionary character.

References

1. *Materialy XXVII s"ezda KPSS*, Moscow, 1986, p. 146.
2. V. I. Lenin, *Polnoe sobranie sochinenii*, vol. 27, p. 98.
3. *Materialy XXVII s"ezda KPSS*, p. 47.
4. Ibid., p. 39.
5. Ibid., p. 31.
6. Karl Marx and Friedrich Engels, *Sochineniia,* vol. 47, p. 606.
7. Ibid., vol. 36, p. 369.

PETR O. AVEN

The Distribution Mechanism and Social Justice

[From the editors of *Kommunist*]:
> *Our journal's editors receive numerous letters whose writers reflect on the economic and social problems of restructuring, suggest various ways of solving them, and agree or disagree with various points in published articles. Of special interest to readers are questions falling in the "zone of direct interests" of the people—the interface of economic, moral, and social issues relating to the reform and improvement of the distribution mechanism, the use of social consumption funds, and more broadly, the level of social protection of people. We asked an economist to study this mail and to comment on it in the pages of our journal.*

The June Plenum of the CPSU Central Committee noted that the main and most crucial aspect of restructuring is its relevance to the people's economic interests and its consideration of these interests, which should impart new dynamism to our economic system and to all economic work. Success will depend largely on the concept of social justice—a key indicator of economic interests and the way society's members perceive social justice and the avenues of securing it.

The greatest reader response was generated by three groups of proposals that were raised for discussion in one way or another in the journal's pages: expansion of the sphere of paid medical services; differentiation, and in some instances raising, of apartment rents, and changing proportions between the public, cooperative, and individual housing sectors; and altering prices, including retail prices, on food and services and bringing them into line with socially necessary costs.

Analysis of the letters makes it possible, if only approximately, to depict the interests of different social groups, to weigh the readers' pros

Russian text © 1987 by "Pravda" Publishers. "Mekhanizm raspredeleniia i sotsial'naia spravedlivost'," *Kommunist*, 1987, no. 15, pp. 115–22.

Petr Olegovich Aven holds a candidate's degree in economics and is a senior research associate at the All-Union Scientific Research Institute of Systems Research.

and cons regarding the above-mentioned problems, which, while different in their content and avenues of resolution, nevertheless are connected by a deep-running bond that influences people's general social feeling, their living standards, their social activism, and ultimately—the fate of restructuring.

Health care

A draft of the "Guidelines for the Development of Health Care for the Population and Its Restructuring in the USSR During the Twelfth Five-Year Plan and the Period Ending in the Year 2000" was presented for public discussion. It clearly confirmed the inviolability of the basic principle in the organization of Soviet health care—the general availability of free medical care, which is among our society's fundamental and constitutionally guaranteed values. We emphasize that this is a principle that no one has any intention of repudiating; on the contrary, it will be affirmed in the future as well and will continue to be the main, decisive principle. At the same time, judging by the journal's mail and proposals published during discussion of the draft in the pages of the press, there is the question of the admissibility and feasibility of *supplementing* free medical care with paid services. This question also generates heated debate.

Characteristically, the basic arguments in favor of expanding the sphere of paid services were made primarily by physicians themselves. First among them was the argument that our health care system's resources are used wastefully and ineffectively even though they are in short supply, which aggravates the shortage of certain types of medical care. Physician *Artem'ev*, for example, writes from Petrozavodsk that "the result of free hospital care is that the nation's hospitals are filled with an extremely large number of people that have practically no need for hospital care." On the basis of his personal experience, he believes that the work of "emergency aid" stations involves a large number of calls for cases that are not emergencies; each call costs the health care system between six and twenty rubles; if, following the example of certain socialist countries, at least partial payments were instituted for "emergency aid," the number of unjustified calls would be significantly decreased; in any event, he believes that the client should be charged for "deliberately false calls." (To be sure, it is not clear which calls, with the exception of prank calls, can be classified as "deliberately false'': for example, a case of heart failure or tachycardia has passed by the time the ambulance arrives; there is a sharp rise in blood pressure followed by a return to normal. What should be done in such a case? It is not easy to answer such questions.)

The second argument in favor of partial payment for medical services is the careless attitude that many people have toward their health. *E. Kissel'*, a doctor of economics living in Zhukovskii, emphasizes in particular that such carelessness is encouraged by the fact that, in his opinion, in our country it is sometimes more profitable to be sick than to work. Readers note the need for a differentiated approach to different groups of patients and diseases. They cite the following example: patients who have "earned" cirrhosis of the liver as a result of the abuse of alcohol spend up to 1.5 months undergoing treatment in the hospital; the cost of diagnosis and therapy alone is more than eleven rubles a day; would it not be just to compensate such costs from personal income?

The need for differentiation of state spending on medical care for "those who try to improve their health and those who rashly ignore it" was the main topic of letters to the editor from professors *V. Ermakov*, *I. Lavrova*, and *V. Alekseeva*, candidate of medicine, from Moscow. The authors note that polyclinics, sanitoria, and preventoria frequently encounter patients who do not observe the specified regimen or the physician's prescriptions, and "is it not just that these people repay the people's money that is spent on them?"

Some readers even propose the complete discontinuance of payments for sick-leave certificates for illnesses directly connected with [a person's] life style, emphasizing that this will on the one hand encourage people to abandon harmful habits and on the other will help to curb abuses of sick leave. However, we should note that our health and diseases are an extremely subtle, delicate topic. In reality, it is very difficult to distinguish between people who take care of their health and those who ruin it. Arbitrariness is almost inevitable here. It would thus seem that the principal reserves of our health care system should not be sought here.

The third argument concerns the attempt to give every citizen a real possibility of receiving care and advice from a physician with the highest qualifications. Readers note that it is practically impossible for the majority of patients to be received by a prominent, well-known specialist and all the more so to be systematically treated in a leading clinic. At the same time, a person wants to be certain that he has done everything possible to protect his health or the health of those close to him.

The partial use of the working time of the best physicians for a fee (even quite a high fee) appears entirely justified. The authors of many letters believe that this will not only make high-quality care available to patients but that it will also rid medicine of corruption and bribes. At the same time, it is essential to emphasize once more that the introduction of paid consultations naturally does not mean abandoning the existing system of free consultations when so directed by district polyclinics and hospitals.

Finally, there is one more argument in support of partial payment for medical services—the need to eliminate leveling [uravnilovka] in the pay of medical personnel. Naturally, it is also possible to combat leveling by improving the organization of pay system in hospitals, polyclinics, and [medical] institutes. This could be facilitated, for example, by giving patients the right to choose a physician in a polyclinic in their place of domicile, and by making the level of pay directly dependent on the number of patients a physician serves. However, the introduction of such a practice into the existing health care system may be protracted for a long while owing in particular to the inevitable resistance of the less-qualified [medical] personnel. Many readers believe that partial payment for [medical] services would be instrumental in singling out the best physicians. The real possibility of realizing additional lawful earnings would make it possible to ascertain and connect the results of the physician's activity, his qualifications, and his qualities as a person more effectively. This right should probably be conferred only on specialists whose work has been beyond reproach for a specified period of time.

Of course, it is naive to assume that treatment "for money" will always be better than treatment free of charge. At the same time, the authors of the letters believe that the choice of physician and partial payment for his services make relations between patient and physician more personal and make the specialist responsible for the health of each individual patient (which is clearly insufficient today). The present organization of health care is to a considerable degree oriented toward "indicators" and "statistics." Patients indeed pass the physician as if they were on a conveyor, and the physician, as on any conveyor line, sometimes thinks about numbers rather than the individual person. With such a statistical approach, there will inevitably be a "permissible percent of flaws," even though "flaws" are absolutely inadmissible here. Is the reason why some physicians do not devote the proper attention to the most difficult cases the fact that their impact on statistics, on "gross output," is negligible while they are time-consuming? Partial payment and assured compensation (including monetary) for errors in treatment are a real means of abandoning the statistical approach.

Readers opposed to partial payment for medical services also have very weighty arguments.

The first such argument stems from the fear that the removal of certain types of medical care from the "free medicine" sector will artificially "push" patients from the free to the paid sector, and will cause an unjustified lowering of real incomes and standards of living. This must be prevented by a strict distinction between minimum health care services provided free of charge and additional care on a fee basis. However, the readers first of all note the vagueness of the very concept of "minimum." "Is it indeed possible to establish some minimum medical care given such immeasurable, unforeseen diversity for each person and for the population of the entire nation?" ask, for example, Ermakov, Lavrova, and Alekseeva.

Another argument in favor of health care entirely free of charge is the pressing nature of many types of medical care. This point is addressed in particular by *V. Golovin* of Voroshilovgrad, who believes that medical services "can be postponed only at the price of the loss of health. This is what results from charging for medical services. We witness countless examples of people refusing medical services even when they are free. But if a charge is imposed for these services, even fewer people will consult a physician. The number of sick can only increase as a result."

Finally, readers adduce one more very important argument against introducing charges for medical services: the possibility that the quality of work in the basic, free sector will deteriorate still further because society's attention inevitably is transferred in some measure to the development of paid services (being of higher quality, they will also seem to be more desirable and prestigious), and the most socially active and demanding citizens will be reoriented toward paid health care. People in the low income brackets who cannot afford the services of the paid sector will be the losers.

A number of letters proposed the adoption of entirely paid medical care but also suggested that every person receive corresponding monetary compensation. However, as *A. Zamotaev* from Moscow observes, "monetary compensation would inevitably be oriented toward a certain average statistical person. And this means that chronically ill, debilitated people who are illness-prone would be in the worst situation." Nor is the problem solved by exempting pensioners, children, veterans, etc., from the payment of fees. In such case, the ones doing most of the paying would be able-bodied people who practically never use physicians' services. But this makes the very idea of charging [for medical care] almost pointless.

Thus, it is obvious that the partial payment of medical services is a problem to which there is no simple, unequivocal solution. A differentiated approach to various groups of patients and diseases is required. Strictly speaking, that is the whole idea. After all, the point is to pay only for that which goes beyond the framework of a certain standard— consultation by highly qualified specialists, the creation of comfortable conditions in hospitals, intensive nutrition, etc.

Moreover, such measures cannot be separated from other key tasks in the development of our health care system: increasing the share of national income going toward maintaining and improving the population's health; restructuring the system of medical education; developing pharmacology, medical instrument making, etc. Unfortunately, the result of the practice of residual allocation of funds for social needs has been that the share of spending on health care and physical culture in our country's national income has not increased in the last twenty-five years and still amounts to approximately 4 percent (at the same time, the share of health care spending in the U.S. gross national product has doubled; in Japan, it has more than doubled). Without a radical change in this situation, all organizational restructuring, including restructuring connected with the introduction of charges, will hardly lead to the desired results: reduced mortality, longer life expectancy, and the improved health of the population.

Free medical care and the across-the-board improvement of its quality will be the main direction in the development of our health care in the years ahead. This will not be easy to achieve. It will be necessary to allocate significant additional resources to this end, to use them more effectively, to not postpone addressing this problem in spite of the complex resource situation in the national economy. Paid medical care can only be an adjunct to an effectively functioning system of free medical care, otherwise the already difficult social problems in this sphere might only intensify.

Housing and payment for it

That the housing problem in our country continues to be strained is also confirmed by the readers' letters. Many of them speak of difficult housing conditions, of spending many years waiting for a separate apartment, and also of abuses and violations of social justice in the distribution of living space. It is fitting that there is also discussion of the principles of our housing policy, which is based on free housing for most of the needy and low apartment rent.

Discussing the first of these principles, *R. Livshits* from Komsomol'sk-na-Amure, holder of a candidate degree in philosophy, notes in particular that "if free housing is a principle of social policy, it should be universal. . . . However, more than 20 percent of newly commissioned housing is the product of cooperative and individual construction: in other words, society gives four out of five persons an apartment free of charge while one person in five has to pay for it completely." Moreover, there is essentially no objective, socially determined criteria for indicating who may receive an apartment free of charge and who must buy it. This opinion is shared by engineer *A. Medvedev*, candidate of economics *S. Il'in* from Moscow, *V. Konishchev*, a doctor of geology and mineralogy from Minsk, and a number of other readers.

The situation is exacerbated by the low rent charged for apartments received from the state fund. At the present time, the subsidy for the maintenance of this housing is 9.8 billion rubles a year. The subsidy is paid in the face of the most extreme differentiation in housing accommodations: while the average total living space per person is 14.9 square meters, millions of families do not have even a third of this area and live in hostels. On the other hand, there are many cases where the living area per person exceeds 20–30 square meters. As a result, writes *I. Krichevskii*, a doctor of economics from Moscow, "some people receive a large permanent subsidy from society, while others are deprived not only of the subsidy but of normal housing as well. Practically speaking, the former group receives hidden additional income at the expense of other groups, primarily those with low incomes."

To this it should be added that there is essentially no differentiation in rent depending on the quality of housing. Leningrader *A. Berlin* notes: "Today the situation is such that the rent for a magnificent apartment with all amenities in the most prestigious part of town and for a room in a communal apartment without any amenities somewhere on the outskirts of town is practically the same.''

The social injustice of the existing situation in which half of the population living in state apartments pays less than one-third of the current costs while the other half pays not only all the capital but also all the current housing maintenance costs, is beyond question. And it seems just that monetary compensation be paid to those who live under relatively marginal conditions or who are forced to pay for housing by those who have a qualitative or quantitative surplus of free housing.

There are some who object to this proposition. Judging by the letters, most of these objections stem from equating the present imperfect system of housing distribution and rent with socialist principles. Typical in this sense is the question of *V. Ustinov* from Semipalatinsk to the editors: "How shall we propagandize the Soviet way of life if we abandon totally free health care and low payments for communal services?" It would appear that the reason for such questions is the absolutization of certain principles in the organization of socialist society that are justified and socially just in certain stages of its development but that are unjustified in others. Writes R. Livshits in his letter:

> Under certain historical conditions, free housing corresponds to the striving for social justice, while under other conditions it is appropriate to charge for housing. In the thirties and fifties, at a time when there was no mass housing construction program in our country and the population simply did not have the funds with which to purchase housing, its distribution free of charge was entirely just and was the only acceptable and unburdensome avenue open to the state. By the mid-eighties, the situation was radically different. The vast scale of housing construction dramatically increased the load on the state budget. The increase in the population's well-being created the prerequisites enabling the population to use its own funds to participate more actively in the solution of the housing problem. A paradox has developed: millions of people are prepared to give their money for an apartment, but the state does not wish to take it and at the same time is unable substantially to expand the scale of construction in a short time. The free distribution of housing, instead of being an effective means of solving the housing problem, has become a brake on development: under modern conditions, it is unjust and burdensome to the state.

But it is quite obvious that a restructuring of the system of housing distribution and rent is a very complex problem that affects the interests of all the people. Ill-conceived solutions are absolutely inadmissible here. There arise difficult questions to which there are no unequivocal answers. This is also reflected in the mail. One such question: Should a charge be made for all housing or for only living space that exceeds the established minimum? Opinions differ on this point. Most readers consider it self-evident that rent should be paid only for housing in excess of a certain quantitative and qualitative limit. Others, however, believe that such payment will just be one more palliative: in particular, it will not enable the state to obtain all the money it needs to expand housing construction.

Of course, the question of drawing upon the population's resources in resolving the housing problem must not be underestimated. In terms of the number of apartments under construction per 10,000 population in 1960, the USSR occupied second place in the world (121 apartments), but in 1980—only eleventh (75 apartments). The growth rate of living space has not increased in the last twenty years. It was 0.22 square meters per person a year in 1961–65 and 0.2 in 1981–85. If this rate continues, it will take us more than fifty years to reach the present level in the German Democratic Republic (26 square meters per person). At the same time, capital investments in housing construction total more than 30 billion rubles a year. These investments are at present growing very rapidly. But it is difficult to finance this growth from the state budget. The most important way of increasing capital investments for this purpose is to draw upon the population's monetary resources.

However, it would seem that an increase in the state's monetary revenues cannot be regarded as the goal of housing reform. The most important thing is to increase the effectiveness of social guarantees in this sphere, which today is apparently inseparable from free housing within the framework of the guaranteed minimum. Apartment rent must analogously be increased primarily for housing in excess of the limit.

From the standpoint of social guarantees, the compulsory purchase of apartments from the state housing fund, on which certain readers insist, seems unjustified. Can such payment be considered just for state apartments that have already been issued to pensioners, especially if they have no surplus area? The basic reserves should not be sought here. What is more, imposing on citizens the obligation to pay for that which was given free of charge cannot increase confidence in the state. The law, as the saying goes, is not retroactive. And no manner of compensation and benefits will save the situation in the given instance.

At the same time, a well-conceived system of benefits is essential in order to implement feasible measures for increasing the volume of housing that is paid for (raising the share of cooperative construction, increasing the rent for living space in excess of the minimum, etc.). It seems to us that special benefits should be provided for young families acquiring housing. A large part here could be played by loans partially cancelled by the state following the birth of each child. Such a mechanism will help to make payment for housing an active lever of demographic policy, whereas the present apartment allocation system is a powerful brake on raising the birth rate. Making apartments available to young families on a credit basis would substantially raise the stimulative role of wages and would give rise to progressive changes in the structure of consumption.

It would appear that a system of rational benefits can reduce to a minimum the number of those who would lose from the introduction of the new principles of payment for housing. It would be wrong to think that there will be no losers whatsoever. This will primarily affect people who are in an unjustifiably privileged [housing] situation today. The relatively disadvantaged, however, will gain. Society will gain.

The problem of prices

Price reform, including retail price reform on foods, is another extremely urgent problem in which the readers show a keen interest.

Let us briefly present the viewpoints expressed in the letters.

The first argument in favor of raising retail prices is the shortcomings in food distribution. Indeed, when certain products are scarce, the more the price of a commodity deviates from the equilibrium price, from the price that balances demand and supply, the greater is the role played by the rationing of consumption. Today, substantial unevenness in the food supply of different areas, regions, cities, and districts of the nation has been the consequence of such distribution. Scarcity has led to numerous "closed distribution" channels, to unjustified benefits and abuses. (A. Aleksandrov from Irkutsk writes in particular about the injustice of "territorial," "official," and "departmental" benefits in food distribution). Of course, it can be said, taking the cue of economist F. Bokov from Moscow, that the unequal accessibility of inexpensive food products, like other differences in the standard of living, is determined by the law of distribution according to labor, which "excludes the equality of all people with respect to their financial status." But—"according to labor." There is hardly anyone who will venture to say that the inhabitants of capital cities work harder and better than, let us say, the working people in Saratov or Novosibirsk. To be sure, some readers (including associate professor *V. Chevnenko* from Pavlodar and candidate of economics *D. Sorokin* from Moscow) believe that the situation can be remedied by improving the system of "rationing," in particular by expanding the rationing of scarce meat and dairy products purchased for existing state retail prices throughout the entire nation. In their opinion, the introduction of "good rationing" is preferable and more effective than raising prices and introducing compensatory payments. Other readers, in contrast, maintain that the very orientation toward "rationing" unjustifiably rewards certain social groups at the expense of others.

The second argument in favor of raising prices is the uneconomical consumption of food products. Numerous examples of feeding baked bread to livestock are well-known; they are also cited by the readers. Unfortunately, the letters note that all appeals for thrift are not having the proper effect. There is an obvious need for economic measures (Doctor of Economics *A. Khairullin* of Ufa writes about this in particular).

One more argument "pro": low prices, readers believe, cause the scarcity of certain products. In particular, our country leads the world in total production of butter. However, this does not prevent butter (the retail price of which is 2.5 times lower than the state's average cost of producing it) from being one of the extremely scarce foods (this is noted by candidates of economics *O. Saenko* and *Iu. Sheviakhov* from Moscow). At the same time, excess demand for food resulting from the adverse structure of the working people's expenditures results in insufficient demand for nonfood commodities. Higher prices on many products of light industry and other branches (that compensate for the low food prices), observes candidate of economics *V. Parasochek* from Moscow Region, lead to their diminished consumption and to the accumulation of surpluses of certain commodities.

Other proposals on price reforms concern imperfections in the existing system of subsidies for consumer goods. As is known, their sum grows much faster than the volume of retail trade turnover. Thus, between 1966 and 1986, subsidies for meat and dairy products increased 16-fold while their sale increased only 2.7-fold. This growth is based on the increase in the enterprise cost of production of virtually all agricultural products. In twenty years (from the Eighth through the Eleventh Five-Year Plan), the average annual rate of increase in the enterprise cost of production for cattle was 5 percent, and for milk—4 percent. It is becoming increasingly difficult for the state to pay for this increase.

The distribution of subsidies squares poorly with the principles of social justice. Subsidies are only felt by those who buy their food through the state trade network. But these are by no means always the neediest. Often, precisely the reverse is true. Many readers express the opinion that the compensated increase in prices on food will be a gain for the population's high income groups and that low prices are in keeping with the interests of people in the low income brackets. Indeed, as a result of the system of territorial priorities in consumption, the distribution of food at the workplace without regard to family size, and the existence of "closed distribution" channels primarily for persons with relatively higher incomes, judging by budget studies workers' and employees' families with a monthly income of less than fifty rubles per person pay 1.3 times more for a kilogram of meat than families with an income in excess of one hundred fifty rubles per person. In other words, pensioners and large families today buy meat for much higher prices than high income persons employed in management, science, and material production.

The weightiest argument in favor of the restructuring of retail prices is that preservation of the present system of subsidies contradicts the logic of the incipient economic reform and the principles of the new management mechanism. This is written about by many readers who consider that the deviation of retail prices from cost deforms the system of purchase prices, disorients enterprises and the population, inhibits the formation of an optimal food product mix, and makes it impossible to judge the effectiveness of individual branches of the national economy objectively.

At the same time, attention is also merited by the arguments of those who speak out against raising food prices. Chief among them is disbelief in the possibility of making such compensatory payments as would prevent losses by the least affluent population from higher prices. D. Sorokin, in particular, writes about this. He notes in his letter that the "liberation" of prices under the conditions of self-financing and self-recoupment and their orientation toward the enterprise cost of production or consumer demand could lead to further uncontrollable price increases, to the actual "encouragement" of the cost mechanism (this fear is also shared by doctor of economics *N. Berkov* from Kiev).

The essence of the other "con" argument is expressed in Sorokin's question: "Is there any certainty that after state retail prices have been raised on meat and dairy products, the per capita supply of these products in state retail trade will be the same in Moscow as in Iakutsk? If not, are we not deceiving ourselves with [our claim to be] establishing social justice?"

The raising of retail prices on food will unquestionably be justified if and only if we as a result achieve a balanced market, i.e., a situation in which the question of the supply per resident of Moscow or Iakutsk will have no meaning and regional differences in the sale of products will be determined by the differentiation of consumer demand. A most important task, the realization of which would, strictly speaking, justify the wholesale price reform is specifically the elimination of the "nationwide scarcity of them." The realization of this task would greatly reduce the gap between state and market prices as a function of the drop in the demand for products sold outside the trade network. To put it simply, the market would have a competitor in regions where virtually no competition exists today. This is attested to, in particular, by the experience of the major retail price reforms in the thirties and forties.

Finally, one more argument for price stabilization is determined by ideological factors. In the opinion of a number of readers (for example, candidate of economics *V. Pasechnik* from Kiev), raising retail prices "will cause dissatisfaction among the population and will undermine the people's faith in the party's plans, in restructuring." Of course, such warnings cannot be ignored. The formation and support of social forces interested in change are a most important condition to the economic reform. However, we should not underestimate the ability of people to realize the necessity for certain forced and not entirely pleasant measures. It seems to us that one of the tasks of our social scientists is to reveal this necessity rather than to propagandize the rejection of expedient changes. Many years of reluctance to openly discuss, and all the more so apply "difficult" measures that were known to be unpopular constitute one of the reasons why many do not understand the total complexity of the present stage of development of Soviet society (which is also reflected in the letters). There are occasional hints that ill fate is taking from people what rightly belongs to them; they express the desire to have more without looking at the source.

Naturally, we are all in favor of a high level of consumption. But it can be secured only by an adequate level of production. This is obvious. Other possibilities of increasing income, as candidate of philosophy *B. Shaptalov* writes from Magnitogorsk, entail "stealing from future generations."

Many letters express the apprehension that higher prices will not in any way be instrumental in improving the activity of *Gosagroprom* [the State Agro-industrial Committee], in increasing labor productivity, and in reducing the enterprise cost of production. *I. Ivanov*, a resident of Moscow, writes for example: "The product will continue to be exceedingly dear, while the incorporation of actual costs in prices without the serious reform and modernization of the *Agroprom* mechanism and its external relations may only create the appearance that all is well. . . ."

The fact that the high enterprise cost of food production reflects the insufficiently effective use of resources by the agro-industrial complex is obvious. Of course, no change in retail prices itself will solve this problem. "The only way we can correct the situation," emphasizes reader N. Berkov, "is to raise labor productivity and reduce the enterprise cost of production on that basis." Unless the adverse dynamics of production costs are overcome, even after the price increase agricultural products will once again be unprofitable to society. There is need for a basic restructuring of the system of management, for substantial change in the priorities of investment policy, i.e., for the consistent implementation of measures already indicated by the party. It is their realization that will make it possible to satisfy demand with favorable price dynamics. It would be wishful thinking to believe that success can be achieved instantaneously by a single spurt or a one-time action.

But the question of prices plays no small part here. Based on data on the consumption of meat and meat products in the most "fortunate" regions, it can be concluded that to saturate the market with any real increase in the volume of production and with the retention of existing state prices is a task that cannot be resolved in the foreseeable future. It is this, and not a one-time increase in subsidies (which are widely employed in both socialist and capitalist countries), that explain the need for retail price reform. And if, as a result of the reform, it is impossible to balance the market, the reform will lose much of its meaning.

There is one more fear that permeates many of the letters—that measures to reduce the population's real income will be carried out under the banner of the struggle for social justice. Of course, in actuality the change in the standard of living will be characterized first of all by other factors: by the dynamics of effectiveness of social production, by the distribution of national income between the consumption fund and the accumulation fund, and by the change in the share of spending on the nation's defense capability. Policy in the area of prices, wages, and social consumption funds only determine how the created consumer goods and services are distributed between various groups of the population. However, it would be fundamentally wrong to shrug off on this basis the apprehensions that are generated by the possibility of restructuring the retail price system. People are entitled to know and should know what will be undertaken in such a case to protect their standard of living, to prevent the adverse impact of these measures on the real incomes of different population groups.

Only if the restructuring of the economy leads directly to the improved well-being of the people can one count on an increase in social activism, on the strengthening of the social base of the reforms. The letters received by *Kommunist* offer convincing proof of this point once more.

Any socioeconomic reform is possible only when the forces interested in it "outweigh" the forces interested in preserving the *status quo*. Typically, readers discussing the first steps of restructuring also write about its opponents and about those who vacillate or are indifferent to the innovations. This confirms the urgency of the need for the objective illumination of the course of the reforms. At the same time, a number of socioeconomic and political problems cannot fail to emerge or intensify. As experience shows, it is impossible to forecast all "contingencies" with exhaustive precision. And there is nothing terrible in this if there is a ready "feedback" system that makes it possible to resolve the most acute problems, if society, without hoping for a miracle, knows beforehand the kind of changes that will come and how they will affect the standard of living of different social groups of working people.

The reproach of "historical narrowness," expressed in particular by A. Voitolovskaia from Novosibirsk against the authors of several articles published by *Kommunist*, has a direct bearing on this. In her opinion, the restriction of the analysis to quite a narrow time frame hinders the release of the masses' creative energy and the "spiritual uplifting of the people." Other readers, by contrast, believe that abstract discussions of the distant future and unjustified promises of the type that "the present generation of Soviet people will live under communism" prevented and continue to prevent the sober analysis of the current state of affairs and the development of the most effective proposals on changing the existing situation.

Many years of mistakes in the forecasts of the social sciences, excessive absorption with "scholastic disputes on the legitimacy of commodity-monetary relations, mathematical economic methods, the development of personal household plots, etc., under socialism" (as assistant professor *I. Povarich* from Kemerovo writes) and the over-abundance of wishes of the type "must develop" and "must create" (noted by Minsk sociologist *E. Skorobogatyi*) undermine confidence in social scientists (which is the subject of letters by *V. Kozlov* of Tbilisi, *V. Savin* of Gor'kii, and other readers). The situation can only be corrected by public discussion of the given reforms (without oversimplifying them), by examining the mechanism by which they are prepared and implemented.

Without a knowledge of the interests, orientations, and priorities of all social groups, it will be difficult to hope for the success of measures [aimed at eliciting] the ideological, political, and moral support of the reforms. The consolidation of social forces supporting the restructuring in society is the guarantee of its success.

Barriers
to Reform

P. O. AVEN AND V. M. SHIRONIN

The Reform of the Economic Mechanism

The Realism of the Projected Transformations

Political support for the reform and the "system of correctives"

We no longer require proof for the need noted at the Twenty-seventh CPSU Congress for the "deep restructuring of the economic mechanism."[1] Nor are the basic directions of the future reform—the increased economic independence of enterprises; strengthening of the role of economic stimuli and levers; gradual transition to wholesale trade in the means of production, etc.—the subject of serious discussion. The consensus is essentially that the transition must be made from predominantly administrative to predominantly economic methods of regulation of economic life.

However, while supporting the dominant ideas regarding the general direction of the reform, many economists have doubts that it can be successfully brought about in a short time, or that economic science is ready for such a restructuring of the economic mechanism that must be the "deepest and most radical [restructuring] since the construction of socialist society began."[2]

Russian text © 1987 by "Nauka" Publishers. "Reforma khoziaistvennogo mekhanizma: real'nost' namechaemykh preobrazovanii," *Izvestiia Sibirskogo otdeleniia Akademii nauk SSSR. Seriia ekonomika i prikladnaia sotsiologiia*, no. 13, issue 3 (September 1987), pp. 32–41.

The authors are affiliated with the All-Union Scientific Research Institute of Systems Research, USSR Academy of Sciences, Moscow; and the Institute of Economics of the USSR Academy of Sciences, Moscow.

What are the grounds of such pessimism, of this skeptical attitude toward the reform's designs? First and foremost, it is the failure of previous attempts by the USSR and foreign socialist countries to reform their economic mechanisms. Suffice it to mention attempts in the USSR at wholesale reform in 1965 and at partial reform in 1979, attempts at radical reform in Czechoslovakia in 1965–69, in the mid-seventies in Poland, etc. Practically speaking, the transition from War Communism to NEP and the new stage in the reform of the economic mechanism in Hungary that began in 1979 are the only examples of a consistent transition from "administrative" to "economic" regulation.

The question naturally arises: What basis is there for the hope that the newly commenced reform of the economic mechanism in the USSR will succeed? In order to answer this question, it is necessary to understand the factors in the previous failures and to determine the degree to which these factors have been eliminated today. Unfortunately, the history and theory of economic reform under socialism have not been sufficiently discussed in Soviet scholarly literature. At the same time, many authors write about the need for restructuring while emphasizing the complexity of the existing situation in the economy and the impossibility of securing "good" development by old methods. There is the *de facto* assumption in this that the reforms will come automatically when the situation itself guarantees the reality of the planned reforms.

Notwithstanding the dearth of Soviet works on the history of the 1965 reform, the general consensus is that it gradually "eroded" primarily because powerful social groups, and especially the "apparatus," were not interested in reform. It is impossible to disagree with this statement—the success of any reform is possible only when the social forces interested in reform outweigh the forces that are interested in stagnation. And this means that in order for a reform to be successful, it is necessary not only to analyze the array of social forces, but also to make provision in the restructuring program for winning over those who are opposed to it.

The economic interests of social groups in Soviet society have not been sufficiently investigated to date. Essentially this problem has only been formulated.[3] At the same time, without understanding the interests, aspirations, and priorities of social groups, it is difficult to hope for serious proposals on garnering political support for the reform, on consolidating the forces potentially interested in the reform. The formation of the "necessary" array of forces is the principal task in preparations for the reform.

This task is broader and more defined than the task of "clearly identifying and then neutralizing those economic interests that are counteracting the planned measures and those interests associated with the striving to maintain everything as it is."[4] This statement contains an actual appeal to exert "powerful pressure" on opponents of the reform, even though it is not clear who can and should become the object of such pressure.

In proposing their programs without any awareness of the interests of different social groups, the authors of reform programs essentially foist "their own" economic mechanism on those who will live and work under it. This perpetuates the tradition of the existing economic mechanism, in which the separation of the economic decision-making process from the agents that implement those decisions is one of the major shortcomings. Such foisting appears more than strange in view of the striving for substantial democratization of economic life that distinguishes all serious proposals regarding the reform. The point is not the involvement of the broad masses in the formulation of various aspects of the future economic mechanism, but the necessity of considering the interests of the various social groups in this formulation.

In discussions of the unconsoling results of past attempts at economic reform, one frequently hears the thesis that "good" economic science proposed a rational reform program but that "bad" practice was unable or unwilling to make use of this program. We do not believe that such an assertion can withstand criticism. When it proposes a reform program, science has the obligation of considering the "practical" reaction, which, like any reaction in society, is determined by the corresponding interests. At the same time, there is a need not for individual measures but for a system of measures—moreover, a system that provides for feedback and reaction to various problems that may arise in the process of restructuring of the economic mechanism. The experience of preceding reforms convincingly shows that it is impossible to forecast all problems and all potential surprises with exhaustive precision. And there is nothing terrible in this if there is a ready "feedback" system, a system of correctives, a system for damping (attenuating) the most complex problems. From what we can see, such a system is lacking in the current reform proposals, even though it is eminently compatible with the plan for instituting consistent reforms and itself constitutes a reform, a program for making the transition away from the present economic mechanism to a special, target-oriented [*tselevoi*] mechanism. The study of foreign experience must be directed primarily toward the construction of such a "system of potential answers" and not toward the development of a model of the special mechanism. Indeed, the absence of such a system threatens the viability of the proposed reforms.

The "command economy" and the "consensus economy"

Any program for restructuring the economic mechanism must consist of three basic parts: a) a description, or "portrait" of the existing economic mechanism; b) a model of the special mechanism; (c) a plan of transition from the existing to the special mechanism.

The imperfect nature of the transitional plan was discussed above. To what degree have the two other parts of the program been elaborated by economic science?

In our opinion, the fact that scientific forecasts of the consequences of local changes in this mechanism are often wrong convincingly attests to the deficient understanding of the logic of the existing economic mechanism. Many examples of such errors could be cited. What is the worth of many years of "playing with indicators" when the replacement of the "gross" indicator [*val*] by commodity output and later by realized or normative net output has each time been substantiated and presented as the next panacea for all economic disorders. What is more, the authors of such substitutions soon became their first critics. It was specifically the proposals by economic science directed toward expanding the independence of enterprises to market their produce that facilitated the authorization of agricultural enterprises in March 1986 to sell up to 30 percent of the planned purchases of potatoes, vegetables, fruits, and berries to consumer cooperative organizations and on the collective farm market. Collective and state farms interested in higher prices must exercise the right extended to them. However, the farms surprisingly did not (or were not able to) take advantage of the new possibility—according to preliminary data, only 2 percent of the planned harvest in 1986 was sold outside the state procurement system.[5]

This is not the only example of a result that was almost the reverse of what was expected. It seems to us that all such "surprises" are based on the oversimplification of the "working" model of the existing economic mechanism. As is known, the modern economic mechanism was shaped in the thirties. It was at that time that the normative model of this mechanism, which can be characterized as a "command economy," was formed. This model is based on: (1) the relatively objective view of higher links of management regarding the potential of lower links; (2) the formation of orders and commands for the realization of the indicated possibilities on this basis; and (3) the relatively rigid responsibility for nonfulfillment of these commands.

It may be assumed that in the early years of its existence, the actually functioning economic mechanism did not differ too much from the norm. However, the situation changed radically in more recent years. The modern economic mechanism is substantially different from the mechanism of the thirties and from the general normative model. The basis of this distinction is the vastly increased complexity of the economic system, as a result of which the prerequisite "of having an objective knowledge of the possibilities" is usually not operative. In this connection, the system of orders [*prikazy*] cannot function—the "command" economy is gradually being replaced by the "consensus economy" ("bargaining economy") in which the relations of higher and lower are not only (and not so much) the relations of subordination as the relations of exchange. Material-technical resources, money, norms, various incentives for managers, etc., are the resources (arguments) of the higher-situated participants in this "bargaining"; the fulfillment of production targets (or promises to do so), participation in periodic campaigns (especially in agriculture), etc., are the resources of the lower-ranking participants. It is natural that responsibility for the nonfulfillment of assumed obligations gradually diminishes in the face of the unclear potentiality of the lower participants in the "bargaining" situation.

In one of the rural raions of the Altai, we asked farm directors the following question: "Why do you carry out the commands of the raion leadership concerning sowing and harvesting schedules even if you do not consider these schedules optimal?" The three possible answers were: (1) orders from the top must be obeyed; (2) the nonfulfillment of such orders will affect your career; (3) if you accept the leadership's demands today, the leadership will help you later (for example, in the distribution of material-technical resources).

The absolute majority of agricultural enterprise managers who believed that they were violating optimal sowing and harvesting schedules tended to choose the third response. Thus, the participation in periodic campaigns is perceived as a resource for which the enterprise will later be compensated.

Of course, the idea of "bargaining" is not new. However, it is necessary to call attention to two circumstances. First, while proposing measures for the restructuring of the economic mechanism, some economists continue to proceed from the model of the "command economy" in the belief that the economic "center" can stipulate the new rules of management and that the economic agents will begin to live obediently according to these rules.

The second and more important point is that the actual "consensus economy" remains practically unstudied, as do the procedures for reaching agreement and the "weights" of various resources in the "bargaining." Without determining such "weights" as well as the "weights of material-technical resources" in horizontal exchanges, it is impossible to determine the real degree of scarcity of a product or to make a reliable forecast of the consequences of reduced administrative pressure and of the introduction of economic incentives and levers. The question of the closeness and difference of such "weights" in different regions of the nation is a question of special interest. Without studying this question, it is impossible to forecast the future behavior of the market (under "economic" regulation), its potential unity and possible fragmentation. The latter is especially important: consideration of the importance of being able to monitor the market with the introduction of economic regulators played an enormous role in the successful introduction of the new economic mechanism in Hungary. As is known, previous attempts to restrict the single market in our country in an effort to be able to monitor and control it were unsuccessful, and commodity-monetary relations quickly broke through the established boundaries—this also happened in 1914 when the system of "taxation" was introduced and in 1921 when attempts were made to restrict trade to the framework of "local circulation."[6] However, the question of the possibility of such restriction remains open at the present time.

The simplistic "model" understanding of a number of key aspects of the existing economic mechanism is connected with the view of the "command" nature of the economy. Without setting ourselves the goal of "cataloging" these oversimplifications, we shall merely point to certain of them. Thus, the place of money in the modern mechanism is frequently interpreted simplistically. It recently has been common practice to exaggerate the significance of the "monetary" motivation, the enterprise's striving to maximize its income, and to exaggerate the actual role of commodity-monetary relations. The following statement is typical: "The material interest of enterprises . . . is created in the process of self-recoupment by the compensation of expenditures by means of the enterprises' own income. The more products and the better quality products the enterprise gives society, the more monetary resources will it have at its disposal. Consequently, it will be materially interested in the results of its work."[7] Of late, the contrary point of view that money "is not necessary," "is not a scarce resource," etc., has become widespread. It is improbable that either of the extreme points of view reflects the existing situation. Of primary significance today is the distribution of centrally allocated material-technical resources, for which the enterprise always has money in the event they (resources) are allocated. Indeed, most loans to enterprises are unsecured, the repayment of debts is deferred, debts are written off (for example, loans to agricultural enterprises for production expenditures are made irrespective of their indebtedness during the entire period of preparation for field work), etc. However, all this does not entirely detract from the significance of money, the existence of which is, for example, an additional argument of the lower-standing participants in the "bargaining" for resources. The striving for profit is not altogether absent; rather, it tends to be "nonlinear"—depending on the current conditions, the branch of production, and the problems to be solved, it is more advantageous to the enterprise either to be poor (just as it is better to be a state farm operating at a loss than a state farm with a slight profit) or to get rich fast. Such nonlinearities, their conditions and results, and the factors influencing the relative value of money in the "bargaining" of higher and lower participants remain unstudied.

Yet another oversimplification that arises naturally from the conception of the "command" nature of the existing economic mechanism is the hypothesis of the standardization, of the unity of rules of management actually existing in different regional and branch systems. Indeed, if we assume that these rules, like all other "commands," come down from the upper echelons of management and are carried out without discussion down below, and if we consider the fundamental unity of the normative documents articulating these rules, then the conclusion that "local" economic mechanisms are similar will be indisputable. However, in actual fact the rules of management are also the subject of "bargaining," of independent reform, and the actual economic mechanisms in operation in different regions and branches form under the influence of specific conditions and are thus substantially different from one another.

We attempted to determine the similarities and differences of economic mechanisms in the agro-industrial complexes of two rural raions of Saratov Oblast'. Accordingly, all collective and state farm managers in these raions were asked, in particular, to evaluate on a four-point scale the degree of influence that certain leaders at the raion level have on decisions taken regarding the previously mentioned economic issues. It turned out that, notwithstanding similarities in production conditions, historical traditions, etc., the "power structures" in the chosen raions differ substantially—managers occupying the same positions play different roles. Thus, in one raion, almost 50 percent of the farm managers declared that they did not participate in the compilation of five-year plans for the sale of their enterprises' produce (1 and 2 on the influence scale); in another raion, this situation described only 23 percent of the managers. In the first raion, 77 percent of the respondents believed that the chairman of the raion planning commission greatly influences the compilation of the five-year plans (four and three points); in another raion, fewer than 25 percent of the managers emphasized the role of the raion planning commission in planning. In the first raion, only 30 percent of the respondents took note of the participation of the first secretary of the raion party committee in deciding routine issues; in the second—77 percent, etc.

It does not appear that anyone disputes the substantial differences in "local" economic mechanisms. At the same time, the proposal to standardize the real rules of management is implicit in all cases where problems of individual enterprises, regions, or branches are declared to be general and are extended to the entire economy. Such approximation is not only exceedingly crude but is also frequently wrong. This concerns, in particular, the popular conception of the general striving of economic managers for independence. Of course, very many enterprise managers feel a "shortage of freedom." However, dramatic differences in the real possibilities of managers predetermine the different degrees to which they feel this shortage, and moreover we can be sure that many managers do not strive for this independence, that, having declared this striving, they only say what people want to hear. The special importance of studying factors influencing the striving of the economic manager for independence and of studying actual differences in the rules of management stems from the fact that the special economic mechanism based on "normative economic" regulation essentially presupposes a sufficient uniformity of the existing rules (the "same" money, uniform norms governing deductions from profits, etc.). Thus does the separate problem of "reducing diversity" arise.

Associated with the simplistic understanding of the existing economic mechanism is the constant striving to introduce the normative principle into this mechanism. As a rule, this striving has up until now ended in failure. In our opinion, this is determined, first, by the frequently fundamental impossibility (or lack of readiness) to formulate "correct" norms within real periods of time. Second, given the existing imbalance in the economy and mandatory, address planning, there can be no serious hope for the stability and unity of a number of norms (the formation of the wage fund, for example). When the production program is conveyed on a mandatory basis [to the enterprise], the excessively rigid norms preclude changes in the plan, and hence the burden of excessive rigidity lies entirely on the enterprise's shoulders. Under these conditions (and also under the ordinary conditions of indeterminacy regarding the quality of the norms), "bargaining" for the parameters of the normative mechanism and their individualization—Hungary's economic practice is rich in such procedures[8]—become inevitable. It is not surprising that current attempts at introducing uniform norms in our country are ending in failure.[9] Otherwise, the use of the normative mechanism can only be of a formal nature—in our opinion, this is the very future that awaits the normative distribution of resources. Given the acute shortage of a number of resources and a situation where central allocation is the "main control," abandonment of the usual "bargaining" for resources allocated against the promise of future output seems unlikely at the present time. The normative mechanism will evidently be used effectively only for the distribution of nonscarce, i.e., relatively abundant resources, whereas scarcity will continue to be the object of "bargaining."

Due to the constraints placed on economic thought by the "command economy" model, many processes occurring in real economic life remain unstudied. This applies, for example, to the distribution of material-technical resources. The "command economy" model presupposes that the economic "center" knows the most effective way of distributing a limited quantity of certain resources and knows how to effect this distribution. When they learn that in economic practice there is frequently no knowledge whatsoever of the proportions of the most effective distribution, some economists merely state that resources are distributed "poorly" and "incorrectly," and others do not even take the trouble to study the real rules of distribution, concentrating their efforts on "correcting" the existing situation, on proposing new methods of "optimal" resource distribution, on the "objective" determination of needs, etc. However, all these methods and various supply norms usually play a formal role while the actual central allocations are subject to entirely different laws. (At least three different resource-distribution rules can be assumed. First: based on maximum effectiveness. Second: based on equalization of the supply of different recipients. Third: based on the sequence in which the orders are received.) In practice, of course, all possible rules become "intermingled." At the same time, it can be assumed that these rules play a different role and have different "weights" in different situations. Determination of the factors influencing the "weights" and the procedures for establishing them are of exceptional importance in characterizing the existing economic mechanism.

The special mechanism and
the trajectory of the transition

The model of the special economic mechanism is the most highly developed of all the parts of the reform program. It may even be possible to speak of the existence of a "standard special model," the basic features of which are repeated in discussions of what is "proper" by quite a large number (if not the majority) of economists. This model, which has remained essentially unchanged since the sixties, is characterized by:

—the realization of the state plan primarily with the aid of economic norms and levers (prices, taxes, rates, payments for resources, etc.), with a relatively restricted role for mandatory address targets;

—the differentiation of methods for coordinating current production activity and methods of managing the "growth mechanism," with concentration of the interests of the "center" on investment policy;

—the distribution of material-technical resources not by central allocations, but on the basis of other horizontal ties and wholesale trade;

—the normative (or residual) formation of the wage fund given predominantly tax-type control over its distribution;

—the broad development of intraproduction democracy, etc.

On the whole, this model is marked by the extent to which both the general conception of the future mechanism and its individual elements have been developed and conceptualized. At the same time, this model also raises a number of questions.

They stem above all from the fact that the choice of the optimal model of the economic mechanism must be preceded by a precise definition of the goals of the country's socioeconomic development. A. Balassa, in a monograph translated into Russian, shows the different consequences that the choice of one of the three "principal goals"—"effectiveness," "equilibrium," or "growth"—should have (in selecting a model of the economic mechanism and determining the basic directions of economic policy).[10] In the Soviet scientific literature, such comparison of goals is usually simplified and reduced to the dichotomy "economic effectiveness *vs.* social justice." The constant attention of a number of authors to the construction of criteria of "socioeconomic effectiveness" instead of purely "economic" effectiveness attests to the popularity of just such a comparison. Without going into the question of the "correct" determination and comparison of the goals of economic development, we can nevertheless note that there is no doubt about the very multiplicity of potential goals. At the same time, in order to provide an operational definition of one, it is necessary to know the values of a multitude of different indicators, the most important of which are economic growth rates, parameters of the population's standard of living, and characteristics of the differentiation of personal incomes.

It can be said that the special [*tselevye*] values of many of the corresponding magnitudes have not been determined with sufficient clarity, and that even though they were cited in a number of scientific works or documents (for example, in the Comprehensive Program for Scientific-Technological Progress and its Socioeconomic Consequences), they are still a subject for discussion. Advocates of retaining the present system of management debate with the proponents of reform essentially about the goals and not about the type of economic mechanism that is required to attain them. The open clarification of the frequently "special" character of the debate on the economic mechanism and the involvement of the broad masses of working people in this debate is necessary both for the clear determination of the sought-after goals and for the design of the appropriate mechanism.

The problem of making the transition from the present mechanism to the special economic mechanism is directly connected to the indeterminacy of the goals. The fact of the matter is that in the process of this transition there will be certain inevitable "losses" that may be of all different types. Thus, during the economic reform in Czechoslovakia, the actual rise of prices exceeded the expectations in industry by 1.5-

fold and in construction by 2-fold, and the annual increase in industrial output declined from 7 percent in 1966 to 5.5 percent in 1969.[11] The economic reform of 1965–67 in Yugoslavia produced high growth rates of effectiveness but "aggravated a number of economic problems— unemployment, the deficit balance of trade, nonliquidity of firms, structural disproportions."[12] In practice, the unexpected appearance of such problems and society's unpreparedness for the inevitable losses resulted in the halting of the reforms and the return to the "tested" methods of administrative regulation. To avoid such an outcome, they needed to determine the limits to the possible deviations before- hand and the permissible "sacrifices." Without this it was impossi- ble to design a plan and a trajectory of transition to the new eco- nomic mechanism and to determine the duration of the period of transition.

In the present economic reform situation in the USSR, the problem of determining the trajectory of the transition is aggravated first by the fact that the very model of the special economic mechanism requires more precise definition. Second, even if one believes that the future mechanism can correspond entirely to the "standard special model," it is easy to see that this mechanism will differ greatly from the present mechanism. We would like to make a number of comments in this regard.

1. In the "standard special model," the economy is regarded as consisting of three levels: the center, the enterprise, and the worker. However, today there is at least one more intermediate level in the branch (subbranch) or region. As T. I. Zaslavskaia has noted in par- ticular, at this level there arise specific interests that do not coincide either with national economic interests or with the interests of the enterprises. The inevitability of the existence of such a level stems from the division of roles necessary for our country where the enterprise must engage in production proper, the branch must articulate long- range policy in the corresponding direction, and the national economic center must provide general coordination. The combination of the functions of branch development and the maintenance of general bal- ance in the center is obviously possible only on the scale of a relatively small country (Hungary, for example). This is also suggested by the existence of an analogous intermediate level in the economies of devel- oped capitalist countries—this role is performed by large firms and corporations, which number several hundred in the United States, for example. In branches where production is typically small-scale, the

same role is played by territorial, supply-sales (such as the syndicates during NEP), or financial organizations. In the "standard special model," the corresponding level was lost from view and merged with the economic center. (Known proposals on the amalgamation of kindred branch ministries are also "working" in the same direction).

2. The "standard special model" comes in two colors: the "mandatory-planning color" and the "market color." Essentially, its authors, proceeding from the model of the "command economy," propose restricting "commands" to their "natural" sphere—to questions of national economic importance (or the coordination of investment activity, or only the elaboration of basic structural measures); in current operations at the lower levels of the economic system it is assumed that the second "classical" mechanism—the commodity-monetary mechanism—will be used. However, the question of combining two "polar" systems of regulation, of the readiness of the "mandatory" level to make peace with the existing market down below, remains open. As is known, the specific interests of the intermediate link noted above transform the commands and rules that go today from the "center" to the enterprises—the theme of branch legislation has already become the talk of the town. What guarantees are there that the intermediate level will not begin to play the same role of transformer in the new economic management mechanism, too? This essentially is a question of eliminating the exclusive position that bureaucratic hierarchies have occupied in the economy (and in society in general).

In order to resolve this issue, in order to ensure the nonbureaucratic control of economic processes, it is necessary, first, to secure the combination of the interests of all levels of management. Thus, the branch level can be oriented either toward a specific product mix or toward the maximization of the income of subordinate enterprises. In the first instance, the harmonious combination of interests is hardly possible. Local legislation, the formal observance of all-union rules, etc., become inevitable here. Under the conditions in our country, such processes are extremely difficult to control—it is this, like the inability to monitor the market, that distinguishes the Soviet from the Hungarian market. Second, the rights and potential of enterprises must be substantially expanded. Third, the very problem of "market and plan" is in large measure transformed by replacement of the view of the existing economic mechanism as a poorly functioning "command economy" by the view of it as a "consensus economy." Given such replacement, the problem of the "forceful" introduction of the radical new mechanism is replaced by the problem of changing the "weights" of various resources in various kinds of "bargaining" depending on the specific goals of economic policy.

3. The standard special model assumes that the maximization of profits will be the enterprise's principal work incentive. Automatism in the coordination of economic activity under market conditions is based on the general striving for profits. It is known that this automatism is secured primarily by the tranfusion of capital from branches yielding a low profit to branches where a shortage is felt and prices rise accordingly. But such adaptation in the majority of cases require not only (and not so much) change in the structure of production at a given enterprise, with given production capacities, as much as the creation of new capacities and structural changes based on the criterion of the maximum effectiveness of investments. It is the search for the optimal potential of capital investments that ensures maximum profit, and it is the struggle for the market and not the quest for short-term profitability that is the main driving force behind development under competitive conditions. However, the standard special model presupposes that structural change is the exclusive prerogative of the "center"—the question of the sufficiency of enterprise incentives under these conditions remains "off screen." In particular, the question of the capitalist market and commercial credit has essentially gone unexamined. The very origin of "free" capital is most inevitable—the capital investment process can be effectively managed with the aid of long-range norms only under the conditions of a relatively small economy. In the USSR, the individualization of the norms alone is the alternative to such development of potential "bankers," etc. In any case, it should be noted that at the present time there is not even the embryo of a capital transfusion mechanism, and hence sufficient flexibility in the investment sphere should not be expected in the near future.

4. An orientation toward profits presupposes the existence of a general equivalent—sufficiently universal, liquid money. The absence of such an equivalent today is entirely obvious. Moreover, in addition to numerous types of money, we have a difficult-to-control market of "socialist securities" that includes: title lists, ceilings on capital investments, various authorizations (for example, the appropriation of land), etc. Only the possibility of unifying the money paid for a given article, various securities, and centrally allocated resources can give impetus to new economic activity. Under the existing economic mecha-

nism, various securities are issued by different departments, and little is done to monitor their flows or to coordinate them with one another. At the same time, the exchange and transfer of these "securities" and money (for example, the transfer of funds from one account to another), which could create an adaptive, automatic mechanism for correcting their volume and relative exchange rates, is today regarded as an abuse if not a crime. The imbalance of flows of these "securities" and money, the lack of a corresponding adaptation mechanism, and the general material and financial imbalance aggravate the complexities involved in the restructuring of the national economy and predetermine the inevitable length of the process of attaining equilibrium under market conditions.

It seems to us that the cited considerations confirm the need to examine the "standard special model" not as a prescription for restructuring all aspects of economic life, but as a quality, or more precisely, an indicator of direction or an ideology of reform. But one ideology of reform is not sufficient. The temptation to introduce into the economy ideologically true but technologically untested proposals not coordinated with the existing economic mechanism leads to the necessity of replying with force to resistance to the economic system that tries to reject "foreign" elements. Such force is rarely successful. More frequently, the results of introduction do not correspond to the expectations and sometimes even turn out to be contrary to them. Such failures not only affect the lives of millions of people but even discredit good ideas which are inevitably transformed in the process of their forcible implementation. (Corrections to plans have discredited the very idea of mandatory address planning. In precisely the same way, the individualization or the lack of substantiation of norms discredit the idea of the normative approach.) When they propose any innovations, economists must realize the consequences of the practical introduction of these innovations. (In particular, the implementation of a proposal will increase food prices and the compensatory increase in wages will inevitably lead to the relatively more rapid growth of prices, even though this growth is not presupposed by the authors of the corresponding proposals[13].) The need for the thorough restructuring of the economic mechanism does not require proof. However, the formulation and realization of the reform program require the implementation of a number of exceptionally serious measures relating to political, institutional, scientific, and informational support. Only the purposeful and coordinated realization of these tasks can ensure success.[14]

Notes

1. *Pravda*, March 6, 1986.
2. L. I. Abalkin, "Teoreticheskie osnovy perestroiki khoziaistvennogo mekhanizma," *Problemy nauchnoi organizatsii upravleniia ekonomikoi: Tezisy materialov Vsesoiuznoi konferentsii. 13–15 noiabria, 1986 g.*, Moscow, 1986, p. 11.
3. T. I. Zaslavskaia and R. V. Ryvkina, "O predmete ekonomicheskoi sotsiologii," *Izvestiia SO AN SSSR. Seriia ekonomika i prikladnaia sotsiologia*, 1984, no. 1, iss. 1.
4. Abalkin, *Teoreticheskie osnovy perestroiki*, p. 28.
5. *Pravda*, December 9, 1986.
6. See, for example, L. N. Iurovskii, *Denezhnaia politika sovetskoi vlasti*, Moscow, 1928. In our opinion, this book remains the deepest study of economic problems during the transition from War Communism to NEP.
7. *Politicheskaia ekonomiia: Uchebnik*, ed. A. M. Rumiantsev, et al, Moscow: Politizdat, 1977.
8. See, for example: R. Nyera and M. Tardos, "Enterprises in Hungary Before and After the Economic Reform," *Acta Oeconomica*, vol. 20 (1978), 1–2.
9. Concerning the increasing individualization of norms, see, in particular, N. Ia. Petrakov and E. G. Iasin, "Ekonomicheskie metody tsentralizovannogo planovogo rukovodstva narodnym khoziaistvom," *Problemy nauchnoi organizatsii upravleniia ekonomikoi*, p. 33.
10. A. Balassa, *Osnovy planirovaniia vengerskogo narodnogo khoziaistva*, Moscow: "Nauka" Publishers, 1983.
11. O. I. Anan'in and E. T. Gaidar, "Khoziaistvennye reformy v sotsialisticheskoi ekonomike: nekotorye diskussionnye voprosy," *Teoreticheskie problemy sovershenstvovaniia khoziaistvennogo mekhanizma*, Moscow, 1986, pp. 66 –67.
12. S. A. Vasil'ev, "Ekonomicheskaia sistema 'ob"edinennogo truda' v Iugoslavii: osnovnye osobennosti i problemy razvitiia," *Teoreticheskie problemy sovershenstvovaniia khoziaistvennogo mekhanizma*, p. 91.
13. See, for example, S. S. Shatalin, "Sotsial'noe razvitie i ekonomicheskii rost," *Kommunist*, 1986, no. 14, p. 67.
14. Even though the article was received before the June Plenum of the CPSU Central Committee, the editorial board still considers it to be timely.

Nikolai Shmelev

Economics and Common Sense

I will begin by saying that I fully support the analysis and conclusions V. Seliunin advanced in his article. He does not talk about trifles, about secondary problems and difficulties in our economic life. He talks about the most important thing. We have no need of illusions. The question today really stands the way Seliunin writes: "either the feeble but absolute power of administrators and the inevitable collapse of the economy, or restructuring with good chances of salvation." It is vitally essential to us that the nation's leadership, the middle link, and the entire population be fully aware of the critical nature of the present stage in our history: either we will move forward like a great, mighty, and dynamic power or we will soon (I believe at the beginning of the next century at the latest) turn into a backward, stagnant state that will be an example to the entire world of *how not to* organize economic life.

The crux of the problem—at least today—lies not in economic growth rates, not in gross output, and not in the quantity of output. The time has come to rid ourselves of the "religion of growth rates," of the almost mystical horror of their possible lowering. We have driven ourselves into a corner, into a blind alley: in the inevitable, irreversible choice between the religion and economic rationality, we continue to opt for the religion and to sacrifice the nation's future for the sake of it.

We need high, if you will, "heart-rending" growth rates only in the supernew branches—in the so-called "high-tech" branches. But these branches even in the United States currently produce

Russian text © 1988 by "Znamia" and the USSR Union of Writers.

"Ekonomika i zdravyi smysl," *Znamia*, July 1988, pp. 179-84.

The author is a Professor and holds the degree of Doctor of Economic Sciences.

8-9 percent of the gross national product. Everything else is produced by conventional, traditional branches of production and the service sphere. We do not need more metal: in the entire industrial world the production of ordinary metal is declining, and we alone, blinded by the slogans of the first five-year plans and bound hand and foot by the cost mechanism, continue to increase its production thoughtlessly and do not even ask ourselves why? We do not need to increase the gross production of machine tools (the great majority of them are already technologically obsolete): a large part of our machine tools either stand idle altogether, are operated in only one shift, are undergoing repair, or are operated with such tolerances that it would be better if they were not in operation at all. We need machine tools with different quality. We produce about 800 million pairs of footwear a year (and import another hundred million pairs)—no one else in the world produces so much footwear either in terms of gross output or on a per capita basis. Why do we need any kind of growth in this area? Is it not clear that we must simply produce different footwear rather than increase the production of the present, worthless footwear?

Even in the agro-industrial complex we have no need to increase gross output today: we ruin, spoil, rot, or lose at least 20 percent of our annual production of grain, 60-70 percent of our fruit and vegetables, and 10-15 percent of our meat. We do not need more mineral fertilizers, tractors, and combines: we produce two times more mineral fertilizers than the United States, 6-7 times more tractors, 14-16 times more combines, but as is known, we buy grain from them rather than they from us. Actual demand for tractors, for example, is already one-third less than the volume of production. I agree with Seliunin: if you get rid of coercion, "if you presently obliged combines to find customers on their own, they would probably not be able to utilize even half of their capacities." And even under these conditions, we are still investing billions of rubles in the construction of a new tractor plant in Elabug! Do we not have other things to spend our money on? Or is this simply public tribute to the stubbornness and thoughtless departmental ambitions of the Ministry of Agricultural and Tractor Machine

Building that obviously cannot be kept in check anywhere.

No, it is not necessary and it is ineffective to accelerate everywhere and in all respects. Such acceleration is truly "illusory." The country's main problem today is not "gross acceleration"; it is not here that the basic forces and sources of our forward movement lie. We need a different economic mechanism, a different quality of growth, i.e., a different quality of our output, a different scientific-technical level of production, and finally (and this, I am convinced, is the most important), a different social atmosphere in the country that liberates man's creative powers that have been suppressed by many decades under the pressure of an incredibly inflated administrative pyramid. The atmosphere of "universal strain," of gross output at any price ("going all out") that is built into the Twelfth Five-Year Plan—this is not an atmosphere that will enable us to make progress in the economic reform in actuality and not just in words. This is no paradox, it is the reality of our life. Seliunin is right: "we should relate calmly to the nonobservance of the targets of the current five-year plan—we will consider that we have saved resources instead of wasting them on the production of unneeded items."

What is more, it is specifically the atmosphere of "universal strain," the orientation toward gross output, that explain the sad and extremely alarming fact that the new Law on the Enterprise, in which we place such hopes, is in fact paralyzed. Why? Because ministries are silently, quietly smothering it in its cradle without paying any attention to the moaning and groaning in the press. A state order [*goszakaz*] for 100 or more percent of the product; 85-95 percent withholdings from enterprise profits in favor of the budget and ministries; the impossibility of disposing of centrally allocated resources without permission from above; the lack of possibility for the enterprise to sell its own products and to spend its rubles outside the "supply rationing system"; the increase in the number of mandatory directives that are handed down from above under the hypocritical name of "control directives"—does it take much to turn the law into an empty sound? The technique of the matter was known long ago: it is thus that cost accounting (i.e., independence, self-recoupment, self-financing) was already smothered once in 1965. I once again agree with Seliunin and I am willing to bet that if everything goes on the same way as it is today, "in one or two years there will not be a single square meter of factory floor space available for filling contractual orders." About what kind of cost accounting, market, freedom of enterprises, and liberation of creative forces of production collectives will we be able to talk then?

Of course, I am far from thinking that ministries today are staffed by nothing but villains and incorrigible bureaucrats ready for anything so long as they do not lose power, people who are entirely indifferent to the fate of our country, to the fate of the nation. No, I am certain that most of our bureaucrats are intelligent, decent people. As long as ministries are *responsible* for production, for meeting the targets of the Twelfth Five-Year Plan, as long as none of their functions are actually transferred downward to enterprises and associations, then the market, self-tuning, contractual relations, money, a full-valued ruble will all remain theory, discussion, and the dreams of people who have finally obtained the right to speak but who by virtue of their status are unable to influence events.

Take away the pressing, unreasoning strength of arbitrary, unrealistic plan targets; take away the very strict responsibility of ministries for meeting these targets; take away from departments and local party, soviet, and economic authorities their present main function—to "knock out" a plan at all costs. It will then be possible to say just who our bureaucrat is in reality. I agree that the elimination of functions is much more difficult than the mechanical reduction of the apparatus by one-third or even one-half. But if we do not eliminate functions, we will never break the resistance of departments and local authorities (especially in the countryside) to the economic reform: in reality, they will have no other choice than to resist it.

But this in my belief is the way out of another enormous problem raised by Seliunin: how to achieve an appreciable improvement in the population's standard of living, how to change the present social atmosphere so that people would believe in restructuring and economic reform, so that they would overcome the passivity that has been instilled in them over decades. There is vast potential here.

Seliunin, for example, quite correctly points to the unjustifiably high accumulation norm in our national income (on the order of 40 percent if we eliminate the distortions of our statistics), which serves more and more as a kind of "perpetual motion" or "black hole"—production for the sake of production, without the slightest benefit either to the mass consumer or to the solution of the nation's common social problems and the problem of expanding its social infrastructure. If only for the production of the means of production, this, probably the highest accumulation norm in the world, would probably produce an indisputable effect: if not now, then possibly in twenty or fifty years it would probably affect the standard of living of the common man. But in reality, an enormous part of this accumulation is spent for nothing; it is used only to keep our economic machine "idling." Our inventories, for example, are presently growing five times faster than inventories in the United States, while our total inventory to national income ratio is more than three times higher than the corresponding ratio in the United States. Our output-capital ratio has declined twofold in the last twenty-five years, including a threefold decline in construction. Elsewhere in the world it usually takes 1.5-2 years to build a plant of any size in any area of specialization; in our country—11-12 years or more. We still permit ourselves the luxury of maintaining an entire ministry—the Ministry of Land Reclamation and Water Resources (with an annual budget of approximately 11 billion rubles and a work force of two million persons)—which does nothing but harmful work (which would seem to prove its ineffectiveness). What if it built roads, elevators, bridges, and housing?

The reason for all these phenomena is the flawed nature of the all-embracing system of mandatory planning that puts the brakes on our economic mechanism. There is only one way out: self-tuning, cost accounting, and the market. We will then be able to allocate a much smaller share of national income for accumulation than at present. An enterprise operating on a thoroughly cost-accounting basis will not be able and thus will not (in order to keep from going bankrupt) maintain monstrously large inventories, will not have such unutilized production capacities, and will not build "Egyptian pyramids" that are of no use to anyone in the nation.

And this is only one of the sources of the higher standard of living and of development of branches of the economy that are working for the consumer. There are also many others. The time has come, for example, to have a real discussion of our potential for improving the population's lives by reducing the army and defense expenditures, the system of state security, and [the number of] various law-enforcement agencies. It is clear to everyone that the management apparatus at all links and levels of our economy is incredibly inflated and has in large measure already acquired a purely parasitic nature. We hold the world's record for the manager-to-population ratio. According to our norms, even China, which comes after us, should have not 27 million "ganbus" (and they consider even this number too many) but 70-75 million. The potential here can be seen, as the saying goes, with the naked eye. For example, if we consider drivers of personal automobiles alone, we, a socialist state, presently occupy what is probably the first place in the world in the number of professional servants. And again there is one solution—the elimination of the *functions* of a superfluous administrative superstructure, cost accounting, self-recoupment, and the self-financing of production collectives.

Here is a basic fact: at least 20-25 percent of the work force employed in industry today is superfluous to the production process even according to our technical norms. They are either superfluous in absolute terms or are only kept so that they can be sent out to do the haying, to bring in the harvest, can be sent to the vegetable bases, etc., i.e., for needs that could be satisfied with a smaller work force under the conditions of rational cost accounting. Is this not a reserve for utilizing idle production capacities (Seliunin said that they number more than one-fourth in industry), for expanding production, and for bringing about a corresponding rise in the population's standard of living?

However, in the given stage, it seems to me that something else is of decisive importance. The most important thing is that the ruble is not working. Economic incentives do not work or work badly because there is nothing to buy with basic pay or with various kinds of additional income. Even the existing standard of living and the existing average wage are in large measure a fiction, and they will continue to be such until we succeed in saturating the market with food and manufactured goods, not goods in general, but specifically those that are in demand. I am convinced that this is the main task of restructuring, bearing in mind the mood and vitality of the population and its interest in the success of the economic reform.

I fear that from this point of view the best sequence of reform measures, its best "algorithm," has not been chosen. The earliest return in respect to the saturation of the market (I think within 2-3 years) could be expected from the development of our agriculture and the development of individual-cooperative activity.

No complex constructions and reconstructions are needed here: it is only necessary to remove and break all artificial administrative fetters that continue to hamper our agriculture and the individual-cooperative sector. In the countryside there is no need whatsoever for management by injunction [*administrirovanie*], and hence there is no need whatsoever for any kind of administrative organs with economic functions. There is no need whatsoever for direct or hidden forms of *prodrazverstka* [forced requisitioning of grain during the War Communism period], i.e., mandatory forms of planned deliveries, because there is no way all the produce of the village can leave our country, and even in the case of purely commercial relations, it will for the most part not bypass the state elevators and meat combines.

I am convinced that the individual-cooperative sector should abandon the characteristic habit of our entire present administrative-financial system of counting the money in the pockets of small producers and cooperators and then of counting (if they count at all) what they give to the state, to the market, and to all of us. Let this sector first of all develop and prove itself—for six decades it has been smothered by all manner of devices. It also needs benefits and production-development decisions rather than prohibitive measures that kill any initiative in its embryo if it goes slightly beyond the limits that are arbitrarily set in some office or other where people have long ago lost any conception of what constitutes real life.

But nevertheless there is one question on which I do not entirely concur with Seliunin. This is the question of price reform.

As we know, price reform must resolve at least two problems: (1) it must entirely eliminate deformations that have accumulated in price formation starting with the late twenties, especially artificially depressed prices on fuel, raw materials, food, and services, and the equally artificially jacked up prices on machinery, equipment, and all manufactured consumer goods; (2) it must determine a new procedure as to who will in reality establish prices in the nation—the State Committee for Prices, the ministry, or the market itself in the form of contractual relations between buyer and seller. Seliunin (saying that the effect of the first measure will be short-lived and therefore negligible) in my estimation underestimates the absurdity of the distorted world and the price conditions under which our economy as yet lives; simply put, we today do not really know which is in reality dearer—gold or bricks. We must first of all establish real price proportions approximating those by which the entire world lives today. This can also be done administratively, by explicit edicts from above, naturally while securing the corresponding monetary and other compensation to the population, for which the abolition of state price subsidies will mean a direct loss. And having made this administrative step, having established objective, realistic price proportions, it will also be possible to move forward.

In what direction? This is a difficult question and, judging by the intentions of the State Committee for Prices that filter through to the newspaper page, it is entirely possible that we will once more wind up in the wrong place.

Thus far, the State Committee for Prices evidently adheres to traditional armchair positions: we think up a "good," "intelligent" price that has been carefully calculated by committee girls using computers and then we impose it on real life, i.e., on industry as a directive. This "normative price" will take into account average costs and average conditions in producing a given good (with a certain gravitation to better conditions) while all industry must unconditionally accept it and act in accordance with it. In my view, this is a very dangerous illusion! Once again it is not real life but religious faith in organization, the belief that things are more visible up above, that it is not the "wise heads" that should subordinate themselves to economic reality but the economic reality should be subordinate to them.

How many prices can the chairman of the State Committee for Prices and his staff count more or less carefully, more or less objectively? Using any computer? Scores or hundreds of prices? Hardly more, because thousands and tens of thousands of prices (given the connection of every price with all the proportions and relations in the national economy) physically cannot be objectively "calculated" on any thinking computer. But how many prices do we actually need? We produce 25 million types of products in the nation, and consequently we need the same number of prices. No organization and no computer can calculate them all. I do not speak of flexibility, the mobility of prices, their gravitation toward a state of equilibrium between supply and demand.

No, there is no need for illusions, and we must not deceive ourselves—no State Committee for Prices can cope with this task even if we increase its staff scores and hundreds of times. This can be done only by the market, only by the free movement of demand and supply, only by establishing direct contractual relations between supplier and customer. Nonetheless, we have set ourselves the task of eliminating the monopoly of the producer in our national economy; the absence of a monopoly is a genuine, totally unrestricted market. Not a flea market in Malakhovka, as many understand this word due to their ignorance, but a real market, i.e., the normal state of any reproductive process based on the profound social division of labor and the specialization of production.

It is sad, dear comrades! But when will we finally return to simple common sense, to the basis upon which economic life was built for centuries, and stop dreaming up all kinds of "intelligent" constructions in our offices, each more complex and unviable than the other? Seliunin rightly asks: "Do we ultimately learn from our failures or not? Do we believe in economic management techniques or not?"

It sometimes seems to me that this is the principal philosophical question of the entire restructuring program. Shall we continue to rape life or to help life, to help the healthy, natural forces that are included in it? We are not yet able to answer this question at the top of our voice. But it must be answered because the fate of the nation, the fate of the people, and hence the fate of each of us, are at stake.

About the Editors

ANTHONY JONES, a fellow of the Harvard University Russian Research Center, teaches in the department of sociology at Northeastern University. His most recent publications are *Readings in Comparative Sociology* and the co-edited volume *Soviet Social Problems*.

WILLIAM MOSKOFF is the Ernest A. Johnson Professor of Economics at Lake Forest College. He also serves as the editor of the journal *Comparative Economic Studies*. The author of *Labor and Leisure in the Soviet Union*, in 1988 he published the co-edited volume *Reorganization and Reform in the Soviet Economy*.